CAMBRIDGE
UNIVERSITY PRESS

CAMBRIDGE ENGLISH
Language Assessmen
Part of the University of Cambri

CAMBRIDGE
OFFICIAL
PREPARATION MATERIAL

Cambridge English

Annette Capel
Niki Joseph

Series Editor: Annette Capel

Prepare!

STUDENT'S BOOK

Level 5

Cambridge University Press
www.cambridge.org/elt

Cambridge English Language Assessment
www.cambridgeenglish.org

Information on this title: www.cambridge.org/9781107482340
© Cambridge University Press and UCLES 2015

First published 2015

Printed in Dubai by Oriental Press

A catalogue record for this publication is available from the British Library

ISBN 978-1-107-48234-0 Student's Book
ISBN 978-1-107-49793-1 Student's Book and Online Workbook
ISBN 978-1-107-49792-4 Student's Book and Online Workbook with Testbank
ISBN 978-1-107-49787-0 Workbook with Audio
ISBN 978-1-107-49788-7 Teacher's Book with DVD and Teacher's Resources Online
ISBN 978-1-107-49786-3 Class Audio CDs
ISBN 978-1-107-49789-4 Presentation Plus DVD-ROM

Contents

WRITING	LISTENING AND SPEAKING	EXAM TASKS	VIDEO
A short text Completing a task		Reading part 3	
	Listening Homework project **Speaking** Talking about yourself	Writing part 1 Listening part 3 Speaking part 1	Friends forever
An online comment Suggestions and comments			Fun and games
	Listening Lost on a mountain **Speaking** Talking about past experiences Answering questions (1)	Reading part 5 Listening part 2 Speaking part 1	
A story (1)		Reading part 3 Writing part 3	You made it!
	Listening Matching extracts and pictures **Speaking** Discussing options (1) Expressing opinions	Listening part 1 Speaking part 2	
An informal letter or email (1)		Writing part 3	
	Listening Moving to another city **Speaking** Describing a picture (1) When you don't know the right word	Reading part 2 Writing part 1 Listening part 4 Speaking part 3	Amazing architecture
A short message (1) Checking your writing		Reading part 4 Writing part 2	
	Listening A race with teams of dogs **Speaking** Discussing a topic (1) Taking part in a discussion	Reading part 5 Speaking part 4	Animals and us

WRITING	LISTENING AND SPEAKING	EXAM TASKS	VIDEO
A story (2)		Writing part 3	Off to school
	Listening Announcements **Speaking** Talking about homes, family and school Answering questions (2)	Listening part 3 Speaking part 1	
An online review		Reading part 3	Perfect or real?
	Listening Choices and decisions **Speaking** Discussing options (2) Suggestions and decisions	Reading part 4 Listening part 1 Speaking part 2	
An informal letter or email (2)		Writing part 3	
	Listening Discussing a film **Speaking** Describing a picture (2) Describing what you can see	Listening part 4 Speaking part 3	Let's film that!
A short message (2) Phrases for short messages		Reading part 1 Writing part 2	Getting the message
	Listening An interview with a journalist **Speaking** Discussing a topic (2) Keeping the conversation going	Listening part 2 Speaking part 4	The celebs
An informal letter or email (3)		Reading part 2 Writing part 3	
	Listening Friends talk about their achievements **Speaking** Discussing options (3) Agreeing and disagreeing	Speaking part 2	

Welcome to *Prepare!*

Learn about the features in your new Student's Book

Your profile Start each unit by talking about you, your life and the unit topic

Word profile Focus on the different meanings of important words and phrases

Easy to find exam tasks

Talking points Give your opinion on the topic in the text

Corpus challenge Take the grammar challenge and learn from common mistakes

Prepare to write Learn useful tips to help you plan and check your writing

Video Watch interviews with teenagers like you

Prepare to speak Learn useful words and phrases for effective communication

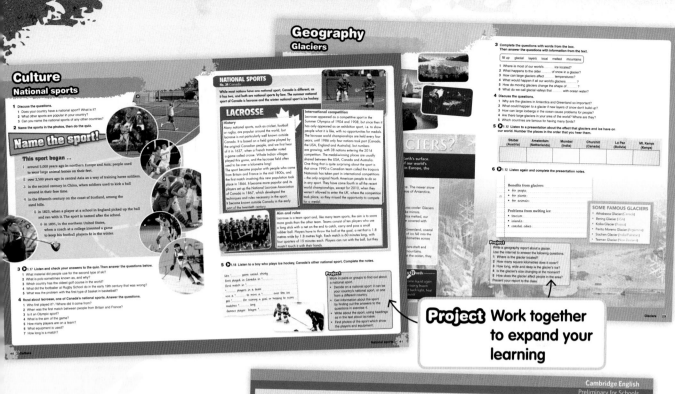

Culture Read useful tips, practise techniques, then try a taster exam task — see excerpts below.

Project Work together to expand your learning

Exam profile Read useful tips, practise techniques, then try a taster exam task

Review Check your progress

Video Watch teenagers doing speaking tasks in an exam situation

Look through your book and do the quiz with your partner.

1 What is the topic of Unit 9?

2 In which unit can you find something that children make with snow?

3 In which unit can you find a photo of a big cat?

4 In which unit can you find out what kind of friend you are?

5 Can you find a famous Portuguese footballer? Who is he? What page is he on?

1 Going shopping

VOCABULARY Shopping

Your profile

Where do you usually go shopping?
Which is your favourite shop? Why?

1 Look at the photos. What different things can you buy in these places? Compare your answers with your partner.

3 ▶1.02 **Complete the sentences with the words in the box. Then listen again and check.**

> change   charge   charges   discount
> online shopping   receipt   refunds
> send … back   serves   shop   spend

1 Eva says that markets are probably her favourite place to .... She says you don't have to .... much money there. If you're a tourist, sometimes they can .... you high prices.

2 Allan thinks that .... is the best thing ever. He says if you spend a certain amount, you don't have to pay the delivery .... If it's not right, you can usually .... the items ....

3 Marty's favourite department store was offering a 10% .... on some games. He says they are really good about ....

4 Elena thinks it's nice when you know the person who .... you.

5 Bonnie likes little shops. She says if you buy something and it's not right, you can .... it. You just have to show them the ....

4 **You are going to ask your partner some questions about the last item they bought. Write the questions using these words. Then ask the questions.**

0 shop / department store
   Did you shop in a department store?

1 get / a receipt

2 how much / spend

3 who / serve you

4 get / a discount

2 ▶1.02 **Listen to five teenagers talking about these different places to shop. Match each speaker to one of the photos in exercise 1.**

Eva

Bonnie

Marty

Elena

Allan

5 **Discuss the questions.**

1 Do you keep the receipts for things you buy? Why? / Why not?

2 How often do you or your parents do online shopping?

3 Do you enjoy going to shops where you know the person who serves you?

4 What was the last time you got a discount?

5 Have you ever sent an item back? Why?

READING

1 Read the title of the article. Why do you think teens aren't allowed in the mall? Read the article quickly to check.

N◯ TEENS ALLOWED

DO YOU go shopping on your own? Lots of teenagers spend Saturday afternoons in shopping malls without their parents, but for some unlucky teenagers, this is going to come to an end. The Store is one of America's biggest shopping malls, popular with local shoppers and tourists from different countries. With a theme park inside it, it's especially popular with young people, but it is no longer going to allow unaccompanied teenagers. If you are under the age of 15, you won't be able to hang out with your friends during quite a lot of the holiday season this year. 'Last year there was quite a bit of trouble with young people during the holiday shopping season,' said Jackie First, who works for Safety First, the security company at The Store. 'So this year we are increasing our parental escort policy (PEP), which says that parents must stay with children and young people inside The Store.'

SO, what does this mean? Well, at the moment the parental escort policy says that no one under the age of 15 can enter The Store on Fridays or Saturdays after 4 p.m. alone. But now they will have this rule on other days, including some school holidays.

Jackie First explained, 'The main problem is that some parents think The Store is a babysitter. There were quite a few kids aged ten here on their own. These kids are just hanging around in the mall, they aren't doing anything and they aren't spending any money.'

The Store will introduce the new rule on Thursday.

Post your comments here

A lot of us teenagers go to shopping malls just to be with our friends, but there are some teenagers who annoy others, and that kind of thing. But that's only a few kids. It's not all of us. It's not fair.

Stacey

There aren't many places for us to go but The Store is great. We can meet our friends, check out the shops, you know, and we usually meet there for birthday parties. It definitely won't be the same if we have to have our parents with us.

Tarah

I don't have much money so if I have to go shopping with my dad, he'll have to pay for things! Cool!

Luke

2 🔵 Read the article again and the comments. Are the sentences correct or incorrect?

1 People from other parts of the world visit The Store.
2 There are only shops in The Store.
3 The PEP means that teens under the age of 15 have to be with someone older.
4 Jackie First mentioned bad behaviour from some teens as a reason for changes to the PEP.
5 Jackie First agrees with parents who allow young children to go there on their own.
6 Tarah and her friends use the mall as a location in which to celebrate something.
7 Luke can afford to buy things when he is out with his father.

3 Match the highlighted words and phrases in the article to the meanings.

1 finish
2 a person who takes care of young children
3 start
4 without anyone else
5 difficulty

4 Read the comments that the teens posted. Who …

1 talks about the reasons for the rule?
2 thinks the new rule will be good?
3 will have to find a different place for special occasions?

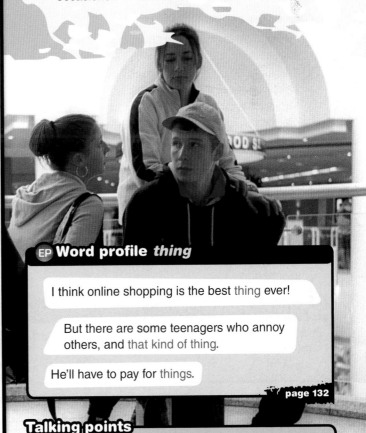

EP Word profile *thing*

I think online shopping is the best thing ever!

But there are some teenagers who annoy others, and that kind of thing.

He'll have to pay for things.

> **page 132**

Talking points

❝ Do you think it is sometimes necessary for malls to not allow unaccompanied teenagers?
Do you think people spend too much time shopping? Why? / Why not? ❞

GRAMMAR Determiners

1 Read the examples and look at the nouns after the bold words. Which are countable and which are uncountable?

1 *Last week my favourite department store was offering a 10% discount on* **some** *games.*
2 *They aren't spending* **any** *money.*
3 **No** *teens allowed.*
4 *It isn't* **much** *fun in the rain.*
5 *There aren't* **many** *places for us to go.*
6 *There are* **plenty of** *sites!*
7 *I have* **several** *store cards, you know, for my favourite shops.*
8 ***A lot of*** *teenagers go to shopping malls just to be with their friends.*

2 Complete the chart with the words. You can use some words more than once.

| ~~some~~ ~~any~~ many much plenty of |
| a lot of no several |

	Countable	Uncountable
Positive	some	
Negative	any	

→ Grammar reference **page 145**

3 Choose the correct words.

1 I want to do *many / some* shopping at the supermarket.
2 There are *much / several* shops here that sell shoes – we call it shoe street!
3 There are *a lot of / any* discounts in stores at the moment.
4 There aren't *several / any* shops that are open late on Thursdays.
5 There are *no / plenty of* mobile phones here that I like – let's try another shop.
6 It isn't *many / much* fun going clothes shopping on your own.
7 Have you got *many / much* discount cards?
8 There are *several / any* places I go to regularly at this market.

⊘ Corpus challenge

Find and correct the mistake in the student's sentence.

I have so much photos on my phone!

---

4 Complete the conversation with the words in the box.

| any many much no |
| several plenty ~~some~~ some |

A: What are you doing?
B: I'm looking for **(0)** ..some.. information about **(1)** .... trainers. I went to the *Sports On* website but there weren't **(2)** .... in my size – not even one pair! So I'm looking again.
A: I'm surprised. There are **(3)** .... of websites for online stuff. Have you tried this one: www.allmytrainers.com?
B: Not yet! I can't see **(4)** .... places that sell these particular trainers – look, there are only one or two.
A: True! But click here. There you are! And it looks like there are **(5)** .... models listed here in fluorescent green like you want.
B: Cool!
A: How **(6)** .... money were they in the shop?
B: About $100, I think.
A: OK, click here for more information. Oh dear!
B: What? Tell me!
A: Well, I'm sorry, but there are **(7)** .... trainers in your size!

VOCABULARY *any*

1 Read the examples. What other words and phrases do you know with *any*? Which uses of *any* have a positive meaning?

1 *They aren't doing* **anything**.
2 *I love shopping* **anywhere***, so I don't really mind where I go.*
3 *Try these batteries. Are they* **any** *good?*

2 Complete the sentences with the words and phrases in the box.

| ~~any~~ any more any longer anywhere |
| anything anyone any better any good |

0 I don't mind about the colour – *any colour will do.*
1 I can't eat .... – I'm full! That was delicious.
2 I can't find my school bag .... Where did I put it?
3 I don't mind what I have – I'll eat .... – I'm so hungry!
4 Has .... got David's number? I need to call him today.
5 Maria doesn't work in this shop ....
6 This book isn't .... – it's so boring.
7 Tony isn't feeling .... today – perhaps you could come back tomorrow.

WRITING   A short text

1 Read about a competition in a magazine. What do you have to write about?

COMPETITION!

Tell us about the last cool thing you bought. Where did you buy it? Why did you choose it? What do your mates think of it? Send us an email at itsallaboutyou@teen.com. We'll include the best texts in our magazine!

Maria, aged 15

Last week I was at the mall and I went into Blue Sky, which is my favourite store. You can find lots of cool things for your room there. I saw these cute money banks in the shape of a camper van! And there was a 10% discount! I'm saving up some money for my summer holiday, so now I've got somewhere to keep it. Now my best friend wants one too!

Rachel, aged 15

Mum was going to get these super trainers for me at the end of the month but I couldn't wait any longer, so I bought them myself. I got them from the local sports shop near my house. Several of my friends already had pink ones but I wanted to be different. So I got some green and grey ones! Plenty of people have asked me where I got them but I'm not telling anyone my secret store!

Mitch, aged 14

Last week I bought some really cool sunglasses from a shop in my town called J&L. J&L is a great shop that sells sunglasses and other things like hats and scarves. There are lots of styles to choose from, but I chose these ones because I just loved them! Several people have already told me I look good in these sunglasses!

2 Read the three texts. Which thing do you think is the coolest?

3 Read the *Prepare* box. Then read Mitch's text again. Underline the sentences that answer the competition questions. What extra information does he add?

Prepare to write—Completing a task

When you write an answer to something:
- answer all the questions.
- add some extra information.
- use a range of different tenses and structures.

4 Read Maria's text again. Underline all the different tenses and structures that she uses.

5 Read about the competition again. You are going to write a short text about something you bought recently. Plan your ideas and make some notes. Here are some ideas to help you.
- What is your cool thing?
- Where did you buy it?
- Why did you choose it?
- What do your friends think?
- Extra information?

6 Write your own short text.
- Use the tips in the *Prepare* box.
- Write about 60 words.
- Remember to check your spelling and grammar.

VOCABULARY   Personality adjectives

1 Read the quiz and choose the five sentences that are most true for you.

Your profile
How important are friends to you?
What makes a good friend, in your opinion?

WHAT KIND OF A FRIEND ARE YOU?

I say 'Well done' to my friends when they do something well.

I love my friends, but I enjoy being on my own as well.

If my friends have a problem, then I'll listen.

I love hanging out with a big group of friends.

I hang out with my friends if I have spare time.

My friends trust me with their secrets.

My friends are sometimes a bit annoying.

I'd do anything to help my best friends.

I love laughing, especially when I feel silly!

I sometimes feel a bit anxious in situations where there are lots of people.

I have lots of best friends – girls and boys!

I prefer to listen to other people's ideas, although I sometimes have good ideas too.

2 Read the descriptions below. Do you agree with what the quiz says about you?

1 Mostly blue
Brilliant best friend

You're a **reliable** best friend. And you're also kind, **honest** and caring, and your friends know how **sensible** you are! You're a sweet person and it's no surprise that you love having people around you.

2 Mostly yellow
The fun friend

You've got loads of friends and you're **easygoing**! You love having fun and you'd never be **cruel** to anyone. People love having you at parties! Go, **sociable** you!

3 Mostly green
The part-time pal

You've only got a few friends at the moment, but that's OK! Be **confident** about making new friends. You're **talented** and **intelligent** – now is the time to get out there and share! Friends can be fun!

3 Match the **words** in exercises 1 and 2 to the meanings.
1 making you feel angry
2 able to learn and understand things easily
3 unkind and unpleasant to people
4 able to be trusted or believed
5 behaving in a careful way that shows a lot of thought
6 enjoying being with people
7 worried and nervous
8 telling the truth
9 relaxed and calm
10 certain about your ability to do things well
11 behaving in a way that does not show much thought
12 having a natural ability to do something

4 ▶1.03 Listen to Eva and Marty talking about the quiz. What kind of friends are they?

5 Discuss the questions.
1 How would you describe yourself? What is your best personal quality?
2 What qualities does your best friend have?

READING

1 Read Eva's profile. How would you describe her?

2 Read Eva's blog post. Tick the points that she makes.

1 Friendships are more important than family.
2 People have their own ideas about friendships.
3 A friend is often someone who has the same interests as you.
4 Some people have difficulty in being friends.
5 Only sociable people have friends.

Hi! I'm Eva! I'm 14 years old and I live in Australia. I love studying science at school and in my free time you can find me on the beach with my friends.

http:ourclassblog.com

a blog by students for students!

Written by Eva, member since 2013. View profile

I did a quiz about friendship the other day. It was interesting and it got me thinking. Some people say the friends that we make at school will always be our friends. But is this really true? And what does friendship mean?

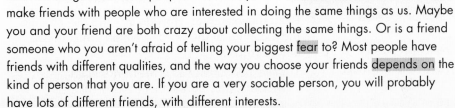

Firstly, who are our friends? I guess friends mean different things to different people. We usually make friends with people who are interested in doing the same things as us. Maybe you and your friend are both crazy about collecting the same things. Or is a friend someone who you aren't afraid of telling your biggest fear to? Most people have friends with different qualities, and the way you choose your friends depends on the kind of person that you are. If you are a very sociable person, you will probably have lots of different friends, with different interests.

However, some people are not very good at being friends. For example, they may get tired of hearing about your problems – especially if they have their own reasons to be anxious.

My best friend and I are really close, and I love imagining that we're always going to be best friends. But I know that as we grow older, we'll develop differently and so we may not always be close friends. She may not live close to me, so I may not see her very often. We'll probably disagree about a lot of things, too. But that's part of friendship, so I'm sure we'll always be friends. Here's a photo of us together!

Wasabiboy
I like this post Eva, and I think you're right. Some people are good at keeping in touch with friends, but other people just don't bother. Nowadays with social media it's really easy to find out how people are and tell them what you're doing. But it's important to remember the difference between social media friends and real friends.

Surfingforever45 @wasabiboy
Yep, I agree with you. I have lots of online pals and we're keen on playing the same online games and stuff, but it's true, they don't really know me. I don't think boys think about friends as much as girls. It's really uninteresting! But I like the way you wrote your ideas Eva!

3 Read Eva's blog post again and the comments. Who says …?

1 I'm sure I'll always be friends with my best friend.
2 I have friends who share the same hobbies as me.
3 It's easier to communicate with friends now.
4 Online friends aren't the same as friends in real life.
5 Having different ideas is part of being friends.
6 Boys aren't interested in talking about friends.

4 Match the highlighted words in the blog post to the meanings.

1 is influenced by
2 friends
3 something you are afraid of
4 don't have the same opinion
5 continuing to communicate with someone through phone, letter, texts, etc.
6 very interested in something

EP Word profile *close*

My friend and I are really close.

We may not always be close friends.

The museum closes at six o'clock.

page 132

Talking points

❝ Do you think that the friends people make at school will always be their friends? Why? / Why not?

What are the differences between online friends and real friends? ❞

GRAMMAR -ing forms

1 **Read the examples and complete the rules with the correct words.**

1 *I love **imagining** that we're always going to be friends.*
2 *Some people are good at **keeping** in touch.*
3 *They are interested in **doing** the same things as us.*

> -ing form   preposition   -ing form

> **a** After some verbs such as *enjoy* and *hate* we use the ....
> **b** Some adjectives are followed by a .... and then by the ....

→ Grammar reference **page 146**

2 **Complete the sentences with the -ing form of the verbs in the box.**

> go   prepare   study   watch   work   visit

1 I don't mind .... to the cinema with my parents occasionally.
2 I love .... action movies.
3 The girls enjoyed .... a presentation together for their English class.
4 David can't stand .... at the café after school.
5 Marcia is interested in .... at a university in her home town.
6 I don't really like .... museums.

3 **Match the sentence halves.**

1 Jo is afraid
2 Mike is good
3 Jackie is keen
4 Nina is crazy
5 Phil is interested

a about playing online games with her friends.
b of disappointing her friends.
c on going to football matches with friends.
d in making music in the school band.
e at listening to other people's problems.

4 ⬤ **Complete the second sentence so that it means the same as the first. Use no more than three words.**

1 My best friend Jake and I really love playing online games together.
 My best friend Jake and I .... on playing online games together.
2 Jake knows how to play online games really well.
 Jake is very good .... online games.
3 He likes to learn about new techniques.
 He's interested .... new techniques.
4 He doesn't like it when he loses more than two games.
 He can't .... more than two games.
5 Jake is crazy about improving his score.
 Jake really wants .... his score.

5 **Complete the sentences about yourself. Compare your sentences with your classmates. Find someone who has similar ideas.**

> *I'm good at scoring goals!*

1 I'm good at …
2 I'm afraid of …
3 I'm keen on …
4 I'm crazy about …
5 I'm tired of …
6 I'm interested in …

⊘ Corpus challenge

Find and correct the mistake in the student's sentence.

We love go out together to the cinema.

VOCABULARY Prefixes: *un-* and *dis-*

1 **Read the examples. How do *un-* and *dis-* change the meaning of the words? Which prefix do we add to verbs?**

1 *Talking about friends is really **interesting**! We'll probably **agree** about a lot of things.*
2 *Talking about friends is really **uninteresting**! We'll probably **disagree** about a lot of things.*

2 **Write the correct negative form of the words.**

1 pleasant
2 appear
3 happy
4 like
5 lucky
6 kind

3 **Read the text and complete it with the words in the box. Add a negative prefix to the words if necessary.**

> agree   appear   interesting
> kind   lucky   pleasant

Online friendships

Many people have an opinion about online friendships, especially parents. It can be really boring and [1] .... to talk about it. They always say the same thing! Last year, Mum had an [2] .... surprise – an old classmate contacted her and started posting old photos of her online. My sister and I thought it was funny, but Mum didn't! Fortunately, Mum just closed her page and the classmate [3] .... Another friend told me about someone who was writing [4] .... things about her on her wall. That's not nice! I'm very [5] .... because nothing like that has happened to me. But I [6] .... when people say you have to be careful about the online world.

LISTENING

1 Look at the photo. What do you think is happening?

2 Read the notes. What are they about? What kind of information is missing in each space?

> **HOMEWORK PROJECT**
> A **(1)** .... Quiz
> Ask friends and **(2)** ....
> Book to choose character from **(3)** ....
> Minimum number of questions to write **(4)** ....
> Date to hand in project **(5)** ....
> Teacher's email address **(6)** .... @school.com

3 ● ▶1.04 Listen and complete the notes in exercise 2.

SPEAKING Talking about yourself

1 ▶1.05 Listen to an interview with Anne-Marie and Faisal. Tick the questions that they answer. Do they just answer *yes* or *no*, or do they add more information?

	Faisal	Anne-Marie
1 What's your name?		
2 How old are you?		
3 What's your surname?		
4 How do you spell that?		
5 Who do you sit next to in English?		
6 Where do you live?		
7 Do you study English?		
8 Do you like studying English?		
9 Do you listen to music?		
10 What's your favourite kind of music?		
11 Do you get up early or late?		
12 How often do you go to the cinema?		

2 ▶1.05 Read the *Prepare* box, then listen again. Which phrases do Anne-Marie and Faisal use?

Prepare to speak Talking about yourself

Talking about likes and dislikes
I like it because …
I don't like it because …
I prefer …

Talking about habits
I usually …
I sometimes …

Giving your opinion
I think it's …

3 ● Ask and answer the questions with a partner. Use phrases from the *Prepare* box to add more information.

1 What's your surname? How do you spell it?
2 Where are you from?
3 What's your house like?
4 Do you play sports? Why? / Why not?
5 When do you go to bed?
6 Do you read books? Why? / Why not?

Culture
Shopping around the world

1 **Discuss the questions.**

1 When do you usually go shopping?

2 Are there any special shopping days or times in your country? Why are they special?

2 ▶1.06 **These four times of the year are special for shopping in different countries. Can you guess which countries? Listen and check.**

> Cyber Monday   Dubai Shopping Festival   Black Friday   Golden Weeks

3 ▶1.06 **Listen again. When is each special time? What other facts do you learn about each one?**

4 **Look at the photos on page 19. Where do you think each one is? What do you think you can buy there? Read the texts and check your answers.**

5 **Read the texts carefully and choose the correct place or places.**

Where can you shop if you …

1 want the most fashionable things?

2 don't want to spend a lot of money?

3 want to have something to eat?

4 want to shop in the evening?

5 want to shop during the night?

6 don't want to spend time with tourists?

7 don't want to get wet in the rain?

8 want to have some entertainment as well as shop?

6 **Answer the questions and underline the words in the texts that give you the answer.**

1 Can Jintana only buy new things at Saphan Phut market?

2 Do you think that Villaggio Mall is cheaper or more expensive than the other places?

3 Does the Grand Bazaar have a roof?

4 Does Esen buy anything that she can use in cooking?

5 Why don't people drive to Moosonee?

7 ▶1.07 **Listen to a report on teenagers' shopping habits in the United States. Number the questions in the order you hear them.**

a Have you bought anything online in the last three months?

b Where do you usually get the money from when you go shopping?

c How often do you go shopping?

d Do you count shopping as one of your hobbies?

e Do you shop more instore or online?

f What do you buy when you go shopping?

8 ▶1.07 **Listen again and match five of the questions in exercise 7 to the results in the pie charts. Listen again to check.**

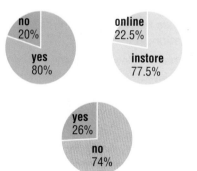

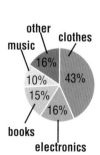

Project

Work in pairs or groups to find out about teenagers' shopping habits in your country.

- Write a short questionnaire. You can use the questions in exercise 7 or make up your own questions.
- Ask at least ten friends or classmates the questions and make notes of the answers.
- Make pie charts or graphs to show the answers.
- Display your results in class. Have you all got the same results?

WE ASKED YOU

TO SEND US INFORMATION ABOUT YOUR FAVOURITE SHOPPING EXPERIENCES AROUND THE WORLD.

HERE ARE JUST A FEW OF YOUR ANSWERS.

JINTANA

1 SAPHAN PHUT NIGHT MARKET

Thailand is well-known for its markets, and in Bangkok you can find a market on almost every street corner! My favourite is Saphan Phut market – it's a night market, so you can have an evening out there. It opens at about six, but is really busy by eight, and doesn't close until midnight. All the local teenagers go to it because it's cheap and it has a lot of second-hand stuff. Also, it isn't a tourist destination (yet!). I usually get my jeans and T-shirts there. It's also really good for its street-food stalls. It's very sociable – great for meeting friends, shopping and eating, all in the same place.

HARUN

2 VILLAGGIO MALL

You have to see Villaggio Mall in Doha to believe it – really! It's a huge shopping mall with all the main international shops, and designer label shops selling luxury goods, but it's extraordinary – it looks like an Italian town; I suppose that's because Italy is the centre of the fashion industry. It's even got a canal running through with Italian boats on it. How cool is that! Of course, it's got cinemas and restaurants too, and there's a new theme park for kids there now. It's open every day, most days from 9.00 in the morning till 11.00 at night, and you can easily fill those hours, believe me.

ESEN

3 THE GRAND BAZAAR

I'm sure you've heard of the Grand Bazaar in Istanbul – it's one of the biggest covered markets in the world. It consists of about 60 streets and about 5,000 shops selling everything you can think of, like antiques, jewellery, carpets and leather. Of course, it has clothes and electronic things, and other usual market stuff, at all prices, and lots of cafés and restaurants. I love shopping at the spice bazaar; it's so colourful and smells wonderful. The bazaar is open from 9.00 to 7.00 every day except Sunday. It gets incredibly busy, though, full of tourists every day. One unpleasant thing is that there are no toilets, but I think they're planning to modernise the bazaar soon.

THOMAS

4 MOOSONEE, CANADA

OK, I guess you're all wondering what unusual shopping experience there is in a tiny seaport with about 3,000 people in the north-east of Canada? Well, there isn't. My shopping experience is online shopping, because I do more or less all of my shopping online. Sure, we have a few shops, but mostly selling necessary things. There's no road access to Moosonee, so everything is brought here by rail or sea. Online shopping is great for everyone – it's quick, it's easy, you can send things back, and the shops are open 24 hours – but it's so important for people in places like Moosonee, where it's the only real opportunity we have for shopping.

3 Fun and games

VOCABULARY   Sports phrases

Your profile

Do you prefer team sports or individual sports? Why?
Which new sport or activity would you like to try?

1 **Look at the photos. Discuss the questions.**

1 Which are individual sports? Which are team sports?
2 Which of these sports can you do at your school?

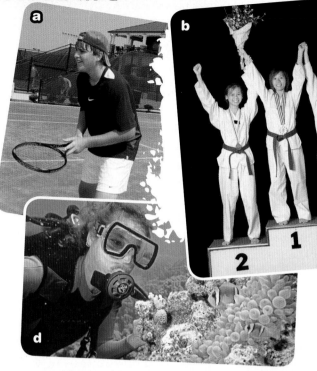

2 ▶1.08 **Listen to three people talking about sport. Which sports do they talk about?**

3 ▶1.08 **Listen again. Choose the correct words to complete the phrases.**

1 **enter** / **join** a competition or tournament
2 **win** / **score** a prize, medal, game or match
3 **have** / **join** a go at something
4 **score** / **win** a goal or point
5 **give** / **lose** a game or match
6 **win** / **beat** the other team
7 **join** / **enter** a club
8 **give** / **join** (someone) the chance
9 **miss** / **enter** an opportunity to do something

4 **Complete the email using some of the words from exercise 3.**

Hi Helen,

I've just got more information about the competition at the tennis club next week. I think I'm going to ¹ .... the .... because I like tennis, and it looks like fun. The competition isn't only for people who already play tennis. They want to ² .... people the .... to play, even if they aren't very good players. Why don't you ³ .... a .... at playing a few matches? It's all friendly and just for fun, so it doesn't matter if you ⁴ .... all your .... But if you do very well, you might ⁵ .... a ....!

I think they're looking for members for their club too. They're offering a 10% discount if you ⁶ .... the .... on the day. I hope you can make it – we don't want to ⁷ .... the .... to take part.

Text me if you want to know more,
Emma

5 **Look at the photos in exercise 1 again. Describe what is happening and what is going to happen in each one. Use the phrases from exercise 3.**

6 **Discuss the questions.**

1 Have you ever scored a goal in a game? How did you feel?
2 When did you last win or lose a match? How did you feel?
3 What new sports would you like to have a go at?

READING

1 Look at the photo and the title of the blog post. What is a buddy? What do you think BuddyBall is? Read the blog post quickly and check your ideas.

THINGSILIKETODO
.blogspot.com

BE A BUDDY

Posted by Pym on July 26th

Here's a picture of my friend Ally doing BuddyBall! I want to tell you about this really cool programme. My best friend and I help with it every summer in the holidays. It's absolutely awesome! We don't get paid, but we don't mind that, because it's fun and we like helping out. We just give them a few hours of our time every week as volunteers for BuddyBall, an organisation that helps kids with disabilities make new friends.

It provides the opportunity for children to take part in different sports. The kids do different sports at different times of the year – so football in autumn, basketball in winter and baseball in spring. In summer, we do lots of different sports with them. The programme works both ways. It gives these kids the chance to do sports which they don't normally have the opportunity to do, and we get the opportunity to try some new and exciting sports and make new friends.

So what does a buddy do? At the moment, I am a buddy for an eleven-year-old called Tom. He is in a wheelchair and is a good basketball player, but just like any kid, it upsets him if he misses a shot or makes a bad pass. He starts to cry and doesn't want to play. Sometimes he gets annoyed and

I can see that he wants to give in. So, as his buddy, I encourage him. At the moment, we're working on our basketball skills together. Now he's more confident. It's great to see how he has improved and he doesn't get upset so easily.

My friend Ally is a buddy for a kid called Clara. She hasn't got many language skills and is also a bit wild! She likes running away. Ally learned how to work with Clara and to get her to join in the games. Now she loves baseball and next week she's playing in a team. Even though she doesn't always pay attention to the coaches, she does well and has a good time. Her parents are extremely happy about the BuddyBall programme and they say that Clara is more confident and sociable after her BuddyBall sessions.

BuddyBall is a great opportunity for everyone! Differences disappear and we realise that we're all just kids who love playing sport. I love doing BuddyBall and it gives me so many rewards because I know I'm doing something really useful!

2 Read the blog post again and choose the correct words.

1 Pym does BuddyBall because *it's part of his school programme / he enjoys doing it.*
2 The sports programme *stays the same / changes* for each season.
3 By doing this programme, the disabled children have the chance to *do different sports / concentrate on a single sport.*
4 The programme gives opportunities for learning to *the disabled children / everyone who takes part.*
5 Tom can *deal with not doing well / score goals* more easily now.
6 Clara still needs to learn to *listen to the instructors / play the games properly.*
7 Her parents say that BuddyBall has helped Clara *win more games / make more friends.*
8 Pym enjoys BuddyBall because he's *helping other people / doing something different.*

3 Match the highlighted words in the text to the meanings.

a good things that you get as a result of doing something
b gives people something they need
c an official group of people who work together for the same purpose
d got better at something
e watch or listen to something carefully

This blog has 533 followers. ➡ Follow this blog.

Talking points

" How important is it to do sports regularly? Why?

Why do some people like taking part in sports competitions?

What are the benefits of using your free time to help others? "

EP Word profile *give*

We just give them a few hours of our time a week.

It gives these kids the chance to do sports.

Sometimes he wants to give in.

page 132

GRAMMAR Present simple and continuous

1 Match examples to the rules.

1 *My best friend and I **help** with it every summer.*
2 *At the moment, we**'re working** on our basketball skills.*
3 *Next week, she**'s playing** in the team.*
4 *Sometimes I can see that he **wants** to give in.*
5 *The organisation **helps** disabled kids.*

> We use the present simple:
> **a** to talk about something that we do regularly.
> **b** to talk about a fact, system or process.
> **c** with state verbs (*want, like, love*, etc.) which describe what we like, think and feel.
> We use the present continuous:
> **d** to talk about things that are happening now.
> **e** to talk about future plans that we are sure about.

→ Grammar reference **page 147**

2 Choose the correct form of the verbs.

1 I *meet / 'm meeting* Maria later today.
2 I usually *am getting up / get up* at about 7 am.
3 My parents *are coming / come* from France.
4 Our class *is visiting / visits* a castle tomorrow.
5 *Do you think / Are you thinking* you really know all your friends on your social media sites?
6 My brother *likes / is liking* the same music as you.
7 *I'm trying / I try* to finish this before dinner time.

⊘ Corpus challenge

Find and correct the mistake in the student's sentence.

I write this letter to invite you to have a picnic with me at the park.

3 Read the poster about a swimming competition. Complete the conversation with the correct form of the verb in brackets.

4TH ANNUAL
BLACKLODGE CHARITY
SWIMMING COMPETITION
Fri–Sat, Nov 29th–30th
$15 per swimmer – pay in advance.
Registration forms from www.blacklodgeswim.com
For more information call: 02-999-98767

A: What [1] .... (you / do) at the moment?
B: I [2] .... (fill) in this form for the swimming competition. The club [3] .... (hold) a competition every year. [4] .... (you / want) to enter too?
A: Maybe. But I'm not a very good swimmer.
B: It doesn't matter. It's for charity. We [5] .... (choose) a different charity each year. This year we [6] .... (help) disabled children. And it only [7] .... (cost) 15 dollars! Come on! There are lots of fun races.
A: Oh well, yes, OK! That [8] .... (sound) like a good thing to do. Pass me a form!

4 Think about a sports hero. Make notes, then present your hero to the class. Try to use a variety of tenses and think about these questions:

Where / from?
Where / live?
Current club / team?
Important games / matches?
Rafael Nadal lives in Majorca. At the moment, he's probably practising tennis.

VOCABULARY Strong adjectives and adverbs

1 Look at the pictures. Which adjective has a stronger meaning?

It's **cold**.   It's **freezing**.

2 Put the adjectives in the right column.

> ancient   bad   big   ~~cold~~   enormous
> exhausted   ~~freezing~~   old   terrible   tired

Normal adjectives	Strong adjectives
cold	freezing

3 Read the examples and complete the chart.

1 *BuddyBall is a **very** good opportunity for everyone.*
2 *It's **absolutely** awesome!*
3 *Her parents are **extremely** happy about the BuddyBall programme.*

With normal adjectives	.... , ... , incredibly, really
With strong adjectives	.... , really

4 Complete the sentences. Use the adverbs in the chart in exercise 3. More than one adverb is sometimes possible.

1 My brother is .... good at tennis.
2 All the players were .... exhausted by the end of the tournament.
3 The medals that we won were .... big.
4 The crowd at the Cup Final was .... enormous.
5 The weather was .... freezing!
6 Josh is .... unhappy about missing the final.
7 The result was .... terrible – we lost 6–2!
8 The football team played a/an .... brilliant match and won 4–1.

WRITING An online comment

1 Read the advertisement. What other sports do you think would be good for BuddyBall? Why?

BuddyBall

WE NEED YOU!

We want more sports and activities for BuddyBall! Tell us what you would include and explain why it would be good for the kids. Post your ideas online!

2 Read Nat and Zoe's online comments. Then answer the questions.

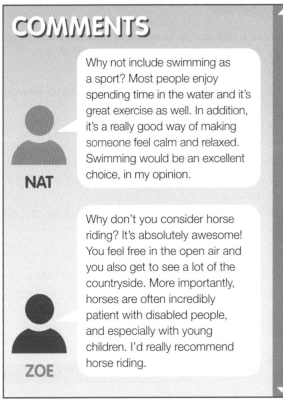

COMMENTS

NAT

Why not include swimming as a sport? Most people enjoy spending time in the water and it's great exercise as well. In addition, it's a really good way of making someone feel calm and relaxed. Swimming would be an excellent choice, in my opinion.

ZOE

Why don't you consider horse riding? It's absolutely awesome! You feel free in the open air and you also get to see a lot of the countryside. More importantly, horses are often incredibly patient with disabled people, and especially with young children. I'd really recommend horse riding.

1 What sport does Nat suggest for BuddyBall?
2 How many reasons does he give for including it?
3 How does he link his reasons?
4 Which activity does Zoe mention?
5 What is her main reason for including it?

3 Read the *Prepare* box. What phrases do Nat and Zoe use to make suggestions? What other phrase could you use to suggest something?

Prepare to write Suggestions and comments

When you post your ideas online:
- explain your reasons clearly and link them: *also ... , ... as well.*
- use different phrases for making suggestions.
- use positive words and phrases to recommend something.

4 Underline the positive words and phrases that Nat and Zoe use to recommend their sport or activity.

5 Read the task below and plan your ideas.

> We're planning a new sports club in this town. We want ideas for sports for teenagers to do.
>
>)(suggest one sport the club should offer for teenagers
> ⚽ explain why you think teenagers would enjoy this sport
>)(say why this sport would be good for the club.
>
> *Post your comments here!*

6 Write your comment.
- Use the tips in the *Prepare* box.
- Write 35–45 words.
- Remember to check your spelling and grammar.

4 From fire to snow

VOCABULARY Extreme weather

1 Look at the photos. What is happening in each one? Which do you think is the scariest? Why?

2 ▶1.09 Listen to three people talking about extreme weather. Match each person to a photo. Which photo isn't needed?

3 ▶1.09 Listen again. Are the sentences true or false?

Speaker 1
1 The speaker didn't listen to the weather **forecast**.
2 There was no **power** in the city for a while.

Speaker 2
3 The speaker saw a fire **tornado**.
4 There was a lot of **lightning** in the sky.
5 The fire **burnt down** more than one building.
6 The high winds **blew** a bus **away**.

Speaker 3
7 The speaker didn't know what to do when there was a **flood**.
8 The river **rose** by three metres.
9 It stopped **pouring** in the evening.
10 Dirty water **flowed** along the street.

4 Match the words in exercise 3 to the meanings.
1 raining a lot
2 destroyed by fire
3 energy, usually electricity, that is used to provide light and heat
4 moved by the wind
5 a report saying what the weather is likely to be like
6 light that appears in the sky during a storm
7 a large amount of water covering an area that is usually dry
8 an extremely dangerous wind that blows in a circle
9 moved along without stopping
10 increased in level

5 Discuss the questions with your own ideas.
1 What should you do in case of a flood or lightning?
2 How accurate are weather forecasts?
3 Has your home or school ever been without power? When?

EP Word profile *case*

No one expected the amount we got in this case.

We all know what to do in case of a flood.

He put the sand bags by the front door, just in case!

page 133

READING

1 Read the article quickly and decide on the best title (a–c). Don't worry about the spaces yet.

  a Firefighters in Australia unable to take a break

  b Canberra's hot weather seems likely to continue

  c Weather conditions create something unusual

Over a four-month period last year, Australian firefighters put out a large **(0)** .... of fires. But a few years earlier, one fire grew so powerful that it **(1)** .... a tornado nearly 500 metres wide. The fire hit the capital city, Canberra, **(2)** .... the summer and destroyed many homes. These houses were situated less than 100 metres from a large **(3)** .... of pine trees planted for business **(4)** .... on the edge of the city.

(5) .... small fires started burning to the west of Canberra around January 9 and, because it was difficult for firefighters to **(6)** .... them, they continued to burn and became stronger each day. Then, on January 18, the wind speed **(7)** .... as the temperature rose to 40°C, **(8)** .... meant that the individual fires joined together. Scientists now **(9)** .... that this was Australia's first 'fire tornado'. It was an extremely rare **(10)** .... that was produced by the thunderstorms accompanying the fire.

2 Look at the example space (0) and the possible answers. The correct answer is A. Why? Complete sentences a–c below with answers B–D.

  0 **A** number   **B** sum   **C** figure   **D** total

  a I don't know the exact cost, but I know it's a six- .... number.

  b They offered me a large .... of money.

  c If you add the numbers together, the .... is 207.

3 ⬤ Choose the correct word for each space (1–10) in the article.

1 A handled	**B** created	**C** presented	**D** developed
2 A for	**B** along	**C** during	**D** since
3 A land	**B** area	**C** size	**D** part
4 A reasons	**B** facts	**C** aims	**D** answers
5 A Plenty	**B** All	**C** Lot	**D** Several
6 A arrive	**B** get	**C** reach	**D** travel
7 A increased	**B** added	**C** lifted	**D** turned
8 A whose	**B** which	**C** who	**D** where
9 A describe	**B** tell	**C** imagine	**D** believe
10 A play	**B** issue	**C** event	**D** matter

4 Read the article again and answer the questions.

  1 Why did so many houses burn down?

  2 Why couldn't the firefighters put out the fires before January 18?

  3 How does a fire tornado happen?

5 Imagine you are reporting a TV news story about an extreme weather event. In pairs, decide what happened. Then follow the instructions below and practise reporting your news story.

Student A (speaking in the studio)

- Start with a dramatic piece of information from the studio.

  All schools are closed today because of …

- Introduce your local reporter.

  And here is … in …

Student B (reporting from the local area)

- Describe what has happened in an interesting way.

  The extreme weather overnight came as a complete surprise. First, there was …

- Say what will happen next.

  The most urgent thing to deal with will be …

- Say who you are and return to the studio.

  This is … and now back to the studio.

Student A

- Thank your reporter and make a final comment about the news story.

  Thank you very much, Ana. Let's hope that …

Talking points

  What kinds of extreme weather cause the most problems for people? Why?

  Will people ever be able to control the weather? Why? / Why not?

GRAMMAR Past simple

1 **Match the examples to the rules.**

1 *Over a four-month period last year, Australian firefighters **put out** a large number of fires.*

2 *One fire **grew** so powerful that it **created** a tornado.*

3 *On January 18, the temperature **rose** to 40 degrees C.*

> We use the past simple to talk about:
> **a** a single completed past action or event.
> **b** something that happened at a particular time in the past.
> **c** things that happened regularly in the past.

→ Grammar reference **page 148**

2 **Underline the irregular verbs in the examples in exercise 1. What are their infinitive forms?**

3 **Read the text. Complete it with the correct past simple form of the verbs.**

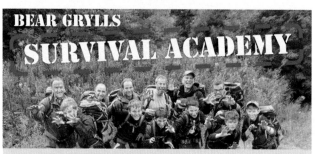

BEAR GRYLLS
SURVIVAL ACADEMY

The 24-Hour Family Course

Mum [0] *booked*. Dad and me on this course as a surprise! I [1] .... (feel) a bit nervous before we [2] .... (get) there, but it was great fun and we both [3] .... (learn) so much. There were five other people about my age, and each [4] .... (come) with one parent – mostly super-keen Dads! The course [5] .... (not begin) until midday on Saturday and [6] .... (include) one night outside under the stars. They [7] .... (give us) our own backpack in which we [8] .... (carry) all the things we [9] .... (need). We [10] .... (hike) through some difficult countryside and we even [11] .... (cross) a river at one point. They [12] .... (teach) us how to build and light a fire. We [13] .... (dig) for food, [14] .... (build) our own basic sleeping accommodation, and they [15] .... (tell) us how to protect ourselves in extreme weather. We all [16] .... (sleep) really well because we were exhausted! The next morning was all about 'self-rescue' – they [17] .... (split) us up into different groups and we [18] .... (find) our way back to the main building, where they [19] .... (give) us a badge and a certificate. Dad and I both [20] .... (say) this experience was the best present ever!

⊘ Corpus challenge

Find and correct the mistake in the student's sentence.

I meet him when I was on holiday last year.

used to

4 **Read the examples and the rules. Match each example to a use, a or b, in the rules.**

1 *My family **used to live** just outside Canberra.*

2 *As kids, we **used to spend** every August with our grandparents.*

3 *How **did** people **used to keep** warm during the long, cold winters?*

4 *Summers in Britain **didn't used to be** as wet as they are now.*

5 *Nick **didn't used to come** snowboarding with us, but now he loves it.*

> We use *used to* to talk about:
> **a** something that happened or didn't happen regularly in the past.
> **b** a permanent situation in the past that is no longer the case.
> For questions and negative forms we can use either *used to* or *use to*.

→ Grammar reference **page 148**

5 **What things did/didn't you used to do when you were ten years old? Write six sentences that are true for you. Use phrases from the box.**

> belong to a sports team
> do my homework on time
> go to shopping centres alone
> hang out with different friends
> play loads of computer games
> text friends
> stay in every night
> watch a lot of TV
> wear make-up

VOCABULARY Phrasal verbs

1 **Complete the sentences with the correct form of the phrasal verbs in the box.**

> blow away   burn down   come out   hang out
> put out   split up

1 The shop we used to go to for sweets .... in a fire last month and they aren't going to rebuild it.

2 When we were camping, we didn't used to .... our camp fire .... overnight, but it was quite safe.

3 I left my essay on the wall outside for a minute and all the pages .... in the wind!

4 I used to be in a bigger class, but they .... us .... into two groups.

5 It was pouring earlier today, but then the sun .... again.

6 How often did you use to .... with friends instead of studying?

2 **Write three sentences using phrasal verbs from exercise 1. Read your sentences to a partner.**

LISTENING

1 Look at the photo of Mt Bachelor in Oregon. Imagine you got lost in the snow. What would you do?

2 ● ▶1.10 You will hear an interview with a teenage boy called Jake, who got lost on a snowy mountain in Oregon, USA. Read the six questions. Then listen and try to answer the questions, choosing A, B or C.

1 What happened to Jake's skis?
   A He carried them down the mountain.
   B He left them where they came off.
   C He hid them both in the deep snow.

2 Jake stopped walking down the mountain because
   A it was too dark for him to reach the bottom.
   B there was still a lot of snow falling from the sky.
   C he couldn't remember what to do from the TV shows.

3 What was good about Jake's snow cave?
   A It was built on flat ground.
   B It allowed him to remove his gloves.
   C It kept him completely out of the wind.

4 Who was out looking for Jake that evening?
   A a single helicopter
   B groups of people on foot
   C both of his parents

5 What part of Bear Grylls' advice did Jake follow in the woods?
   A search for tracks in the snow
   B look for lights to aim at
   C walk on your hands and knees

6 While Jake was missing, his mother
   A tried to contact him on her cellphone.
   B thought that not enough people were looking for him.
   C managed to stay positive by thinking about him.

3 ▶1.10 Compare your answers with a partner. Then listen again and check.

4 Do you think Jake did the right thing? How brave was he?

SPEAKING   Talking about past experiences

1 ▶1.11 Read the questions. Then listen to Mariann's answers. What verb forms does she use to talk about her past experiences?

1 What was your favourite outdoor activity as a child?
2 How much time did you spend outdoors when you were younger?
3 Tell us about the things you did during good weather.

2 ▶1.11 Complete the text with the missing verbs. Then listen again and check.

Mariann ⁰ *...used to live...* in the mountains. She
¹ .... in the snow, and every winter, she ² ....
a snowman with her friends. In the summer, she
³ .... with her grandparents, who had a farm.
When the weather was good, she ⁴ .... in the river
and ⁵ .... flowers in the fields.

3 ▶1.11 Read the *Prepare* box. Then listen to Mariann's answers again. Which phrases does she use?

> ## Prepare to speak — Answering questions (1)
>
> **Asking when you are not sure you have understood**
> Do you mean … ?
> **Gaining time to think about your answer**
> Let me think. Um …
> Let me see. …
> Well, …
> **Adding more information**
> … that kind of thing.
> … , actually.

4 ● Ask and answer the questions in exercise 1. Say as much as you can about your own past experiences. Use phrases from the *Prepare* box.

Geography
Glaciers

1 Look at the photos. Then answer the quiz questions about glaciers.

1 **How much of our world's ice is in mountain areas?**
   a 5%   b 10%   c 15%

2 **Where can we find ice that is 2 kilometres deep?**
   a the Himalayas b Antarctica c the Andes

3 **Without glaciers, our world would be …**
   a colder.   b drier.   c warmer.

4 **Icebergs form when coastal glaciers …**
   a break up.   b build up.   c freeze.

5 **A fjord is a coastal … that fills up with water.**
   a beach   b hill   c valley

2 Read the fact-file about glaciers. Check your answers to the quiz in exercise 1.

WHAT ARE GLACIERS?

Glaciers are large, thick areas of ice. They cover about 10% of Earth's surface. About 95% of this ice is in Antarctica and Greenland. The rest of our world's glacial ice is located in cold, mountainous regions, like the Alps in Europe, the Himalayas in Asia, and the Andes in South America.

HOW DO GLACIERS FORM?

Glaciers form in very cold areas when snows build up over a very long time. The newer snow presses down on the older snow and changes it into solid ice. In some areas of Antarctica, the ice is more than 2 kilometres thick.

HOW DO GLACIERS AFFECT OUR PLANET?

❄ Glaciers have an effect on local climate because they keep local temperatures cooler. Glaciers also slow down global warming because they reflect sunlight into space, like mirrors.

❄ Without glaciers, the world would be a wetter place. If all the ice in Antarctica melted, our oceans would rise about 60 metres. Low islands and coastal areas would be covered with water.

❄ When glaciers melt, the water flows into rivers and lakes. In Antarctica and Greenland, coastal glaciers also break up in warmer weather. When this happens, large pieces of ice fall into the ocean and become icebergs. The largest icebergs can travel thousands of kilometres across the ocean before they finally melt.

❄ Glaciers can change the shape of the land under them. When it's warm, glaciers melt and move. When this happens, they can break down large rocks, hills and even mountains.

❄ Glaciers also cut valleys into the land when they move. If these valleys end at the ocean, they can also fill up with water. We call these underwater valleys *fjords*.

Did you know?

➤ Glaciers contain about 69% of our fresh water. The rest is in lakes and rivers or deep under the ground.

➤ Ice caps are glaciers that cover a large area. If they cover more than 50,000 km² they're called ice sheets.

Key Words

melt become liquid again after being frozen

reflect send back light, heat or sound

3 Complete the questions with words from the box.
Then answer the questions with information from the text.

> fill up   glacial   layers   local   melted   mountains

1 Where is most of our world's .... ice located?
2 What happens to the older .... of snow in a glacier?
3 How can large glaciers affect .... temperatures?
4 What would happen if all our world's glaciers .... ?
5 How do moving glaciers change the shape of .... ?
6 What do we call glacial valleys that .... with ocean water?

4 Discuss the questions.

1 Why are the glaciers in Antarctica and Greenland so important?
2 What could happen to a glacier if new layers of snow don't build up?
3 How can large icebergs in the ocean cause problems for people?
4 Are there large glaciers in your area of the world? Where are they?
5 Which countries are famous for having many fjords?

5 ▶1.12 **Listen to a presentation about the effect that glaciers and ice have on our world. Number the places in the order that you hear them.**

Stubai (Austria)	Amsterdam (Netherlands)	Mumbai (India)	Churchill (Canada)	La Paz (Bolivia)	Mt. Kenya (Kenya)

6 ▶1.12 **Listen again and complete the presentation notes.**

Benefits from glaciers:
• for people:
• for plants:
• for animals:

Problems from melting ice:
• tourism:
• islands:
• coastal cities:

SOME FAMOUS GLACIERS
• Athabasca Glacier (Canada)
• Bering Glacier (USA)
• Kolka Glacier (Russia)
• Perito Moreno Glacier (Argentina)
• Siachen Glacier (India/Pakistan)
• Tasman Glacier (New Zealand)

Project

Write a geography report about a glacier.
Use the internet to answer the following questions.
1 Where is the glacier located?
2 How many square kilometres does it cover?
3 How long, wide and deep is the glacier's ice?
4 Is the glacier's size changing at the moment?
5 How does the glacier affect people in the area?
Present your report to the class.

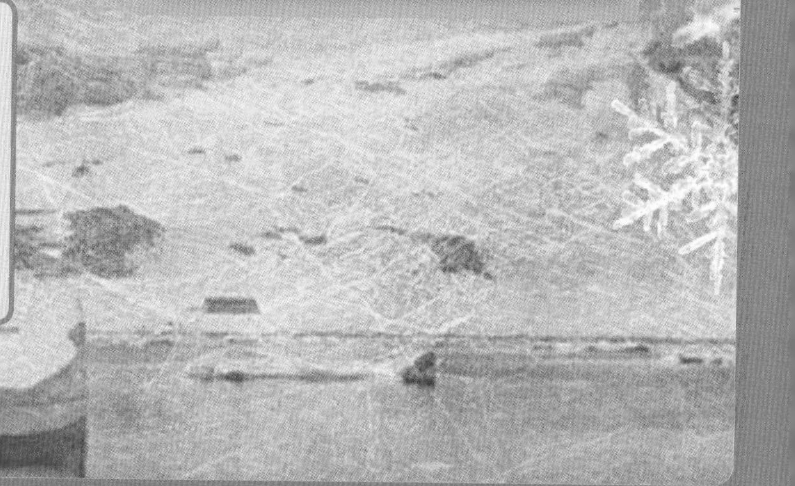

Review 1
Units 1-4

VOCABULARY

1 Match the sentence halves.

1 The shop changed the item
2 We scored a goal in the last minute and
3 The young tennis player was confident
4 It rained all night and I'm not surprised that
5 Mike is a talented chess player
6 I didn't receive the letter in time, so

a and she won a medal.
b there were a lot of floods.
c I missed the opportunity to go on the trip.
d we beat the other team.
e because I had a receipt.
f and he's just entered an international competition.

2 Complete the sentences with the words in the box.

> honest   lightning   refund
> send back   sociable   tornado

1 There was a really bad storm, with thunder and
   ....
2 I took the item back to the store and got a ....
3 You have to believe what he says. He's very ....
4 We had to .... the DVDs because they didn't work
   on our DVD player.
5 The .... caused a lot of damage to buildings.
6 Tess loves being with other people – she's very ....

**3 Complete each conversation with the correct form
of one of the pairs of words in the box.**

> burn down / cruel   charge / online shopping
> forecast / sensible   give / pour   join / serve
> miss / offer

1 **A:** Does the supermarket .... for delivery?
   B: Not if your .... order is over $100.
2 **A:** Did you see the .... on TV last night?
   B: Yes, it would be .... to take an umbrella.
   It's going to rain.
3 **A:** Did you know the girl who .... you in the shop?
   B: Yes, she .... the tennis club last week.
4 **A:** That's the house that .... last week.
   B: I know. I think someone did it deliberately. That's
   really .... !
5 **A:** That shop .... discounts to students on
   Thursdays.
   B: Well, we'd better go there. We don't want to ....
   the opportunity of a bargain!
6 **A:** It .... with rain all day on Sunday, didn't it?
   B: Yes, and it .... me the chance to do my
   homework.

**4 Unscramble the words and complete the
sentences.**

> caergh   eols a mtcah   eliltnetnig
> lrliebae   wopre   srie

1 If Mel says she'll do something, she will. She's very
   ....
2 Angela always knows the answer – she's really
   ....
3 Our team is the best – we didn't ....
   .... last year!
4 Everything went dark when the .... went off
   during the storm.
5 There was an extra .... for the store to
   deliver to our house.
6 It rained for days and we watched the water
   .... and get closer to our house.

GRAMMAR

**5 Choose the correct words to complete the
sentences.**

1 Lucy didn't buy *any* / *much* shoes on Saturday.
2 Sophia wants to buy *some* / *any* new pens for
   school.
3 There are *plenty* / *many* of places that sell
   accessories for phones.
4 I've haven't got *much* / *many* time – I have to go in
   10 minutes.
5 How *much* / *many* exercises do we have to do?
6 *Any* / *No* teens under the age of 18 can watch that
   film – it's for over-18s only.

**6 Complete the sentences with the *-ing* form of the
verbs in the box.**

> do   drive   eat   join   spend   visit

1 Jason considered .... a football club.
2 My mum couldn't stand .... sports when she
   was at school.
3 Jasmine and her mum enjoyed .... time
   together.
4 My Australian friend recommended .... the
   Sydney Opera House.
5 My brother doesn't mind .... me to your house.
6 She imagined herself .... an ice cream.

7 Complete the sentences with the correct forms of the verbs. Use the present simple or present continuous.

1 Mara .... (enjoy) going for a run every morning.
2 Look! The weather .... (get) worse.
3 I .... (know) the answer to the question.
4 It's a really expensive bike. It .... (cost) over $400.
5 She .... (read) an eBook on her phone at the moment.
6 Marcia and Maisy .... (meet) their friends at the shopping centre on Saturday.

8 Complete the article with the past simple forms of the verbs in the box.

> affect   be (x2)   burn   die   help
> lose   post   take   work

EVERY YEAR IN AUSTRALIA there are a lot of bushfires. In 2013, there [1] .... a particularly bad one that [2] .... an area called the Blue Mountains, very close to Sydney. My friend Olivia lives there and her house was very close to the fire. She said that the fire [3] .... for a long time and lots of people [4] .... their houses. Sadly, some animals [5] .... too. But the fire services [6] .... amazing and they [7] .... long hard hours to try to stop the fires. Olivia [8] .... lots of photos during the fires and she [9] .... them on her social media pages. She also [10] .... raise money to give to the people who lost their homes in the fire.

Corpus challenge

9 Tick the two sentences without mistakes. Correct the mistakes in the other sentences.

1 I have so much friends that I can't count them, but my best friend is Marina.
2 We don't have free time this weekend.
3 I'm writting to you to tell you that I have a new dog.
4 I like spending time with my friends.
5 He have a dog and a cat.
6 I'm sending you this letter to tell you about my holiday.
7 We go to the park last weekend.
8 She meet me at the cinema yesterday.

10 Read the text below and choose the correct word for each space.

ONLINE SHOPPING

Most people think that shopping **(0)** .... the internet is a recent development. However, an inventor called Michael Aldrich **(1)** .... the *Teleputer* in 1980. This **(2)** .... used a telephone, a TV and a computer, but it wasn't widely available until the invention of the World Wide Web in the **(3)** .... 1990s.

(4) .... of people began their online shopping experience by buying a book or a DVD, and it was **(5)** .... convenient. Goods arrived quickly and people could **(6)** .... items back if there was a problem.

But what **(7)** .... local shops? Do they have fewer customers? **(8)** .... who visits a shopping mall on a Saturday morning would say the opposite. The shops are usually **(9)** .... with people buying clothes or presents, and the cafés and restaurants full of friends **(10)** .... a coffee together.

0 (A) on	**B** in	**C** at	**D** by
1 A dreamed	**B** directed	**C** developed	**D** decided
2 A course	**B** way	**C** type	**D** service
3 A first	**B** early	**C** new	**D** top
4 A Several	**B** Lot	**C** Plenty	**D** Many
5 A enough	**B** extremely	**C** too	**D** absolutely
6 A change	**B** send	**C** return	**D** get
7 A like	**B** among	**C** about	**D** for
8 A Anybody	**B** We	**C** Nobody	**D** They
9 A active	**B** ready	**C** awake	**D** busy
10 A making	**B** giving	**C** having	**D** doing

11 Here are some sentences about a girl who likes tennis. For each question, complete the second sentence so that it means the same as the first. Use no more than three words.

1 Diane and her sister really enjoy playing tennis.
Diane and her sister are .... on playing tennis.
2 Diane and her sister play tennis every evening except Sunday.
Diane and her sister play tennis every evening .... from Sunday.
3 Diane's new tennis racket is much better than her old one.
Diane's old tennis racket was not .... her new one.
4 Diane became a member of a tennis club last year.
Diane has been a member of a tennis club .... last year.
5 Diane wants to play in the summer tournament.
Diane is interested .... in the summer tournament.

VOCABULARY Verbs for making things

Your profile

Do you like making things? Why? / Why not?
Do you think you are a creative person? Why? / Why not?

1 Look at the photos and describe what you can see. Which objects do you think are recycled?

a

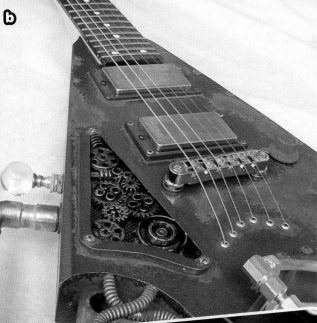

b

2 ▶1.13 Listen to three people, Mark, Leah and Sam. Match each speaker to one of the photos.

3 ▶1.13 Match the sentence halves. Listen again and check.

Mark

1 My brother Jake was **mending** the bike
2 When we **create** something new
3 We all know it's important

a to **recycle**.
b a couple of years ago.
c from something old, it's really satisfying.

Leah

4 We had to **customise** them,
5 First, we thought about the **design**
6 While I was **sticking** the beads on,

d and how we wanted to **decorate** the shoes.
e I decided to **sew** some bits of material on.
f you know, make them our own.

Sam

7 I was helping to **rebuild**
8 You **fix** a problem,
9 I **invented**

g a teen news app.
h the school website.
i but also make something new.

4 Work in pairs. Choose one of the photos and explain how you think the thing was made. Use some of the **words** from exercise 3.

5 Ask and answer the questions.

1 Have you created anything recently?
2 What object would you like someone to invent?
3 Who generally fixes things in your home?
4 Have you ever decorated or customised any of your possessions?
5 Do you think it is important to recycle things? Why? / Why not?

c

d

1 Look at the title of the article and the photos. What do you think the article is going to be about? Read the text quickly and check your ideas.

From *hobby to job*

Yesterday at the Minnesota Fashion Week, the 15-year-old designer Rachel Giddings amazed the fashion world when she showed her clothes for the first time. Everyone agreed that they looked beautiful and that the attention to detail was surprising from one so young.

Rachel Giddings taught herself to sew when she was just seven years old. 'I didn't like my own clothes and I wanted to customise them, so I usually added things – like pockets or zips. Or I made them shorter! My Mom used to get a bit worried about all the scissors and pins lying around,' laughs Rachel. Then during the summer holidays one year, she was looking for something to do when she decided to do a summer course at a fashion and design school located in the heart of her home town, Woodbury, just outside Minneapolis.

At the summer school, Rachel learned many tips and techniques from her teacher, Canadian-born Joan Lo. When Rachel was 12, Joan invited a few teenagers to join her at the famous Toronto Fashion Week. 'I loved it,' said Rachel. 'It was just amazing and I knew that I wanted to be there'. She completed more fashion courses with Joan, and later attended a Fashion Week with her

successful first designs from her collection. Rachel's Mum says that this came as no surprise. 'It's what she has always wanted,' she says. At the Minnesota Fashion Week, Rachel looked absolutely fabulous in her smart leather jacket which had a decoration of a small blue butterfly on it. 'That was hard. I looked for the right material for a long time.' The result was perfect because it looked like a real butterfly.

'It's such a fun thing to do,' says Rachel. 'I think more people should make their own clothes – or at least change their clothes to make them their own, if you see what I mean!' People at the event were making plenty of positive comments about her skill and designs. She sold all of her items and the money went to her own favourite charity, a local children's hospital. 'My little sister was there for a few weeks last year and the staff were just wonderful. I know that they need money to make the children's stay in hospital as comfortable as possible.'

Rachel admits that making and designing the clothes for the show was a lot of hard work. 'At that time, I did all my work on the clothes after dinner, as I had a busy timetable at school and loads of homework as well. But it was worth it.' When asked about her plans for the future, she says she is looking forward to a short break and then the preparations for next season's collection will begin.

2 ⚫ Read the sentences. Decide which are correct and which are incorrect. Write the words in the text which helped you decide.

0 Rachel's clothes surprised many people at the Minnesota Fashion Week.
Correct – amazed the fashion world

1 Rachel used to change how her clothes looked from a very young age.

2 The sewing school that Rachel once attended is in the centre of Minneapolis.

3 Rachel's Mum expected her to go to the Fashion Week when she was 15.

4 Rachel found the material for the blue butterfly without difficulty.

5 Rachel thinks that more people would enjoy making their own clothes.

6 Rachel sold her clothes at the fashion show and gave the money away.

7 While Rachel was studying during the day, she was also sewing at night.

8 Rachel has already started working on the clothes for next season.

3 Match the highlighted words in the text to the meanings.
1 a particular or special way of doing something
2 an ability to do an activity or job well
3 a group of objects of one type
4 one of the four periods of the year

EP Word profile *look*

I looked for the right material for a long time.

Rachel says she is looking forward to a short break.

She looked absolutely fabulous.

It looked like a real butterfly.

page 133

Talking points

❝ Do you think it's important to learn skills to make and mend things? Why? / Why not?
What other creative hobbies are there?
What kind of hobbies can lead to a career? ❞

GRAMMAR   Past simple and continuous

1 Match the examples to the rules.

1 She **was looking** for something to do when she **decided** to do a summer course.

2 In fact, my brother Jake **was mending** the bike a couple of years ago.

3 At that time, I **was studying** during the day and sewing at night.

4 Rachel Giddings **showed** her clothes for the first time.

- a We use the past simple to talk about completed actions and things that happened in the past.
- b We use the past continuous to talk about actions and situations in progress at a certain moment in the past.
- c We can also use the past continuous to describe the background to a story.
- d We can use the past continuous for an action in progress that is interrupted by a short action in the past simple.

→ Grammar reference **page 149**

2 Choose the correct verb forms.

1 My Dad *fixed / was fixing* my computer for me last night. Now it works!

2 I *was walking / walked* along the road when it *started / was starting* to rain.

3 Freddie *spent / was spending* three months in Nepal last year.

4 A new shoe shop *was opening / opened* in my town last week. I want to check it out!

5 I'm sorry I didn't call you sooner but I *was studying / studied* all afternoon.

6 I *was waiting / waited* for the bus when I *saw / was seeing* Paul.

3 Complete the description with the correct form of the verbs in brackets.

I ⁰ _found_ (find) some interesting shells when I ¹ .... (walk) along the beach. I ² .... (pick) them up and ³ .... (put) them in my pocket. Then I noticed that my dog ⁴ .... (run) to me with a piece of wood in his mouth. When he got to me, he ⁵ .... (drop) it and of course, wanted me to throw it again.

But while I ⁶ .... (look) at it, I realised that it was a leg from an old chair. By the time I was ready to go home, I ⁷ .... (have) quite a collection of things from the beach! While I ⁸ .... (clean) them later, I ⁹ .... (have) the idea of creating a piece of art with them. I ¹⁰ .... (take) a photo of the finished piece and uploaded it to the internet – a lot of people really liked it!

Corpus challenge

Find and correct the mistake in the student's sentences.

I saw some of your friends in the youth club. They played games on the computers.

4 Think of a time when you found an interesting object. Answer the questions.

1 Where were you when you found it?

2 What were you doing?

3 What did you use it for, or what did you create?

VOCABULARY   Time adverbs

1 Read the example. How many actions are there? Which adverbs tell us when each action happened?

*She completed the fashion course, **then** she worked for a small company. **Later,** she started her own business.*

2 Choose the correct adverbs.

I wanted to make a birthday card for a friend. ¹First / Suddenly I went shopping and bought the card and other materials, and ²finally / then I looked at some magazines and decided what I was going to do. ³Next / First I drew a picture of a cat because my friend loves them. I was doing this when ⁴finally / suddenly there was a knock at the door. It was my friend! I had to hide everything quickly! I finished making her card ⁵later / next, after she went home. I ⁶next / finally gave her the card on her birthday and she loved it!

3 You are going to tell a partner about something interesting or exciting that happened to you. Prepare your ideas. Use the adverbs in the box and the ideas below, or your own ideas.

finally	first	later	next	then	suddenly

a visit to a city	a problem that you solved
a difficulty with a friend	a surprise from a friend
a trip to the cinema or a concert	

4 Tell your partner what happened to you. Use adverbs from exercise 3.

WRITING A story (1)

1 Do you enjoy reading stories? What makes a story interesting?

2 Read Marilyn's story quickly. What is the title of the story? How many people had the same sunglasses?

'The same sunglasses' by Marilyn

Last week, my brother and I went shopping for sunglasses. We were planning a holiday to a sunny place and we wanted some good sunglasses. We were walking past our favourite shop, when I saw they had a sale! First, we tried on lots of pairs of designer label sunglasses. Next, we each picked out a pair of sunglasses. We both chose the same pair of really cool sunglasses. When we were leaving the shop, we saw our best friends, Margie and Jason. Suddenly we started laughing at each other because we were all wearing the same pink and blue sunglasses! It was very funny!

3 Read the notes. Then read sentences 1–3 below. Do they come from the beginning, middle or end of Marilyn's story? Read the story again to check.

- At the beginning of a story, you can introduce the characters, say what they were doing, and describe the place or the weather.
- In the middle you describe all the events that happened.
- At the end, you describe the final event. Often the final event solves a problem, or is surprising in some way. Say how the characters felt at the end.

1 We were all wearing the same sunglasses.
2 We each picked out a pair.
3 We were planning a holiday to a sunny place.

4 Read the *Prepare* box. Then read Marilyn's story again. Find:

1 three verbs in the past simple
2 three verbs in the past continuous
3 three adverbs which say when things happened

Prepare to write – Writing a story (1)

A good story:
- has a beginning, a middle and an end.
- uses a range of verb forms to describe the background and the main events.
- uses adverbs to say when things happened.

5 Read the task. Then plan your ideas and make some notes. Use the ideas below to help you.

- Your English teacher asks you to write a story.
- This is the title of your story:
  The New Trainers
- Write your **story**.

- What is the background to the story?
- Who are the characters?
- What are the main events?
- What happens in the end?

6 Compare your ideas with a partner. Can you improve your plan?

7 ⬤ Write your story.
- Use the tips in the *Prepare* box.
- Write about 100 words.
- Remember to check your spelling and grammar.

6 Take good care of yourself

VOCABULARY   Health

Your profile

What do you do to stay healthy?
How often do you exercise?
What kinds of food do you think are good for you? Why?

1 Look at the photos. What do they show you about health?

2 Read the quiz. Check the meaning of the words.

---

1 If you're suffering from a bad stomachache, you should …
   A take an aspirin.
   B drink some milk.
   C eat a big meal.

2 The place where a doctor operates is an operating …
   A room.
   B cinema.
   C theatre.

3 If your nose starts to bleed, you should …
   A put your head back.
   B put your head forward.
   C blow your nose.

4 Your friend has a high fever. To reduce the fever, you should …
   A wrap your friend in a blanket.
   B give your friend lots of water to drink.
   C tell your friend to eat lots of vegetables.

5 To prevent mouth and tooth problems, you should …
   A brush your teeth twice a day.
   B eat an apple before you have dinner.
   C eat lots of sweets.

6 If you injure your foot while you are playing football, you should …
   A change your shoes.
   B continue kicking the ball.
   C stop playing and get an adult to check it.

7 Your friend complains of headaches when he has to read the board. He should …
   A always take an aspirin before going to class.
   B get his eyes tested – perhaps he needs glasses.
   C do nothing – the headaches will probably go away.

8 You notice that your friend avoids eating any food with fat or sugar in. You should …
   A talk to your friend about the importance of eating a balanced diet.
   B tell your friend he or she should follow this diet all his or her life.
   C tell your friend to also stop eating fruit and milk.

---

3 Do the quiz with your partner.

4 ▶1.14 Listen to a podcast and see how many answers in the quiz you got right.

5 Complete the sentences with the correct form of words from the quiz.

   1 My father often .... of headaches in the evening.
   2 My brother .... from breathing problems.
   3 Elsie's health isn't very good and she .... going out to places with lots of people.
   4 My sister is trying to .... a strict diet, to lose weight.
   5 My little sister fell over and cut her knee. It .... for ages.
   6 The doctors decided to .... on the young boy and saved his life.
   7 When I was playing basketball, I fell over and .... my foot.
   8 By eating healthy food and doing exercise, you can .... many illnesses.
   9 My wrist was hurting and so I .... it in a bandage.
   10 She's getting better. The doctor wants her to .... the number of pills from three to one.

READING

1 What is an *allergy*? Are you *allergic* to anything?

2 Read the title of the article. Which of the topics do you think it will discuss? Read the article quickly to check your ideas.

what he can/can't eat
where he sleeps
his mobile phone
a short description of where he lives
his exercise routine

He's allergic to
MODERN LIFE!

A Quite a few people suffer from food allergies of one kind or another, but if you are allergic to nuts or wheat, you can avoid eating the food that makes you ill and continue to live a perfectly normal life. Allergies to certain metals can be more difficult to deal with, as they generally have an unpleasant effect on your skin. However, most allergies are not dangerous to human life, just rather annoying.

B But some allergies are much more serious and are extremely difficult to handle. Per Segerbäck has one such life-threatening allergy. He will never be able to live surrounded by other people in a big city and, instead, spends his days alone in a cottage in the Swedish countryside north of Stockholm.

C Segerbäck has to live like this, but why? The answer lies in modern technology – he can't have anything to do with people, especially those he doesn't know. The technological items they are carrying would make him seriously ill. Out on a walk last summer, Segerbäck met one of his few neighbours and during their chat, the man's mobile phone rang. Segerbäck suddenly felt sick and within seconds, he fell to the ground unconscious.

D Segerbäck suffers from a condition called EHS (electro-hypersensitivity), where the energy waves from things like computers, televisions and mobile phones have a very serious effect on the person's body. Phones that are switched on, but are not sending or receiving, usually aren't a problem, but when one is in use, Segerbäck's skin feels as if it is burning and he gets a bad headache immediately. He also complains of feeling sick, being unable to sleep and forgetting things.

E Sweden is the only country in the world so far to recognise that people with EHS have real difficulties and Segerbäck's case has been important in creating a plan to deal with this medical condition. According to government figures, the number of Swedish EHS sufferers is around 250,000, or 3 per cent of the population, and because of this, they are given financial and social support by the government. In the rest of the world, it seems that scientists and governments are only just beginning to understand these unwelcome effects of modern life.

3 Match the summary sentences to paragraphs A–E. There is one extra sentence that you don't need.

1 In order to remain healthy, one man has to live a very quiet life.
2 Only one country is offering help for this modern-day problem.
3 Meeting someone by chance created a health emergency.
4 Research into this problem has found a likely solution.
5 There are some allergies that aren't very serious at all.
6 Segerbäck experiences a variety of health problems when technology is nearby.

EP Word profile *only*

Scientists and governments are only just beginning to understand these unwelcome effects of modern life.

Sweden is the only country in the world so far to recognise that people with EHS have real difficulties.

He only meets a few people.

page 133

Talking points

What difficulties do people with extreme allergies face?
What can other people or governments do to help them?

GRAMMAR Modals (1): Obligation and necessity

1 Read the examples. Then complete the rules with the bold verbs.

1 Segerbäck **has to** live like this.
2 You **shouldn't** take aspirin for a stomachache.
3 You **mustn't** miss lunch.
4 You **ought to** get an adult to have a look.
5 You **don't have to** suffer.

We can use modal verbs to express advice, obligation and necessity. We use:

a *should* and .... to say that something is a good idea.

b *have to* / .... to say that something is necessary.

c .... to say it is very important not to do something.

d .... to say that something is a bad idea.

e .... to say that something is not necessary.

→ **Grammar reference page 150**

2 Look at the pictures and choose the correct sentences.

1 **a** You have to take two tablets every day.
  b You mustn't take two tablets every day.

2 **a** You mustn't park your car here.
  b You should park your car here.

3 **a** You mustn't try this dish.
  b You should try this dish.

4 **a** You don't have to visit this electronics shop.
  b You ought to visit this electronics shop.

5 **a** You don't have to eat in the shop.
  b You mustn't eat in the shop.

3 Rewrite these sentences so that they have the same meaning. Use a modal verb from the box.

> shouldn't   mustn't   ought to   don't have to   ~~have to~~

0 It's necessary to tell someone if you don't feel well.
  You have to tell someone if you don't feel well.

1 It isn't a good idea to eat too many chips.
2 It's important not to eat sweets every day.
3 It's a good idea to do regular exercise.
4 It isn't necessary to go to the gym every day.

⊙ Corpus challenge

Find and correct the mistake in the student's sentence.

I thought we should play outside but Sam's mum told him that he do not, so we played a game inside instead.

VOCABULARY Pronouns with *some, any, every* and *no*

1 Choose the correct word to complete the example. Check your answer in paragraph C on page 37.

*He can't have **anything** / **something** to do with people.*

2 Use words from each box to make new words.

> any   every   no   some

> one   thing   where

People	Things	Places
someone		

3 Choose the correct words.

1 I think *someone* / *anyone* is trying to call you.
2 I spent the morning shopping, but I didn't buy *something* / *anything*.
3 I'd love to live *somewhere* / *everywhere* warm.
4 *No one* / *Everyone* is waiting to hear news about Jo. We're all ready.
5 I'm really hungry, but there's *nothing* / *anything* to eat!

4 Complete the email with the correct words.

Email Auntie May all your problems.
auntiemay@teentroubles.com

Dear Auntie May,
I want to tell you about ¹............ in my class. He used to be really fun and easygoing, but I think that there is ²............ wrong with him. ³............ in my class thinks the same. We had to do a project together and he was annoyed all the time. He didn't seem to have ⁴............ to say and ⁵............ we could say made him feel any better. We don't know what to do. What should we do? Please help us!
Juan

LISTENING

1 You are going to listen to some short extracts. Read the questions and look at the pictures. What words might you hear in each extract?

2 🔴 ▶1.15 Listen and choose the correct picture, A, B or C. Listen again and check.

1 Where is Lola's phone at the moment?

4 What are John's cousins going to send?

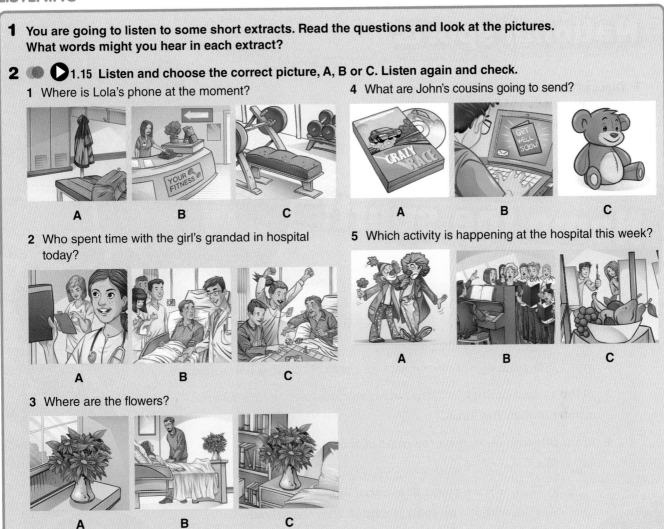

2 Who spent time with the girl's grandad in hospital today?

3 Where are the flowers?

5 Which activity is happening at the hospital this week?

SPEAKING Discussing options (1)

1 Look at the task below. If you were in hospital, what presents would you like to receive?

A young girl is in hospital because she broke her leg. The students in her class want to give her a present. Talk together about the **different** presents and then decide which would be the **best**.

2 ▶1.16 Listen to Ana and Hua talking about the pictures. Do they mention all the possible presents? Do they agree?

3 ▶1.16 Read the *Prepare* box, then listen again. Which phrases do Ana and Hua use?

4 🔴 Turn to page 130.

Prepare to speak—Expressing opinions

Giving your opinion
I think/don't think …
In my opinion …
In my view …

Asking someone's opinion
What do you think?
Do you agree?

Culture
National sports

1 Discuss the questions.
  1 Does your country have a national sport? What is it?
  2 What other sports are popular in your country?
  3 Can you name the national sports of any other countries?

2 Name the sports in the photos, then do the quiz.

Name the sport!

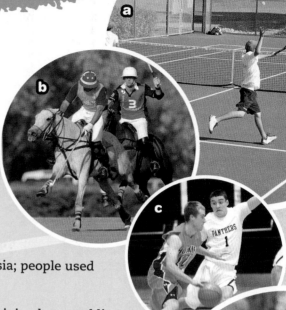

This sport began ...

1 around 5,000 years ago in northern Europe and Asia; people used to wear large animal bones on their feet.

2 over 2,500 years ago in central Asia as a way of training horse soldiers.

3 in the second century in China, when soldiers used to kick a ball around in their free time.

4 in the fifteenth century on the coast of Scotland, among the sand hills.

5 in 1823, when a player at a school in England picked up the ball and ran with it. The sport is named after the school.

6 in 1891, in the northern United States, when a coach at a college invented a game to keep his football players fit in the winter.

3 ▶1.17 Listen and check your answers to the quiz. Then answer the questions below.
  1 What material did people use for the second type of ski?
  2 What is polo sometimes known as, and why?
  3 Which country has the oldest golf course in the world?
  4 What did the footballer at Rugby School do in the early 19th century that was wrong?
  5 What was the problem with the first type of basket in basketball?

4 Read about lacrosse, one of Canada's national sports. Answer the questions.
  1 Who first played it? / Where did it come from?
  2 When was the first match between people from Britain and France?
  3 Is it an Olympic sport?
  4 What is the aim of the game?
  5 How many players are on a team?
  6 What equipment is used?
  7 How long is a match?

NATIONAL SPORTS
No. 24 Canada

While most nations have one national sport, Canada is different, as it has two, and both are national sports by law. The summer national sport of Canada is lacrosse and the winter national sport is ice hockey.

LACROSSE

History

Many national sports, such as cricket, football or rugby, are popular around the world, but lacrosse is not particularly well known outside Canada. It is based on a field game played by the original Canadian people, and we first hear of it in 1637, when a French traveller noted a game called crosse. Whole Indian villages played this game, and the lacrosse field often used to be over a kilometre long!

The sport became popular with people who came from Britain and France in the mid 1800s, and the first match involving this new population took place in 1844. It became more popular and its players set up the National Lacrosse Association of Canada in 1867, which developed the techniques and rules necessary in the sport. It became known outside Canada in the early part of the twentieth century.

International competition

Lacrosse appeared as a competitive sport in the Summer Olympics of 1904 and 1908, but since then it has only appeared as an exhibition sport, i.e. to show people what it is like, with no opportunities for medals. The lacrosse world championships are held every four years; until 1986 only four nations took part (Canada, the USA, England and Australia), but numbers are growing, with 38 nations entering the 2014 competition. The medal-winning places are usually shared between the USA, Canada and Australia. One thing that is quite surprising about the sport is that since 1990 a Canadian team called the Iroquois Nationals has taken part in international competitions – the only original North American people to do so in any sport. They have come fourth in all the recent world championships, except for 2010, when they weren't allowed to enter the UK, where the competition took place, so they missed the opportunity to compete for a medal.

Aim and rules

Lacrosse is a team sport and, like many team sports, the aim is to score more goals than the other team. Teams consist of ten players who use a long stick with a net on the end to catch, carry and pass a small rubber ball. Players have to throw the ball at the goal, a net that is 1.8 metres wide by 1.8 metres high. Each match is 60 minutes long, with four quarters of 15 minutes each. Players can run with the ball, but they mustn't touch it with their hands.

5 ▶1.18 Listen to a boy who plays ice hockey, Canada's other national sport. Complete the notes.

like ¹.......... game called shinty
first played in Canada in ²..........
first match in ³..........
⁴.......... players in a team
use a ⁵.......... to move a ⁶.......... over the ice
get ⁷.......... for scoring a goal or helping to score
matches ⁸.......... long
famous player: Wayne ⁹..........

Project

Work in pairs or groups to find out about a national sport.

- Decide on a national sport: it can be your country's national sport, or one from a different country.
- Get information about the sport by finding out the answers to the questions in exercise 4.
- Write about the sport, using headings as in the text about lacrosse.
- Find photos of the sport which show the players and equipment.

VOCABULARY Music

Your profile

How important is music to you?
What's your favourite kind of music?
When and where do you listen to music?

1 Look at the photos. Where do you think the people are? What are they doing?

2 ▶1.19 Listen and match the speakers to the photos.

3 ▶1.19 Complete the sentences with the words in the box. Listen again and check.

> celebrity   concert hall   DJ   festival
> guitarist   live   music channel   musicians
> production   sound technician   studio
> video clip

1 I'm .... Mike playing your favourite music.
2 And this morning, Lola is in the .... with us.
3 I guess you could say I've been a .... at home for about three years now.
4 I can hear the amazing bass .... , can't you?
5 And it's all recorded anyhow – not even .... !
6 They shouldn't call this event a live music .... !
7 We are live from the Sydney Opera House – a .... that is familiar to our regular listeners.
8 And this is VVTV – the only TV .... that plays your music.
9 Let's take a look at a .... from EE's latest video.
10 Like me, you probably think the .... record their music and that's it.
11 I've just come back from the London Sound Studio where I spoke to .... Bobbi Jackson.
12 She has introduced me to a whole new world: the world of sound ....

4 Ask and answer the questions.

1 Have you ever been to a live music festival? Would you like to go? Why? / Why not?
2 Which music channels do you watch or listen to?
3 Who are the most famous celebrities in your country?
4 Which musicians do you admire? Why?
5 Describe your favourite music video clip.

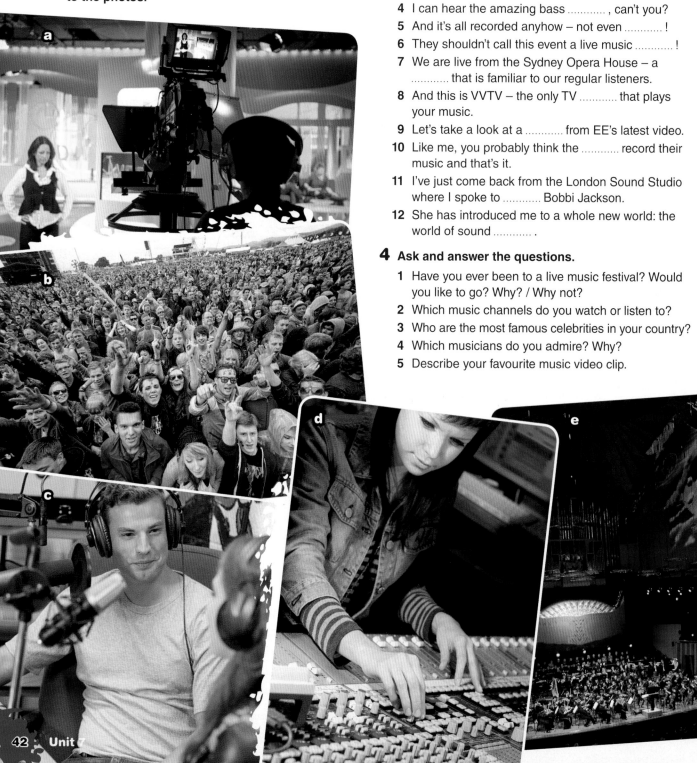

READING

1 Read Allan's profile. How would you describe him?

2 Read the link that Eva has shared with Allan. Answer the questions.

  1 What is the advertisement for?

  2 What do you learn on the course?

  3 Would you like to go on this course? Why? / Why not?

Hi, I'm Allan. I'm 14 years old and I'm from Australia. I enjoy anything with music – listening, playing, mixing, making. I play a few musical instruments and I have guitar lessons once a week.

Eva **shared** a link
Hi, Allan. I think this is just right for you! Eva

Sound Bites

Interested in music, but not in the instruments? How about learning how to record music in a professional studio? Or maybe you'd like to join the backstage crew on a two-day tour?

Does this sound like you?

Come and join us for a one-week course in our studio in Sydney. You'll learn new skills and make new friends! If you're aged 12–18 and you want more information, go to **www.soundstudio.com**

3 Allan is now on the course. Read his email to Eva. Which topics does he mention?

things he's learning about   difficulties on the course
his teachers   a trip to a concert hall
homework he has to do   his friends on the course

4 Read Allan's email again and answer the questions.

  1 How long has Allan been on the course?

  2 What surprised Allan about the singer?

  3 How does Allan describe his instructors?

  4 Why did Matt send Allan a text?

  5 How did Matt help the band?

  6 What is Allan doing with the sound track tomorrow?

  7 Why didn't he finish it today?

  8 What does he say about the course overall?

5 Match the highlighted words in the texts to the meanings.

  1 equipment and knowledge used in science and industry

  2 difficult to understand

  3 group or team of people

  4 add some new information

Hi Eva!

I just wanted to tell you about that course you shared on Facebook with me. I've been here since last Thursday and it's going really well. I haven't had so much fun learning for a long time.

Every day we do something new. We've already learnt how to record a singer – really hard to get the sound right. We had to do so many retakes. That's when they make mistakes or forget their words, and you have to do it again. There was a singer yesterday and she simply didn't know her words! I had to write them out on a piece of paper for her! I couldn't believe it! Crazy!

The instructors are cool though. Matt, the technology instructor, has just sent me a text about a technology app I was trying to find. He's really helpful. He thinks that there has never been so much music technology around on the net, so he isn't surprised that we're all finding it hard to choose which apps to use. It can be really confusing sometimes. He also told me that a band has just come into the recording studio and they are re-recording because there were lots of problems with a volume program they had used. He spent a long time sorting that out.

Tomorrow I think we'll finish a sound track, you know, a song. We've just about finished recording the instruments and we've nearly finished recording the voices. After we have done that, we need to 'master' it. Have you ever heard of mastering? Before I came here, I hadn't either. It's the final stage, when you put the tracks together and check the sound quality, for example, make sure the volume is the same right through the song. You don't want to listen to a track and have to turn the volume up and down the whole time! That's what mastering is. I wanted to finish it today, but I haven't had time yet. I'd like Matt to help me to check it first.

So all in all, the course is just great and I've learnt loads of new skills. I love it because it's technical and fun! Anyone who wants to go into the music industry should definitely do it. Anyway, I'll update Facebook soon, but thought you'd like to hear how I'm getting on!

By the way, have you started your school project yet? If you need any help, give me a call. I'm going to do mine on music!

See you soon,
Allan

EP Word profile *just*

I think this is just right for you.

Matt has just sent me a text.

We have just about finished recording the instruments.

Just listen!

page 133

Talking points

" Do you think music sounds better live or when it is produced in a studio?

What's the best way to encourage people to learn how to make music? "

Sound checks   **43**

GRAMMAR   Present perfect and past simple

1 Match two examples to each rule.

1 *I've been here since last Thursday and it's going really well.*

2 *There was a singer yesterday and she simply didn't know her words!*

3 *He spent a long time sorting that out.*

4 *I've learnt loads of new skills.*

> a We use the present perfect to talk about something in the past that has a link to the present.
>
> b We use the past simple to talk about completed actions in the past. It only refers to the past.

→ Grammar reference **page 151**

2 Complete the sentences with the past simple or present perfect of the verbs.

1 Mike .... (buy) his ticket for the music festival two months ago.

2 He .... (pay) a lot of money for it.

3 He .... (not / see) his favourite band live before and so he's excited.

4 Mike's mum wants to help, so she .... (offer) to take him to the stadium.

5 Mike doesn't need a lift from his mum because he .... (organise) a lift with a friend.

6 Mike .... (call) his friend last night to make the final arrangements for their trip.

3 We often use the adverbs *just, already* and *yet* with the present perfect. Read the examples and complete the rules with *just, already* or *yet*.

1 *Matt has **just** sent me a text.*

2 *We've **already** learnt how to record a singer.*

3 *I haven't had time **yet**.*

4 *Have you started your school project **yet**?*

> With the present perfect, we use:
>
> a .... when something has happened at some time before now.
>
> b .... when something happened a short time ago.
>
> c .... in questions and negative sentences when something has (possibly) not happened.

4 Read the examples in exercise 3 again. Which adverb is used at the end of a sentence? Where are the other adverbs used?

Corpus challenge

Find and correct the mistake in the student's sentence.

I have just buy a new book.

5 Complete the sentences with the present perfect form of the verbs and put the adverbs in the correct place.

1 I .... an advertisement for the X Factor – I think I'll apply! (see / just)

2 Some of the singers .... in front of a large audience. (sing / already)

3 They .... who the judges are. (not announce / yet)

4 It's two hours to show time and the performers .... their costumes on. (put / already)

5 Jake .... in public. (not perform / yet)

6 Our town .... its annual music festival. It was last week. (have / just)

VOCABULARY   Word families

1 Look at the bold words in the examples. What part of speech are they?

*I'd like Matt to **help** me to check it first.*
*He's really **helpful**.*
*If you need any **help**, give me a call.*

2 Complete the table.

Noun	Verb	Adjective
music / musician	–	1 ....
performance / performer	2	performing
3	to advertise	–
entertainment / entertainer	4	5 ....
6	achieve	–
7	record	–

3 Complete the sentences with words formed from the bold words.

1 The person who **performs** on stage is a ....

2 The people who play **music** are called ....

3 When you want to **advertise** a concert, you can put up an ....

4 Someone who **entertains** people is an ....

5 When you **record** something, you make a ....

6 If you **achieve** a high grade in your exams, you should celebrate your ....

WRITING An informal letter or email (1)

1 Read part of a letter that Miina receives from her friend Toby. Then read Miina's reply. Does Miina answer all Toby's questions?

> Last night, Mum took me to an awesome concert in our town. It was amazing!
>
> Tell me about a concert you enjoyed. Where did it take place? What was it like? Who did you go with?

Dear Toby,

It was our school concert last week! And our band played!

It took place in the school hall and there were loads of great performances from different year groups. As you know, I've always been into music. I've played the keyboard since I was six and I've been in a band for about two years now.

I went to the concert with my band mates. When I first walked on stage, it was dark and scary – you can't imagine how nervous I felt! Then the lights came on and we played our music. It was awesome! We had such a cool time and I've never seen so many people clap – for us! We recorded it, so I'll send you a recording.

Write soon, Miina

2 Read the *Prepare* box. What phrases does Miina use to begin and end her letter?

Prepare to write — An informal letter or email (1)

In informal letters and emails:
- use an informal phrase to begin your letter: *Dear …, Hi …, Hello …*
- use an informal phrase to end your letter: *Write soon, Love, See you soon*
- use short forms: *I've, won't, we'll*
- use informal language: *amazing, great*

3 Find six short forms in Miina's letter.

4 Rewrite the sentences using short forms.
1 He has never been to a music festival.
2 We are going to give Amy a lift at 8 pm.
3 Do you know who is going to perform next?
4 I would really like to see a live classical music concert.
5 They have not bought their tickets yet.
6 Dan and Gemma could not find a place to park near the concert.

5 Match the highlighted informal words in Miina's letter to the meanings.
1 lots
2 frightening
3 very good
4 friends
5 enjoyed

6 Read Toby's letter again. Plan your reply and make some notes. Here are some ideas to help you.
- Where was the concert? Was it in a concert hall, or outside?
- Which singer/band did you see?
- Did they perform well?
- Who did you go with? Friends? Family members?
- What did you enjoy most about the concert?
- Were there any problems? What were they?

7 ● Write your letter to Toby.
- Use the tips in the *Prepare* box.
- Write about 100 words.
- Remember to check your spelling and grammar.

8 Amazing architecture

VOCABULARY Describing buildings

Your profile

Do you prefer old or modern buildings? Why?
What is your favourite building? Why?

1 Look at the photos and find examples of the words in the box. Describe each building.

> apartment block   fifth-floor window
> ground floor   upstairs room

2 Match the descriptions to the buildings in the photos. Which description isn't needed?

1 The house on top is much more **recent** than the **original** tower.
2 This glass building seems to be **brand new** and its **fresh** design is **spectacular** to look at.
3 The central part is like a **traditional** cottage, but the large rocks on either side are very **unusual**!
4 It's a **classic** example of a **historic** country house from the seventeenth century.
5 This **modern** building is incredibly narrow, but it could be quite **cosy** inside in its limited space!

3 Complete the chart with the **adjectives** from exercise 2.

Age	Opinion
recent	unusual

4 Look at the photos again. Discuss the advantages and disadvantages of living in each building.

5 ▶1.20 Listen to four people talking about the buildings in exercise 1. Do the speakers mention any of your ideas?

6 Discuss the questions.

1 How much space do you need to live in? Why?
2 What is the view from your bedroom window?
3 What else would you like to be able to see from your window?

READING

1 Five teenagers are working on a project about different homes. Each teenager (1–5) needs to include an unusual home in their project. Read the information about each person and underline the key things they are looking for.

1 Marcelo loves all kinds of sport and wants to find a home that has <u>suitable practice areas</u>. He'd like to write about a building <u>situated by the ocean</u> that <u>belongs to someone well known</u>.
2 Gloria is interested in old buildings. She is hoping to find one in the countryside that is available to rent for short periods.
3 Harry wants to find out about a famous architect and include a building where they used to live in his project. He also wants to get information about classic furniture.
4 Sofie is keen to find a building that is the smallest of its kind. She wants something in a city, so that she can also write about the neighbourhood where it is located.
5 Kurt wants to learn about a recently-built home that is better for the environment than others and has done well in competitions because of its original architecture.

2 Read the descriptions of eight unusual homes (A–H) quickly. Which two are shown in the pictures on this page?

3 ⬤ Read the descriptions again and decide which home would be the most suitable for each teenager to choose.

UNUSUAL HOMES
AROUND THE WORLD

KERET HOUSE

No other house is as narrow as this one! A Polish architect living in the capital, Warsaw, walked past the empty site between a house and an apartment building on his way home and decided to develop it. It's the least suitable house for families, but someone living alone should find it easier.

CROSSWAY

Situated in beautiful countryside, this prize-winning modern home was designed by architect, Richard Hawkes, who lives there with his family. It is one of the first 'passive houses' in the UK and uses energy from the sun to produce all its electricity. Local materials were used to build it and it has a living 'green' roof.

HOUSE NA

The firm of architects who built this house had an unusual starting point, creatures who lived in trees long ago! They imagined them being able to move from one branch to another and communicate easily. These original thoughts produced a modern house made of glass in a quiet neighbourhood in Japan's capital.

FRESTON TOWER

This historic tower has lasted 400 years. There are six floors with a single room on each. From the top, you can see the river and the fields beyond. If four adults share the cost, it is cheaper than £25 a night to stay here. That's less expensive than some youth hostels!

PAS HOUSE

This modern private house is designed for skateboarding. Situated near the beach in California, it is divided into three separate spaces, each ideal for skateboarding, as the floor, walls and ceiling join into one enormous tube. You can even use the furniture to skate off! The owner is a former world champion.

OLD LIGHT LOWER/UPPER

Located on Lundy Island, this is the perfect place to relax. Once a working lighthouse that warned ships at sea of the nearby rocks, the building is now divided into two flats, both offered for rent for short periods. The lower flat has a cosy living room with a real fire.

GROPIUS HOUSE

Other architects may be more famous, but the buildings Walter Gropius created are among the most important of the last century. He designed this as his family home in the USA. The house has an original collection of chairs and many of the Gropius family's belongings remain.

PELOTTI PALACE

This recently-built house in peaceful countryside has amazing facilities, including tennis courts. A well-known footballer lived here last. Available to rent by the month, whoever moves in will have to buy new furniture, but the kitchen is fully equipped.

EP Word profile *last*

A well-known footballer lived here last.

His buildings are among the most important of the last century.

This historic tower has lasted 400 years.

I live in the last house on the left.

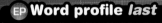

Talking points

" In what ways are some modern buildings better for the environment?
What makes a good family home, in your opinion?
How important is it to have local facilities like parks and shops near your home? "

page 134

GRAMMAR Comparative and superlative adjectives

1 Read the examples and write C for comparative and S for superlative.

1 This is the world's **thinnest** house.
2 Someone living alone should find it **easier**.
3 Decide which building would be **the most comfortable** to stay in.
4 It is **cheaper** than £25 a night to stay here.
5 It's only 122 cm at its **widest** point.
6 Kurt's choice is **better** for the environment.
7 Other architects may be **more famous**.
→ Grammar reference **page 152**

2 Write the comparative and superlative forms of the adjectives in the boxes. Then answer the questions.

> cheap   thin   wide   easy   famous

> bad   far   good

1 Which adjectives are irregular?
2 What do we add to regular adjectives with one syllable?
3 What happens to adjectives like *thin* and *big*?
4 What happens if a one-syllable or two-syllable adjective ends in *-y*?
5 How do we form comparatives and superlatives for most adjectives with more than one syllable?

3 Complete the sentences with the correct form of the adjective in brackets.

1 This café is much .... (cosy) than the old one.
2 Our library has just won a prize for the ....
   (original) building.
3 Is your brother's bedroom .... (big) than yours?
4 This is the .... (good) house to live in.
5 That apartment block is the .... (ugly) one I've
   ever seen.
6 Have you ever seen a .... (spectacular) view
   than this?
7 Living conditions in the past were .... (bad)
   than they are now.
8 This flat is nicer, but it's .... (far) from the city
   centre than the other one.

Ⓒ Corpus challenge

Find and correct the mistake in the student's sentence.

Smaller schools are more nicer and quieter than larger schools in the centre of town.

4 Complete the sentences with examples of *less, least* and *not as ... as* from the text on page 47.

1 No other house is .... this one.
2 That's .... some youth hostels!
3 It's .... house for families.

5 ● Complete the second sentence so that it means the same as the first. Use no more than three words.

1 Monica has just moved to a bigger apartment.
   **Monica's last apartment was not ....
   .... the apartment she is in now.**
2 Monica's home cost less than any other in the
   new apartment block.
   **Monica's home is the ....
   expensive in the new apartment block.**
3 A very close friend of Monica's lives here.
   One of .... friends lives here.
4 Monica's journey to school is shorter than it
   used to be.
   **Monica's journey to school is
   .... far than it used to be.**
5 Monica much prefers where she lives now to
   her old place.
   **Monica thinks that her new place is a lot
   .... where she lived before.**

VOCABULARY Prepositional phrases for location

1 Look at the photo of Dalston House. How do you think the artist created it?

2 Complete the description of the photo with the prepositions in the box.

> above   behind   beside   from   in   on (x2)   to

A man looks as though he's upside down ¹........... the
front door of the house. A boy in a blue top seems to
be hanging ²........... the window, but really he's lying
³........... the ground. Some adults and children are
standing ⁴........... the right of the piece of art, waiting
to have a go. A woman in a pink jumper is standing
⁵........... the front door. There's a modern building
⁶........... the background of the picture. It's ⁷...........
a wall which has graffiti ⁸........... it.

LISTENING

1 How would you feel if your family had to move away from where you live? Think about friends, school, and free time activities.

2 ▶1.21 You will hear a conversation about moving to another city. Read sentence 1 and listen. Is the sentence correct or incorrect? Use the underlined words to help you decide.

  1 Helena is <u>very disappointed</u> with her new school.

3 ⬤ ▶1.22 Listen to the rest of the recording. Choose A for YES (correct) and B for NO (incorrect). Use the underlined words to help you decide.

  2 Helena <u>thinks</u> her father's new employer has been <u>unhelpful</u>.
  3 Helena <u>wishes</u> she had longer before having to leave.
  4 Tom <u>tries to convince</u> Helena that she won't be that far away.
  5 Tom <u>is certain</u> that his sister would allow Helena to stay.
  6 Helena <u>agrees with</u> Tom that the city she's moving to has a lot to offer.

4 Write three pieces of advice to give Helena. Complete the sentences with your own ideas.

You should …
You shouldn't …
You ought to …

SPEAKING   Describing a picture (1)

1 Look at the photo below of skateboarders inside Pas House. How would you describe it?

2 ▶1.23 Listen to Julia. Does she mention any of your ideas from exercise 1?

3 ▶1.23 When you describe something, use adjectives to make your description interesting. Which adjectives in the box does Julia use? Listen again and check.

| awesome | big | comfortable | large | lovely |
| normal | perfect | soft | strange | unusual |

4 Read the examples and the chart. Then put the adjectives in the correct order in the phrases below.

an awesome black chair   *comfortable square cushions*   *cool Californian guys*

Order of adjectives						
QUALITY	SIZE	SHAPE	AGE	COLOUR	NATIONALITY	MATERIAL
awesome	large	square	old	black	Polish	leather

  1 a .... sofa (leather / brand new / gorgeous)
  2 some .... bowls (little / beautiful / glass)
  3 a .... table (square / big)
  4 some .... chairs (red / comfortable / large)

5 ▶1.23 Read the *Prepare* box. What phrases does Julia use? Listen again and complete the sentences below.

Prepare to speak — When you don't know the right word

It looks (a bit) like …	that kind of thing
It looks more like …	something like that
It seems to be …	some kind of

  1 I can see a room in what .... a house.
  2 It's got designer lights and ....
  3 The floor doesn't .... level.
  4 He's sitting on .... seat.
  5 Not pillows exactly, but .... pillows?
  6 It .... a bed, actually.
  7 I guess it's made of wood ....

6 ⬤ Work in pairs. Turn to page 130.

Biology
Hearing

1 Read the text. What does the cochlea send to your brain?

THE EAR AND SOUNDS

Your ears sense different sounds around you and send that information to your brain. Do you know how your ears do this?

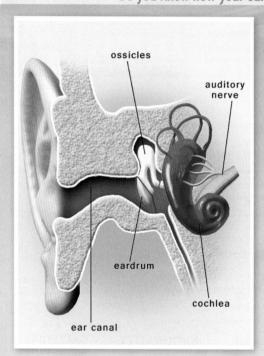

The parts of the ear

The **outer ear** is the part that you can see. It also includes the **ear canal** on the inside. The **middle ear** includes the **eardrum** and three tiny bones, called **ossicles**. The **inner ear** includes a special spiral-shaped structure called the **cochlea**.

How the parts work

1 When sound waves enter the ear canal, they hit the eardrum and make it vibrate. This means it starts to move back and forwards very quickly, with very small movements.

2 When that happens, the three tiny ossicles start to vibrate too.

3 The cochlea senses that the ossicles are moving and it sends electrical signals to the brain through the auditory nerve.

Sound waves, volume and pitch

Your ears detect or sense the volume and pitch of different sounds. The volume of sounds is how loud or soft they are. Pitch is how high or low sounds are. To understand this, we can look at different sound waves.

The distance between the top and bottom of a sound wave is the **amplitude**. This tells us the **volume**.

The distance from the beginning to the end of a sound wave is the **wavelength**. This shows the **pitch**.

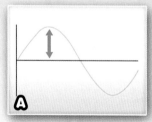
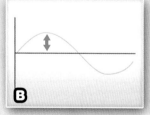
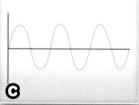
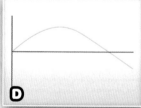

- **Sound A:** the amplitude of each sound wave is larger. This is a loud sound.
- **Sound B:** the amplitude of each sound wave is smaller. This is a soft sound.
- **Sound C:** the wavelength is shorter, so the waves are more frequent. This is a high-pitch or high-frequency sound.
- **Sound D:** the wavelength is longer, so the waves are less frequent. This is a low-pitch or low-frequency sound.

KeyWords

auditory	to do with hearing
nerve	a part of your body that carries electrical signals to your brain
sound waves	the form that sound takes when it travels through the air
vibrate	make very small movements back and forwards

2 Complete the descriptions with the words and phrases in the box. There are two extra words or phrases.

> auditory nerve   cochlea   ear canal   eardrum   ossicles

1 The .... starts to make small, fast movements when sound waves hit it.
2 The .... are tiny bones that move when the eardrum moves.
3 The .... detects the movements of three tiny bones in the ear.

3 Discuss the questions.

1 What is amplitude? Name one sound with a high amplitude and one with a low amplitude.
2 What is pitch? Name one sound with a high pitch and one with a low pitch.
3 How do you think that loud sounds can damage your ears?

4 We measure sound in decibels. Match the words in the box to the photos.
Which sounds are louder? Guess and complete the chart.

> busy traffic   ~~fireworks~~   hair dryer   light rain   rock concert   whispering

Sounds		Decibels
1	jet airplane	140 dB
2	fireworks	130 dB
3	ambulance	120 dB
4	....	110 dB
5	motorcycle	100 dB
6	....	90 dB
7	alarm clock	80 dB
8	....	70 dB
9	normal speech	60 dB
10	....	50 dB
11	refrigerator	40 dB
12	....	30 dB
13	leaves moving	20 dB

a
b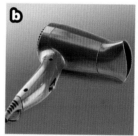
c
d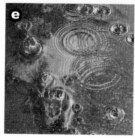
e
f

5 ▶1.24 Listen to a safety message about loud music.
Answer the questions.

1 What happens sometimes after we hear a loud noise?
2 How many decibels can MP3 players produce at full volume?
3 What should people do when they go to a loud concert?
  Why?
4 Why are old-fashioned headphones better than earphones?
5 When you use earphones, what should you ask people around you?

Project

Download a free decibel meter app for your mobile phone.
Use the decibel meter to measure sounds around you:
- typical sounds in your house
- the volume of your MP3 player
- the traffic near your school
- a busy classroom at school
- a quiet library or public park

Take notes about your measurements.
Present your notes to the class.

Review 2
Units 5-8

VOCABULARY

1 Complete the sentences with the words in the box.

> design   invent   mend   rebuild   recycle   sew

1 Jake offered to .... my bike because it wasn't working properly.
2 The button on my coat fell off. I'll have to .... it back on again.
3 I think it's really important to .... rubbish, to help the environment.
4 For a school project, I have to .... an original cover for a mobile phone.
5 I want to .... a machine that will do my homework!
6 When their house burnt down, they had to .... their whole life.

2 Match the sentence halves.

1 I had an injection to prevent
2 The doctors had to operate
3 It took me a long time to recover
4 I need to wrap my arm in
5 I suffer from
6 She took some medicine to reduce

a headaches when I don't wear my glasses.
b a bandage because it hurts.
c the disease.
d on her leg after the accident.
e the high fever.
f from the illness.

3 Complete the adjectives in the conversation.

Anna: Do you know the ¹ h...........c town of Samport?
Fred: I think so. It's a ² t...........l English town, isn't it?
Anna: Yes. Most of the buildings are in an old, ³ c...........c design but there are some quite ⁴ m...........n buildings too.
Fred: There's a ⁵ b...........-n...........w art gallery there, isn't there? I think it opened last month.
Anna: That's right. There's a ⁶ s...........r exhibition on at the moment that includes lots of different art forms. Everyone says it's amazing!
Fred: Oh, yes, I read about it. It includes things like ballet and paintings. It sounds really ⁷ un...........l and different. I'd like to see it!

4 Read the clues and complete the puzzle.

Across

1 someone who is famous, especially in the entertainment business
5 a series of special events and performances that takes place over several days
6 someone who plays a musical instrument, often as their job
7 a room where TV or radio programmes are made

Down

1 a TV or radio station
2 someone who plays the guitar, often as their job
3 a kind of TV or radio programme that is seen or heard as it happens
4 a short video or audio recording
8 someone who plays recorded music on the radio or at live events

GRAMMAR

5 Complete the sentences with the correct form of the verbs. Use the past simple or past continuous.

1 The weather was awful at the festival – it .... (rain) and I .... (not have) my umbrella.
2 Justine .... (watch) TV when she .... (receive) a text message.
3 At the park last week, Magdalena .... (text) while I .... (read) my book.
4 Yesterday Alex .... (miss) the bus and .... (forget) his homework.
5 Hannah's mum .... (decorate) her birthday cake in secret, but Hannah .... (see) it in the cupboard.
6 Jack .... (listen) to music when his mum .... (call) him for dinner.

6 Complete the sentences with the modal verbs in the box.

> don't have to   have to
> mustn't   ought   should

1 I think you .... study tonight – you have a test tomorrow.
2 When you are in class, you .... use your mobile phone – it's against the rules.
3 It's OK, you .... do the shopping – I'll do it later.
4 That doesn't look good – you .... to go to the hospital and see a doctor.
5 I .... be at home for dinner tonight – my aunt is coming.

7 Choose the correct form of the verbs.

1 Sophia *visited / has visited* England last year.
2 Mark *ate / has eaten* sushi before. It isn't his first time!
3 I *just bought / 've just bought* a ticket for a concert next month. I'm so excited!
4 Mr Johnson *didn't give / hasn't given* us our biology homework back yet.
5 My cousin *has added / added* me to his Instagram account yesterday.

8 Complete the sentences with the correct comparative or superlative form of the adjectives in the box.

> fresh   good   narrow   reliable   thick

1 It's a really small shop, and it's in .... street I've ever seen!
2 Jessica is .... than Emma. You can always trust her to arrive on time.
3 The water at the top of the stream is .... than the water at the bottom.
4 I'm .... at sports than Jo.
5 It's so cold that I am wearing .... jumper I have!

Corpus challenge

9 Tick the two sentences without mistakes. Correct the mistakes in the other sentences.

1 My last holiday was great.
2 I go to Spain last year.
3 I musn't forget to bring my school bag.
4 There was a game in our school and I have to play with my classmates.
5 I have just buy a new phone.
6 I haven't read your email yet.
7 What we do moust together is play video games.
8 What I most like is hanging out with friends.

10 ⬤ Read the text below and choose the correct word for each space.

Blogs

Throughout history, people have **(0)** .... written about what they did and how they did it. In the past, many people wrote diaries and with the **(1)** .... of these documents, history experts have been able to understand important events.

(2) ...., though, few people keep diaries. A more popular form of writing about your **(3)** .... of life is a blog. There are several differences between a blog and a **(4)** .... diary. To **(5)** .... with, you just need a computer, the internet and a topic that interests you. Next, you have to decide if you want people to be able to **(6)** .... comments. The **(7)** .... of a blog is also important and you should definitely think about photos. This is **(8)** .... to do if you have a mobile phone with a camera.

So now you just have to write! There are **(9)** .... individuals who have become famous by writing blogs, and even if you don't achieve this, your blog today may be of great **(10)** .... to people in the future.

0 **(A)** always	**B** besides	**C** never	**D** anyway
1 **A** help	**B** skill	**C** ability	**D** advantage
2 **A** After	**B** Before	**C** Presently	**D** Nowadays
3 **A** style	**B** way	**C** system	**D** method
4 **A** previous	**B** modern	**C** traditional	**D** historical
5 **A** open	**B** go	**C** follow	**D** begin
6 **A** make	**B** do	**C** have	**D** say
7 **A** show	**B** form	**C** appearance	**D** entrance
8 **A** ready	**B** simple	**C** regular	**D** sensible
9 **A** lots	**B** much	**C** plenty	**D** several
10 **A** amount	**B** meaning	**C** importance	**D** fashion

11 ⬤ Here are some sentences about a boy who has guitar lessons. For each question, complete the second sentence so that it means the same as the first.
Use no more than three words.

1 Jacob started playing the guitar three years ago.
Jacob has played the guitar .... years.
2 Jacob's classes take place near his house.
Jacob's house is not very .... his classes.
3 Jacob's teacher says it is a good idea to practise at home.
'You .... at home,' says Jacob's teacher.
4 Jacob's friend suggested joining his class because it was smaller.
Jacob's friend said, 'Why .... join my small class?'
5 Jacob believes that enjoying your classes and understanding the teacher are both important.
Jacob believes that enjoying your classes is just .... understanding the teacher.

9 The future is now

VOCABULARY   Technology: nouns

Your profile

Which electronic goods do you use every day?
What do you use them for?
Which is the most important to you?

1 Read the information about Project Loon. Why do you think this project is necessary?

Project Loon aims to provide reliable wireless internet across the southern hemisphere, starting with Australia, New Zealand, Chile and Argentina. This amazing **invention** uses giant balloons 32 km above the Earth, which only require the **power** of the sun and natural weather conditions to work properly. The first **experiment** took place in New Zealand in 2013.

2 Read the quiz and guess the answers.

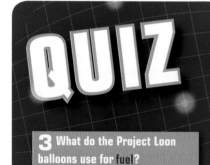

QUIZ

1 Approximately what percentage of the world's population currently have cheap internet **access**?
- **A** 33%
- **B** 66%
- **C** 99%

2 In several countries in the southern hemisphere, an internet **connection** can cost the same as
- **A** a daily cup of coffee.
- **B** a weekly cinema trip.
- **C** a monthly salary.

3 What do the Project Loon balloons use for **fuel**?
- **A** nuclear power
- **B** solar power
- **C** wave power

4 Each balloon uses a **pump** to control the amount of .... it uses.
- **A** air
- **B** electricity
- **C** water

5 What equipment will each balloon carry so that it can work at night?
- **A** a **satellite**
- **B** a **torch**
- **C** a **battery**

3 ▶1.25 Listen to someone talking about Project Loon and check your answers to the quiz.

4 Match the **words** in exercises 1 and 2 to the meanings.
1 a scientific test
2 a substance that is used to provide energy
3 something that moves liquid, air or gas from one place to another
4 something new that has been designed or created for the first time
5 energy that is used to provide light, heat, etc.
6 a piece of equipment that stores electricity
7 a small electric light that you hold in your hand
8 a piece of equipment that is sent into space around the Earth
9 something that joins things together
10 the opportunity to use something

5 Discuss the questions about Project Loon. Use some of the **words** from exercises 1 and 2.
1 What is the project designed to do?
2 What equipment does it use?
3 How will it help people?

6 Discuss the questions.
1 Will everyone have internet access one day? Why? / Why not?
2 What new electronic inventions do you think there will be in the next five years?
3 What fuels do you think we will use in the future?

READING

1 Look at the title of the text. How do you think a car could use social media for fuel?

2 Read the text quickly to check your ideas.

A STUDENT-BUILT ELECTRIC CAR THAT USES SOCIAL MEDIA FOR FUEL

Some American high school students in Kansas City are going to experience a very special journey next week, thanks to an organisation called Minddrive. This charity helps kids who haven't done too well in their education by getting them involved in creative car design after school.

This group of teenagers has worked on a 1967 Volkswagen, replacing the original petrol engine with a lithium-ion battery and adding twenty-first century electronic technology. The project's director, Steve Rees, says, "We want them to say, when it's all over, 'I can't believe we actually did something like this!' It gives them the sense of being able to go back to school and do anything."

Twenty-one students will be driving their car across the States to Washington DC, where they're meeting politicians and talking to journalists about the need for a different kind of education – one that is more 'hands-on', like their car-building experience. To make sure their voices are heard, they've programmed the car's computer to control the amount of electricity used for fuel. The car will only move forward if it gets enough interest on social media – essentially, it'll be using Twitter power for fuel.

The project provides an important lesson for these students: if you want people to care about what you're doing, you have to make sure they know about it. To reach their destination, they'll need a total of 71,040 'social watts', gaining five watts for every new Twitter follower. The car's computer will recognise the hashtag #MINDDRIVE, and posts on Facebook and other social networking sites. Rees thinks collecting this 'social fuel' won't be a problem. He's going to watch their progress carefully, and he is actually expecting huge public support along the route.

3 ⬤ Read the text more carefully and answer the questions. Use the tips to help you.

1 What is the writer doing in the text?
- **A** describing an after-school project in the USA
- **B** complaining about the use of social media
- **C** advising schools on new kinds of technology
- **D** explaining how to repair an electric car

TIP: Think about the whole text and who might read it. Make sure you understand the key verbs in A–D.

2 According to Steve Rees, the purpose of the Minddrive project is
- **A** to persuade problem teenagers to attend their school.
- **B** to give young people a qualification in engineering.
- **C** to encourage a group of students to feel more confident.
- **D** to teach some schoolchildren about petrol-driven cars.

TIP: A question that starts with *According to* is likely to test an opinion or what someone has said. Look out for direct speech in the text.

3 What would someone taking part in this Minddrive project say?

TIP: The final question includes information from all parts of the text. Check that the answer you choose matches the text completely.

A I haven't really enjoyed the experience, as it's exactly how we're taught in school. The drive to Washington will be fun though.	**B** The project's awesome! We're going to tell people in Washington that the lessons we get in school aren't right for everyone.
C I love learning about electronic technology. As I'm already on Twitter, every time I tweet, I'll earn fuel for the car!	**D** It's been cool turning the Volkswagen into an electric car. Steve Rees is going to employ me full time now I've left school.

EP Word profile *actually*

I can't believe we actually did something like this!

Rees is actually expecting huge public support along the route.

Actually, it could be as much as a monthly salary.

▶ page 134

Talking points

66 What can teenagers gain from after-school projects like Minddrive? 99

GRAMMAR Future forms

1 Read the examples. Then complete the rules with *will, be going to* or present continuous.

1 *Rees thinks collecting this 'social fuel'* **won't be** *a problem.*

2 *He's going to watch their progress carefully.*

3 *In Washington DC, they're meeting politicians.*

4 *I'll buy you a new battery.*

We use:

a .... for a definite future arrangement.

b .... for an offer or promise relating to the future.

c .... for a personal plan or intention for the future.

d .... for a general prediction about the future.

→ Grammar reference **page 153**

2 Complete the sentences. Use *will, be going to* or the present continuous.

1 I .... (try) to phone you tonight.

2 Mike .... (borrow) a laptop, so he can play online with us.

3 If you like, I .... (help) you.

4 Our class .... (visit) the science museum tomorrow.

5 Next time we're in Rome, we .... (come) and see you.

6 Jon believes that it .... (be) possible to have driverless cars soon!

Future continuous

3 Look at the examples of the future continuous. Choose the correct words to complete the rules.

1 *The students* **will be driving** *across the States.*

2 *This car* **will be using** *Twitter power for fuel.*

a We form the future continuous with *will + be + -ing* / **past participle**

b We use the future continuous to talk about something that is **certain** / **unlikely** to happen over a period of time in the future.

4 Complete the sentences with the future continuous form of the verbs in the box. There are two extra verbs.

break	drive	hold	make	not see
study	take	wait		

1 I .... for you outside the station tonight.

2 From next week, the class .... American history.

3 We .... a party on New Year's Eve, as usual.

4 My brother .... his university exams in a month's time.

5 Julia .... her friends on Friday.

6 Within ten years, everyone in this city .... electric cars.

5 Choose the correct form of the verbs.

1 Another electronic invention *will be replacing* / *will replace* smartphones one day.

2 How soon do you think we*'ll get* / *'re getting* home after football practice?

3 I*'ll be working* / *'ll work* on Saturday, unfortunately.

4 Ben*'ll sing* / *'s going to sing* in the concert tonight.

5 Don't worry, we*'ll collect* / *'re collecting* your suitcase from the hotel.

6 I need to get to bed early. *We'll leave* / *We're leaving* at six tomorrow morning!

Corpus challenge

Read a student's sentence. Can you correct his mistake with a future form?

On Saturday we go to a football match.

6 Complete the sentences with your own ideas.

1 For my next birthday, …

2 At seven o'clock this evening, …

3 When I'm old enough, …

VOCABULARY enough, too, very

1 Read the examples. Then write *enough, too* or *very* next to meanings a–c.

1 *It will be a* **very** *special journey.*

2 *The car will move forward if it gets* **enough** *interest on social media.*

3 *My little sister thinks this game is* **too** *complicated.*

4 *I'm not fast* **enough** *to be in the swimming team.*

a as much as necessary

b more than is wanted or necessary

c used to make an adjective or adverb stronger

2 Complete the text with words from exercise 1.

Matt Harding was lucky [1] .... to get a job as a video game designer when he was still [2] .... young. At the age of 23, he moved to Australia, and began to realise that he was spending [3] .... much time developing games and not giving himself [4] .... opportunities to see the world and have fun. So he quit his job. While he was travelling in Vietnam, a friend filmed him doing a [5] .... silly dance on a street corner. He thought the clip was [6] .... funny. They did more filming and Matt edited the clips for his blog. Someone saw Matt's video, uploaded it to YouTube and was clever [7] .... to make money out of Matt's crazy dancing – a million people watched that first video!

WRITING A short message (1)

1 Look at the three phones. Which one is the most similar to yours? Describe your phone in two sentences.

2 Read the task and the sample answer. Which point in the task does Jo not cover?

> You are going to buy a new phone. Write an email to your Canadian friend, Sam. In your email, you should:
> - tell Sam why you need to replace your old phone.
> - give Sam some information about the model you're going to buy.
> - ask Sam about the favourite types of phone in Canada.
>
> Write 35–45 words.

> Hi Sam,
>
> Guess what? I'm going to get a new phone. My old one isn't working properly and the screen's tiny. I want a smartphone and I've seen a cool red one with a big screen – really awesome! How's life in Canada?
>
> Love, Jo

3 Add a sentence to Jo's email to answer the final point in the task.

4 Read the *Prepare* box. What kinds of mistake do you usually make in your writing?

5 Correct the underlined mistakes in the sentences. Then match the mistakes to the types of mistake in the *Prepare* box.

1 The <u>batterys'</u> too old.
2 The internet connection isn't <u>enough fast</u>.
3 I dropped my phone and <u>he</u> stopped working.
4 I'd like a smartphone with a <u>fatter</u> screen.
5 What are the most popular <u>Canadien</u> phones?
6 I'm looking forward to <u>hear</u> from you.
7 One of the best phones <u>are</u> made by an American company.

6 Find and correct seven mistakes in the email.

> Hi Sam,
>
> Im going to get another phone becous I have an old one but he is broken. What your favourite kind of phone is? For me, the most important things in a phone is the size of the screen and the number of memory. I enjoy to take photos. Do you?
>
> Luke

7 Read the task below and plan your ideas. Make sure you cover all the points in the task.

> You are going to buy a new video game. Write an email to your English friend, Jackie. In your email, you should:
> - tell Jackie what kind of game you have chosen.
> - explain why you are looking forward to playing it.
> - ask what Jackie's favourite video game is.
>
> Write 35–45 words.

8 ● Write your email.
- Use the tips in the *Prepare* box.
- Remember to add some extra information and use a range of tenses.

VOCABULARY Nature and wildlife

Your profile

How important are animals to you? Do you have any favourite animals?

Which animals in your country are in danger? Why?

1 Look at the photos. Which of these animals is the most in danger today? Give your reasons.

bee

bluefin tuna

tiger

2 ▶1.26 Listen to three teenagers, Daniel, Ruth and Tommy. What problems does each person mention?

3 ▶1.26 Complete the sentences with the words in the box. Then listen again and check.

creatures   crops   environment   humans
jungle   landscape   population   rainforest

1 This problem is as serious as saving the ....
2 The .... of honeybees today is far lower than it used to be.
3 Bees and other insects help our .... to grow in the fields.
4 Some people say that the bluefin tuna is one of the tastiest living .... in the sea.
5 The balance of the ocean .... will be damaged forever.
6 This is all due to the actions of ....
7 The .... where they live is changing, as more and more trees are cut down.
8 The areas of .... are getting smaller.

4 Work in groups. Decide which animal in the photos is the most important to humans. Can you all agree?

5 Discuss the questions.
1 How important is it to protect animals in the wild?
2 What could you do to help?
3 Is enough being done to save the rainforest in your opinion?

EP Word profile *besides*

Besides, without them we wouldn't have nearly as many plants and flowers.

There are other kinds of tuna besides the bluefin that we can eat instead.

Besides being hunted, tigers are facing another challenge.

page 134

READING

1 The photos show the Sumatran orangutan. Read the text quickly to find out at least three facts about this creature. Compare your ideas.

ANIMALS IN DANGER

There used to be orangutans across the whole island of Sumatra and **(0)** .... on Java. This animal lives high up **(1)** .... the trees of tropical rainforests, eating fruit. Unfortunately, because humans have **(2)** .... much of this forest, the Sumatran population is now **(3)** .... to the north of the island. There are only around 7,000 left and this number is going **(4)** .... Unless we do more to help them, they will disappear **(5)** .... People are not allowed to **(6)** .... orangutans as pets in Indonesia. If any are **(7)** .... in private homes, they are taken to a rescue centre. When they are healthy enough, they are transferred to a **(8)** .... area in a national park. **(9)** .... of the orangutans that are rescued in this **(10)** .... end up living happily in the wild and produce babies.

If we protect orangutans now, they will have a future. They probably won't if we do nothing.

2 🔵 **Read the whole text and choose the correct word for each space (1–10).**

0	**A** also	**B** too	**C** yet	**D** still
1	**A** through	**B** among	**C** beyond	**D** inside
2	**A** finished	**B** turned	**C** destroyed	**D** stopped
3	**A** limited	**B** closed	**C** advanced	**D** checked
4	**A** out	**B** down	**C** off	**D** away
5	**A** actually	**B** badly	**C** really	**D** completely
6	**A** have	**B** make	**C** stay	**D** join
7	**A** arrested	**B** found	**C** touched	**D** picked
8	**A** fair	**B** kind	**C** true	**D** safe
9	**A** Both	**B** Many	**C** Lot	**D** Much
10	**A** type	**B** style	**C** way	**D** plan

3 Read the text again and answer the questions.

1 Why are there only orangutans in one part of the island now?
2 Where are orangutans taken if they are found in people's homes?
3 What happens to orangutans that are moved to a national park?

Talking points

❝ Do you think it is fair to keep wild animals as pets? Why? / Why not?

What effect does our lifestyle have on animals in the wild?

Does it matter if certain animals disappear forever? Why? / Why not? ❞

GRAMMAR   Conditional sentences

1 Look at the examples. Which tenses are used in each pair? Match each pair of examples to rule a or b.

1 *If any **are found** in private homes, they **are taken** to a rescue centre.*
   ***When** they **are** healthy enough, they **are transferred** to a national park.*

2 *If we **protect** orangutans now, they **will have** a future.*
   *They **won't have** a future **if** we **do** nothing.*

> a We use the zero conditional for events or situations that actually happen. We use:
>   *If / When* + present simple + present simple.
> b We use the first conditional to imagine what is likely to happen. We use:
>   *If* + present simple + *will / won't*.

→ Grammar reference **page 154**

2 Match the sentence halves. Which sentences use the first conditional?

1 If tigers are better protected,
2 When an area of jungle is cleared,
3 If the area of Arctic ice gets smaller,
4 If an animal is badly injured,
5 If we plant a variety of wild flowers,
6 When more tourism is introduced,

a the land is often used for farming.
b it has many benefits for local people.
c we'll see a lot more butterflies.
d their numbers will probably increase.
e there won't be many polar bears left.
f it isn't able to hunt for food.

3 Complete the second example so that it means the same as the first. What do the examples tell you about the meaning of *unless*?

1 *Unless we do more to help orangutans, they will disappear completely.*
2 *If we .... more to help orangutans, they will disappear completely.*

4 Complete the sentences with *if* or *unless*.

1 Polar bears won't find enough to eat .... we do more to protect their environment.
2 .... we don't protect these animals now, they will die out.
3 Many birds will suffer .... sea levels continue to rise.
4 .... we control whale fishing, there'll be no whales left soon.
5 Elephant numbers will go on falling .... governments do more to protect them.
6 .... enough money is collected, the organisation will open a second rescue centre.

Second conditional

5 Read the examples and the rule. Which example uses the second conditional?

1 *If bees **disappear** completely, we **will** all **suffer**.*
2 *If bees **disappeared** completely, we **would** all **suffer**.*

> We use the second conditional to talk about something that is unlikely to happen. We use:
> *If* + past simple + *would*.

6 Choose the correct form of the verb.

1 If bigger areas of rainforest *exist / existed*, there would be more wildlife.
2 If governments listened to experts, they *will / would* know what to do.
3 Unless the amount of fishing is limited, there *wouldn't / won't* be many bluefin tuna left.
4 If they *don't / didn't* watch documentaries, most people would never see animals in the wild.
5 Unless more areas of forest *are / were* saved, orangutans will not be able to remain.

⊙ Corpus challenge

Find and correct the mistake in the student's sentence.

I would be really happy if you meet Maria.

7 Complete the sentences so they are true for you.

1 If I had the chance to see any animal in the wild, …
2 When I go to bed late, …
3 If I go to the coast next weekend, …

VOCABULARY   Phrases with *at*

1 Read the examples and match the bold phrases to the meanings.

1 ***At least** 95% of wild tigers have disappeared.*
2 *Things are happening **at long last** to protect tigers.*
a finally
b not less than

2 Complete the sentences with the phrases in the box.

> at all   at first   at its best   at least
> at once   at present

1 The amazing filming of wildlife in the Pantanal Wetlands is documentary-making ....
2 When the horse suddenly stopped, I knew .... that something was wrong.
3 It's very dry here .... , but rain is forecast for next week.
4 .... I didn't recognise her, because she looked so different.
5 My brother doesn't know anything .... about looking after animals.
6 The rainforest is disappearing, but .... some of it is protected now.

LISTENING

1 The photo shows someone taking part in a race with teams of dogs called huskies. Read the questions. Try to guess the answers by looking at the photo.

1 In which country does the race take place?
2 How long is the race in kilometres?
3 How many teams enter the race?
4 How popular is it with local people?

2 ▶1.27 You will hear a Skype call about the race between two teenagers, Adam and Berit. Listen and check your answers to exercise 1.

3 ▶1.27 Listen again and tick the three sentences that are correct. Explain why the other two are incorrect.

1 The winners take less than six days to finish the race.
2 None of the dogs is able to run the full distance.
3 Different nationalities are allowed to compete in the race.
4 Some fans like to remain in one place until most teams have passed.
5 Vets at the race are only responsible for looking after sick or tired dogs.

SPEAKING Discussing a topic (1)

1 Read the advice for taking part in discussions. Choose the five pieces of advice which are true. Can you add more advice?

1 Don't be afraid to ask what someone means.
2 Say as much as possible, even if the other person wants to speak.
3 Try to develop your ideas.
4 Make sure you give the other person enough opportunities to join in.
5 Apologise if you interrupt someone, and allow them time to speak.
6 Make links to what you or the other person has said.
7 Talk loudly if another person is trying to speak.

2 ▶1.27 Read the *Prepare* box. Listen to Adam and Berit's conversation again and match the phrases in the *Prepare* box to the functions below.

Prepare to speak — Taking part in a discussion

a Do you mean … ?
b Hang on a moment, when you say …
c Sorry, I don't understand.
d I missed that. Can you repeat that, please?
e Sorry, what were you going to say?
f Going back to …
g Like I said before, …
h On a completely different subject …

1 asking for further explanation if you don't understand something
2 interrupting
3 changing the topic
4 referring back to an earlier topic
5 asking someone to say something again if you didn't hear it
6 encouraging someone to continue after you have interrupted them

3 ● Work in pairs. Look at the picture, which shows another competition involving animals. Discuss the questions, using phrases from the *Prepare* box.

1 Why do you think this event is popular?
2 In what ways is this event different from the race with huskies?

4 Discuss the questions.

1 Why do you think some people enjoy watching animals in competitions?
2 What kinds of event do you enjoy watching on TV?
3 What are the differences between watching events and taking part in them?
4 Why do some people **not** like taking part in competitions?

Culture
Animals as national symbols

1 Look at the photos of animals. Can you name them all? The names are in the box at the bottom of page 63.

2 Read the Animal facts box and complete these comparisons with the animals from exercise 1.

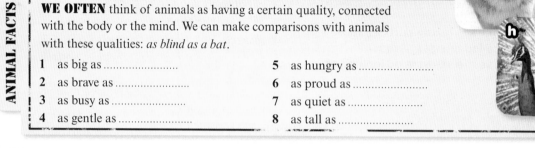

ANIMAL FACTS

WE OFTEN think of animals as having a certain quality, connected with the body or the mind. We can make comparisons with animals with these qualities: *as blind as a bat*.

1 as big as ....
2 as brave as ....
3 as busy as ....
4 as gentle as ....

5 as hungry as ....
6 as proud as ....
7 as quiet as ....
8 as tall as ....

3 Why do you think some countries choose to have an animal as a national symbol on their flag or stamps or coins? Which animals from the list above do you think are national symbols? Why?

4 Read the text quickly to check your answers to exercise 3. Do any of the animals surprise you? Why?

ANIMALS *and* COUNTRIES

If you wanted to show the world your idea of yourself, how would you do it? One way countries do this is with their national symbols, i.e. what they put on flags, coins, stamps, and so on. When an animal is used in this way, it's a national animal.

Click here for a list of national animals

How do countries choose their national animals? Well, they usually choose an animal that comes from their country. The national animal of Tanzania, East Africa, for example, is the giraffe, which lives there as well as in other African countries. But what about the most popular national animal of them all, the lion? The lion's natural environment is Africa, so it is the national animal of a number of African countries, such as Kenya or Liberia. That makes sense. What about England, Belgium, the Netherlands and Bulgaria, though? They all have the lion as their national symbol, but lions don't come from these countries.

In many cases, the main reason for selecting an animal as the national symbol is not because of its natural environment, but because of the qualities we believe the animal has. The lion is the national animal of many countries because we think of it as being strong, proud, honest and brave. These are all qualities that countries like to believe they possess.

Another national symbol like this is the eagle, the symbol of the United States since 1782, and of many other countries, such as Mexico, Egypt and Germany. We see eagles as proud and honest, too, but besides all this – they are free. A lot of birds are national symbols, partly because they show the idea of freedom.

Other national animals include, for example, the elephant, in countries as far from each other as Thailand and Mozambique. This is seen as an honest and hard-working animal. An interesting symbol is the wolf, national animal of Turkey and many southern European countries, such as Portugal and Italy. But don't we see the wolf as a cruel hunter? True, but there are many other opinions of the wolf too. It was believed, for example, that the men who started Rome, Romulus and Remus, were brought up by a wolf. That explains Italy's choice of the wolf. Also, the wolf is a distant cousin of the dog, which has lived and worked with humans for centuries.

The qualities we look for in national animals are mostly those which we value in ourselves and other humans – strength, bravery, intelligence, so how do you explain the national animal of Monaco – the mouse?

5 Match the qualities to the animals. Write the name of the animal next to the qualities.

1 cruel ....
3 proud and brave ....
2 hard-working and honest ....
4 free and proud ....

6 These statements about the article are incorrect. Correct them and underline the part of the text that shows you this.

1 National animals always come from the countries whose symbol they are.
2 Lions originally come from Europe.
3 The main reason why birds are often national animals is because they are proud.
4 The wolf is still seen as a cruel creature.
5 Wolves are closely related to ordinary dogs.

7 ▶1.28 Listen to Sonia giving a presentation to her class and answer the questions.

1 Which animal in particular is her presentation about, and which country?
2 How long has the animal been a symbol of her country?
3 What other animal might you see on some coins?
4 Why didn't Benjamin Franklin want this animal as a symbol?
5 How does Sonia feel about her country's national symbol?

8 ▶1.28 Listen again. Which topics does Sonia talk about?

her country's national animal
when it became the national animal
where it lives
why it was chosen
which other animals were discussed as national symbols
where the symbol appears
how people felt about the choice
how she feels about the choice

9 Sonia makes her classmates laugh in her presentation. What does she say? Why does she do this?

Project

Work in pairs to prepare a presentation about your national animal.
- Find out as much information as you can about your national animal.
- Put the information in a similar order to the presentation in exercise 8.
- If you can, add one or two interesting details.
- Find some pictures to show as examples during the presentation.
- Decide which of you is going to give which parts of the presentation.
- Try to prepare enough information to speak for three or four minutes.

Give your presentation to the class.

a bee **b** mouse **c** lamb **d** lion **e** giraffe **f** wolf **g** elephant **h** peacock

11 Off to school

VOCABULARY School

Your profile

How many hours each week do you spend at school?
How long does it take you to get to school each day?

1 Look at the photos of difficult journeys to school. Which journey do you think is the most difficult? Why?

2 ▶1.29 Listen to a photographer talking about the photos. In what order does she talk about them?

3 ▶1.29 Complete the sentences with the words in the boxes. Then listen again and check.

| grade primary qualifications secondary |

1 The children are very young and go to the .... school.
2 I'm not sure where they will go to school when they are .... school age.
3 I think he was in .... one, so age six.
4 I wonder what .... these children will end up getting.

| attended degree done well |

5 The man was the headteacher of a local school, which he'd .... when he was a boy.
6 He had .... really .... at school.
7 He realised his dream and got a ....

| broke up education done badly |

8 This was the last day of school before the kids .... for the holidays.
9 She thought she'd .... really .... in her exams.
10 I know that .... was important to her.

4 Read the sentences about school. Do you agree?

1 All children should attend school up to the age of 18.
2 Only excellent students should go to university and get a degree.
3 Schools should break up for holidays every four weeks.
4 Children who do badly should never have to repeat a year.
5 Children should start primary school when they are four, and secondary school when they are 12.
6 It's really important to do well at school.
7 Education should be free and available to everyone in the world.
8 Experience in life is more important than qualifications.
9 All children should start learning another language when they're in first grade, when they're six years old.

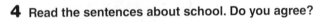

READING

1 What things do you like and dislike about your classroom?

2 Read the three texts. Which classroom (A, B or C) is the most traditional? Which is the most unusual?

CLASSROOMS *around the* WORLD

A **KEL** I decided to apply for a far-away school, but this was definitely further than I imagined! And I never thought that a school classroom could be in a cave! It was a really unusual place to have a school. The families of a Chinese village had built the school, known as Middle Cave Elementary School, in the cave about 50 years before. They had transported the materials for the school furniture up the mountain. It took days and then they made the tables and chairs by hand. Children come from many different places around the area and walk up a stone path to reach the school every day. I arrived at the school in early April to teach English conversation, and I helped the music teacher. Having these lessons in a cave was incredible because of the sound produced inside caves. The classroom made music by itself!

B **CARTER** I wasn't sure what to do in the summer after I left school and before I went to university. I was looking for ideas, and then I found out by accident about the teaching programme for Fiji. I was able to apply because I had had experience of working with children before. So I went to the Fijian island of Nacula for three months. Our classroom was fairly ordinary, with desks and a blackboard. There were hardly any computers, but the walls were covered with colourful pictures and writing, mostly in English. I spent an amazing three weeks at the school helping the class teacher. The teacher had the most beautiful wooden desk that her grandfather had made for her by hand to celebrate her first job. It was a very different school to the one that I had attended back home. I thought that the children all worked really hard and they mostly did well.

C **JADE** I had a very special experience when I went to this school in Cuba a few years ago. Three years earlier, the parents and teachers had built several outdoor classrooms for the summer terms. They had spent a lot of time talking about the design of the classrooms, and eventually they decided to have lots of different 'classroom areas'. There was a classroom in the vegetable garden, there was another one surrounded by trees and there was even a classroom in a rose garden, although there were a couple of sunflowers that someone had planted by mistake! The parents had put a lot of effort into making their children's learning a good experience. I think the children enjoyed it because they didn't feel as if they were in a classroom. However, I was teaching maths and I found I missed having a whiteboard!

3 Read the texts again. Which classroom …
1. was created by parents and teachers?
2. was built by local people about half a century ago?
3. was inside a garden?
4. was inside a big natural hole?
5. had very few computers?
6. was good for music?
7. was challenging for the teacher?
8. had a gift made by the teacher's relative in it?

EP Word profile *by*

The classroom made music by itself!

Her grandfather had made it for her by hand.

There were a couple of sunflowers that someone had planted by mistake!

page 134

4 Find words or phrases in the text to match the meanings.
1. request something in writing or by completing a form (text A)
2. objects that you put into a room or building (text A)
3. not special (text B)
4. do something enjoyable because it is a special day (text B)
5. with things all around a place (text C)
6. energy that you use to do something (text C)

Talking points
" What is important in a good classroom?
What other things help children to learn well? "

GRAMMAR Past perfect

1 Read the example and look at the bold verbs. Answer the questions.

*I **went** to this school a few years ago. Three years earlier, the parents and teachers **had built** several outdoor classrooms.*

1 Which action happened first?
   a the author went to the school
   b the parents and teachers built the classroom
2 Which verb is in the past simple? Which is in the past perfect?

2 Choose the correct words to complete the rules.

> a We use the past perfect to talk about an action that happened *before / after* another action in the past.
> b We form the past perfect with *had + past participle / had + -ing form*.

→ Grammar reference **page 155**

3 Read the sentences and look at the verb forms. Which action came first, a or b?

0 When Jake arrived home, Mark had left the house.
   a Jake arrived home.   (b) Mark left the house.
1 I'd gone to bed when Harriet got home.
   a Harriet got home.   b I went to bed.
2 Martin didn't go to the cinema because he'd seen the film before.
   a Martin didn't go   b Martin saw the film.
     to the cinema.
3 Juliana wasn't hungry because she'd had lunch at school.
   a Juliana had lunch   b Juliana wasn't hungry.
     at school.
4 Paul called me when he had finished his homework.
   a Paul called me.   b Paul finished his
                              homework.

4 Choose the correct form of the verbs.

1 When the police caught the thief, they found five famous paintings that he *stole / had stolen*.
2 Mark *was / had been* late today because he'd missed the bus.
3 I was surprised because I *didn't see / hadn't seen* such an unusual classroom before.
4 Every day Maria *took / had taken* the same route to school as her father had done.
5 The teacher was angry because no one *did / had done* their homework.

⊙ Corpus challenge

Find and correct the mistake in the student's sentence.

Her teacher told her that she got a scholarship to Cambridge University.

5 Read about a school in Norway and complete the text with the correct form of the verbs.

Before I ¹ .... (go) to Norway, I ² ....
(work) all over the world and I ³ .... (see)
many different classrooms. But this ⁴ .... (be)
definitely more impressive than anything I ⁵ ....
(experience) before. I ⁶ .... (not / work) with
a class before in which every child had their
own computer. But I also ⁷ .... (not / go) to
a school before where children had to leave the
island when they ⁸ .... (reach) the age of 16,
to continue their education on the mainland.

VOCABULARY Compound nouns

1 Read the examples and look at the bold words. What kinds of word (nouns, verbs or adjectives) do we join together to make compound nouns?

1 *Our **classroom** was fairly ordinary.*
2 *I missed having a **whiteboard**!*

2 Choose a word from each box to make compound nouns. Write the words next to the meanings.

> bus   fire   foot   head   skate   sun

> ball   board   flower   stop   teacher   work

1 a small object which explodes in the sky and produces bright lights
2 a large yellow flower
3 the place where people get on and off a bus
4 a game in which you kick a ball
5 the person in charge of a school
6 a board with wheels that you can stand on and move forward on

3 You have two minutes. How many compound nouns can you make from the words?

WRITING A story (2)

1 Have you read any stories that take place in school? What happened?

2 Read Alec's story. Choose the best first sentence.

   a It was a really bad day at school.

   b It was the first day back at school after the summer holidays.

   c I was looking forward to the summer holidays.

.... I was sitting quietly in the classroom and feeling very nervous. Before the holidays the teacher had asked us to do some simple homework. I hadn't done it because I'd forgotten all about it. I was really worried that the teacher would be angry. Then the teacher came into the classroom. She took the register, but she didn't mention the homework. She carried on with the class as usual. Finally, at the end of the class she said quickly, 'Don't forget to bring your homework tomorrow.' How lucky! I handed in my completed homework the next day – and I got a good mark!

3 Read the *Prepare* box. Read Alec's story again and find examples of verbs in the past simple, past continuous and past perfect.

Prepare to write — Writing a story (2)

When you write a story:
- use a range of verb forms.
- use adverbs to describe verbs:
  *I was sitting **quietly** in the classroom.*
- use adjectives to describe nouns:
  *I handed in my **completed** homework the next day.*
- check that your story has a beginning, a middle and an end.

4 Look at the highlighted adjectives and adverbs in Alec's story. How do adjectives and adverbs improve the story?

5 Add a suitable adjective to the sentences. Use your own ideas.

   1 A .... man walked into the room.

   2 The teacher gave us some .... homework.

   3 We had a .... day!

   4 The lessons take place in a .... classroom.

6 Add an adverb to each sentence. Use the adverbs in the box or your own ideas. Compare your sentences with a partner.

> angrily   cheerfully   easily   immediately
> quietly   quickly   slowly   well

   0 He shouted at me.
     He shouted at me angrily.

   1 She walked out of the room.

   2 I finished my homework.

   3 We ate our lunch.

   4 He smiled at me.

   5 The teacher answered her questions.

7 Read the task below and plan your ideas, then compare your ideas with a partner. Can you improve your plan?

- Your teacher has asked you to write a story.
- Your story must begin with this line:
  I set off for school as usual that morning.

8 🔴 Write your story.

- Use the tips in the *Prepare* box.
- Write about 100 words.
- Remember to check your spelling and grammar.

VOCABULARY Travel

Your profile

Which is the most exciting form of transport you have been on? Why was it exciting?
Which forms of transport have you travelled on alone?

1 Look at the photos. What forms of transport do they show? What are the different reasons for using them? What other forms of transport can you think of?

2 ▶1.30 Listen to four people talking. Match them to four of the photos.

3 ▶1.30 Listen again. Are the sentences correct or incorrect?

1 The girl's cousin sailed on a cruise ship from New York to Florida.
2 The boy's dad is on board by 7 am every morning.
3 The girl says she and her family will move in a few years.
4 The boy says the public transport he uses is usually on time.

4 Complete the sentences with the correct form of the words in the box.

> abroad   cruise ship   ferry   go away
> harbour   land   on board   public transport
> sail   set out   timetable   tourism

1 Josie's plane .... at 7.28. We should leave now to meet her.
2 .... is an important industry on the island.
3 You can .... from one island to another.
4 We .... really early this morning to catch the plane.
5 Once everyone is .... , the plane can take off.
6 According to the .... , the bus should be here any time now.
7 The .... is enormous – there are three huge swimming pools on it.
8 Do you walk to school or use .... ?
9 The fishing village has a small ....
10 You can catch a .... across the river.
11 You can't go .... if you don't have a passport.
12 We want to .... for a few weeks this summer.

5 Discuss the questions.

1 Have you ever been on board a ship or ferry? Which harbour did you leave from?
2 Would you enjoy a holiday sailing on a cruise ship?
3 Have you ever been abroad? Where and how did you go?
4 Why do some people always go away to the same place for their holiday?

READING

1 Read Elena's profile. How would you describe her?

2 Elena is going to travel abroad alone for the first time. What questions do you think she has?

3 Read Elena's post and compare your ideas.

Hi everyone!
I'm Elena and I'm Australian, but my parents are both British. When I'm not at school, I like doing team sports like basketball and volleyball.

Elena Australia – 12.46 pm

Guys! I'm travelling abroad to visit my aunt in London. But I'm going alone! I'm excited because I've never been to Europe. It's a really long flight and I have to change planes in Dubai. I'm a bit nervous. Is there anything I should know or do before I go? What should I take with me? If anyone has already done a trip like this, could you please post some information? That would be really helpful.

Michael Poland – 1.19 pm

Hey Elena. Firstly, you don't have to think about anything because it's all done for you! But you should definitely find out what the airport at Dubai looks like. You can check it out online. Then you will know what it's going to look like when you get there. The most challenging thing for me was changing planes. But in the end it was all OK. Have a great trip.

Sally NZ – 4.58 pm

Hi Elena! I did a similar trip to that last year on my own. It was really cool because the airline staff checked I was OK, and they provided me with whatever I wanted. They handed me out a range of extra food including sweets! Mum gave me a really cool bag to put my documents in. You hang it round your neck and that way you know where everything is. You should definitely get one of those! Have a good trip!

Max USA – 2.23 pm

Hi Elena! I flew from the US to the UK last year to visit my grandparents. You don't need to worry about who is going to be sitting next to you. They put all the teens together. In fact, my window seat was the best thing on the flight! Also, you should take a travel backpack with your entertainment in – books, iPod, or tablet loaded with films. On my flight last year, the seats didn't have the individual screens, so I was glad I had my own films! Have fun!

Sofia Spain – 4.24 pm

Hi Elena! You need to check what the weather is like, so that you know what clothes to take! I think it's always sunny in Australia, but I live in Europe and it's snowing at the moment. You needn't worry about your bags until you get to London. But obviously remember to pick them up when you get there! Also you have to have a letter from your parents saying that they allow you to travel. You shouldn't forget that letter! A friend of mine didn't have the letter and there was a huge delay. Oh, and don't forget to use the online check-in – you can save a lot of time. Leave plenty of time for the security checks – they're really strict nowadays and they can take a long time. Mind you, as an unaccompanied minor, you shouldn't have to wait too long! Have a good trip – London is amazing!

---

4 Read the comments. Who advised Elena …

1 to find out what the temperature is?
2 to have a document from her parents allowing her to travel?
3 to purchase a special bag for her travel documents?
4 to take things to do on the plane?
5 to allow time for security checks?
6 to find out where she has to go in Dubai before she leaves?
7 to relax about who will sit next to her?
8 that the airline staff were very kind?

5 Read the comments again. Complete the sentences with highlighted words from the text.

1 My grandparents find busy places like airports very ....
2 That bag looks .... to mine, but mine is smaller.
3 Would your parents .... you to fly round the world on your own?
4 Just before getting on a plane, Maria gets really ....
5 It's really frustrating when there's a .... at the airport!
6 The lady at the desk told me where to go. She was really ....
7 On a long flight I don't like a .... because you can't get out easily to go to the toilet.

EP Word profile *check*

They checked in and found their ship.

The airline staff checked I was OK.

Security checks are really strict nowadays.

page 135

6 What advice would *you* give to Elena?

Talking points

“ At what age do you think children should be allowed to travel alone? Why?

What are the advantages of travelling alone, rather than with your family? ”

GRAMMAR Modals (2): Obligation and advice

1 Read the examples. Then complete the rules with the bold verbs in the examples.

1 *You **don't have to** think about anything because it's all done for you!*

2 *But you **needn't** worry about your bags until you get to London.*

3 *You **need to** check what the weather is like, so that you know what clothes to take!*

4 *You **should** take a travel backpack with your entertainment in.*

5 *You **have to** have a letter from your parents saying that they allow you to travel.*

6 *You **shouldn't** forget that letter.*

> We use:
>
> **a** .... and .... to give advice to someone.
>
> **b** .... to say that something is necessary because of a rule or law.
>
> **c** .... to say that something is a personal obligation.
>
> **d** .... , ... or *don't need to* to say that something is not necessary.
>
> Notice the different patterns with *need*:
>
> *You **need to** find out.*
>
> *You **needn't** ~~to~~ worry.*

→ Grammar reference **page 156**

2 Read the notices and messages. What do they mean? Tick a or b.

❶ FREE ENTRY for under 18s

a You needn't pay to get in. ☐

b You should take your money with you. ☐

❷ Suitable shoes only in the gym

a You should wear your trainers for sports. ☐

b You don't have to wear your trainers for sports. ☐

❸ Wet paint DO NOT TOUCH

a You shouldn't sit here. ☐

b You needn't sit here. ☐

❹ Get milk – we've run out!

a You don't have to get any milk. ☐

b You need to buy more milk. ☐

3 Choose the correct modal verbs.

1 If you visit the UK, you *should / don't need to* go to London and visit the Science Museum.

2 You *have to / shouldn't* buy a ticket before you get on the train.

3 I think you *shouldn't / need to* plan this trip carefully if you want it to be a success.

4 If you are travelling alone, you *needn't / should* be scared – the airline will look after you.

5 You *shouldn't / have to* show your passport if an official wants to see it.

6 You *have to / shouldn't* take all liquids in a clear bag when you go through security.

7 You *shouldn't / need to* arrive at the airport too late, or you might miss your flight.

8 You *need to / needn't* get your own drinks because someone will bring them to you.

4 Complete the sentences with your own ideas.

1 My parents tell me I should …

2 When I stay with my grandparents, I don't have to …

3 Right now I need to …

⊙ Corpus challenge

> **Find and correct the mistake in the student's sentence.**
>
> If you come, you will bring a coat because it's cold.

VOCABULARY Phrases with *on*

1 Read the example. What other phrases do you know with *on*?

*He sets out at 7 am and he's **on board** by 8.20 am.*

2 Complete the sentences with the phrases in the box.

> on board   on display   on foot
> on purpose   on sale   on time

1 The children's work was .... on the walls.

2 Some students have to go to school .... because there's no public transport.

3 Finally, my favourite author's latest book is ....

4 If you arrived .... every morning, you wouldn't be in trouble with the headteacher.

5 As soon as you get .... , the airline staff want you to fasten your seat belt.

6 I made the mistake .... , to find out if you were listening to me.

3 Tell your partner about a time when you:

1 were on board a plane or ship.

2 behaved badly on purpose.

3 saw an unusual item on sale.

4 didn't arrive somewhere on time.

5 went somewhere on foot.

6 took interest in something that was on display.

LISTENING

1 Look at the photos. What kinds of announcement might you hear in these places?
Compare your ideas with your partner.

2 Look at the notes. What kind of information is missing? Share your ideas with your partner.

INFORMATION ABOUT THE FLIGHT

Languages spoken by cabin crew: English, Chinese and **(1)** ....
Arrival time at destination: **(2)** ....

ENTERTAINMENT
Comedy shows available on: **(3)** ....

DINNER
Vegetarian option: **(4)** ....
Choice of desserts

GIFT SALES
Special offer this month on: **(5)** ....
Name of airline's magazine: **(6)** ....

3 ● ▶1.31 You will hear an announcement on board a plane. For each question, fill in the missing information in the numbered space.

SPEAKING   Talking about homes, family and school

1 ▶1.32 Listen to Anne-Marie and Faisal talking about themselves. Tick the topics they talk about.

My favourite teacher
My free time
My family
Films I enjoy
My future
My home
My holidays

2 ▶1.32 It's important to add more information when you answer questions. Match two pieces of extra information to each answer that Anne-Marie and Faisal gave. Listen again and check.

1 I have a brother and two sisters.
2 There are lots of films that I like.
3 We usually go to the same place in Italy.
4 I have no idea.

a Next year I'm going to choose my Year 10 subjects.
b I usually watch films on my computer.
c Actually, I want to go to Monaco next year.
d Maybe action films are my favourite because they're really exciting.
e I'm going to study really hard.
f We all love spending time together.
g For example, last weekend we went to the park and played tennis.
h We go there by car every year.

3 Read the *Prepare* box, then look at the sentences in exercise 2 again. Find examples of the phrases and the range of tenses that Anne-Marie and Faisal use.

Prepare to speak Answering questions (2)

Adding extra information
For example …
Actually, …
because …
Using a range of tenses
I usually …
I want to …
I'm going to …
Last weekend, we …

4 ● Read the questions and prepare your answers. Then practise with a partner. Use phrases from the *Prepare* box.

1 Tell me about your home town.
2 Would you like to live in a different country? Why?
3 Can you describe your house or flat?
4 Tell us about your favourite relative.
5 Can you tell us about your favourite teacher?
6 What's your favourite school subject?

Maths
Speed calculations

1 ▶1.33 **Match the photos to the top speeds in the box. Then listen and check your answers.**

Hydroptère

Bugatti Veyron

MV Agusta F4

SR71 Blackbird

Formula Rossa

97 km/h   240 km/h   302 km/h   431 km/h   3,529 km/h

2 **Read the text. Explain the words *speed*, *distance* and *time*.**

Calculating speed

Speed is a measure of how fast something moves. We often calculate speed in kilometres per hour (km/h). That is how many kilometres something travels in one hour. For example, if Car A goes 100 kilometres in two hours, it's travelling at 50 km/h. If Car B goes the same distance in only 30 minutes, it's travelling at 200 km/h.

$$\text{Speed} = \frac{\text{Distance}}{\text{Time}}$$

Car A: 100 km ÷ 2 hours = **50 km/h**
Car B: 100 km ÷ 0.5 hours = **200 km/h**

Converting speed

We can change speeds from kilometres per hour to metres per second (m/s). We multiply by 1,000 (the number of metres in one kilometre) and then divide by 3,600 (the number of seconds in one hour). To convert m/s into km/h, we do the opposite. We multiply by 3,600 (seconds in an hour) and divide by 1,000 (metres in a kilometre).

Car A: 50 km/h x 1,000 ÷ 3,600 = **13.89 m/s**
Car B: 200 km/h x 1,000 ÷ 3,600 = **55.56 m/s**
    13.89 m/s x 3,600 ÷ 1,000 = **50 km/h**
    55.56 m/s x 3,600 ÷ 1,000 = **200 km/h**

Calculating distance and time

If we know a car's speed and the amount of time it travels, we can find out the distance it goes. We multiply the speed and the time.

Distance= Speed x Time

Car C: Speed = 80 km/h
    Time = 2 hours
    Distance = 80 x 2 = **160 kilometres**

If we know a car's speed and the distance it travels, we can calculate the time it takes. We divide the distance by the speed.

$$\text{Time} = \frac{\text{Distance}}{\text{Speed}}$$

Car D: Speed = 50 m/s
    Distance = 5,000 metres
    Time = 5,000 ÷ 50 = **100 seconds**

3 Calculate the speeds in km/h. Then convert them to m/s.

1 A plane travels 2,550 km in 3 hours.
Speed = ... km/h or .... m/s

2 A train travels 450 km in 2.5 hours.
Speed = ... km/h or .... m/s

3 A bus travels 162 km in 1.5 hours.
Speed = ... km/h or .... m/s

4 A person walks 2.25 km in 0.5 hours.
Speed = ... km/h or .... m/s

4 Study the speed chart. Calculate the missing information for distance and time.

	speed	distance	time
1 motorcycle	85 km/h	....	3.5 h
2 bike	4.5 m/s	4,050 m	....
3 helicopter	18 m/s	....	0.25 h
4 speedboat	30 km/h	12 km	....

5  1.34 Listen to a student presentation about the *SonicStar*. Complete the summary below.

SonicStar

The SonicStar is a new aeroplane that will start flying in [1]............ . It will be a supersonic plane, so it will travel faster than the speed of sound which is [2]............ km/h, or Mach 1.

Concorde flew at Mach [3]............ , or about 2240 km/h, but the SonicStar's top speed will be Mach [4]............ , or about [5]............ km/h. The new plane will also fly very high, at an altitude of [6]............ metres. Most planes don't fly higher than 12,000 metres.

The SonicStar will travel from London to New York in [7]............ hours. At the moment, a non-stop passenger flight from the UK to Australia takes about [8]............ hours, but with the SonicStar the flight from London to Sydney will only be about [9]............ . The SonicStar will only carry about [10]............ passengers.

FAMOUS TRANSPORT SYSTEMS

- **High-speed trains:** Shinkansen (Japan), TGV (France), AVE (Spain), KTX (South Korea), THSR (Taiwan), CRH (China)
- **Fast ferries:** Francisco (Argentina), Ocean Arrow (Japan), Tarifa Jet (Spain)
- **Bus Rapid Transit:** Transmilenio (Colombia), MyCiTi (South Africa), TransJakarta (Indonesia), Ahmedabad BRTS (India)

Project

Prepare a presentation about a form of transport. Use the internet and your own calculations to answer the following questions.

1 What form of transport is it?
2 How many passengers does it carry?
3 What is the top speed it can go?
4 How far can it travel in two hours?
5 What advantages does it have?
6 Are there any disadvantages?

Present your report to the class.

Review 3
Units 9-12

VOCABULARY

1 Complete the sentences with *at* or *on*.

1 There were lots of watches .... display.
2 We arrived home .... long last.
3 You see the town .... its best in the summer.
4 I didn't do it .... purpose!
5 There were 200 people .... board.
6 There are no jobs available .... present.
7 I didn't like the film .... all.
8 It isn't far – we can go .... foot.

2 Match the two parts of the phrases.

1	do	a	primary school
2	attend	b	for the school holidays
3	set out	c	badly in an exam
4	carry	d	an accident
5	break up	e	a torch
6	prevent	f	on a journey

3 Read the definitions and write the words in the puzzle. What is the missing word going down?

1 c ☐☐☐☐
2 h ☐☐☐☐
3 e ☐☐☐☐☐☐☐☐
4 j ☐☐☐☐
5 b ☐☐☐☐
6 p ☐☐☐☐☐☐☐☐
7 c ☐☐☐☐☐☐
8 b ☐☐☐
9 l ☐☐☐☐☐☐
10 t ☐☐☐☐☐

1 plants such as vegetables that are grown in large amounts by farmers
2 another word for *people*
3 the air, land and water where people, animals and plants live
4 a tropical forest with large trees growing close together
5 a very rare kind of tuna fish
6 the number of people or animals living in a particular area
7 anything that is living but is not a plant
8 yellow and black flying insects
9 the appearance of an area of land, especially in the countryside
10 large, wild cats with striped fur

4 Complete the sentences with compound nouns formed from one word in each box.

fire	head	skate		board	flowers	phone
smart	sun			teacher	works	

1 I'll call you later on my new ....
2 If students are late for school more than once, they are sent to the ....
3 There was a fantastic display of .... on New Year's Eve.
4 We walked beside a huge field of ....
5 Jonny fell off his .... and cut his arm quite badly.

5 Rewrite the sentences with *enough*, *too* or *very*, adding any other words necessary.

1 The river was too cold to swim in.
   The river wasn't .... to swim in.
2 There wasn't enough information about the trip.
   There was .... little information about the trip.
3 Brian hasn't got enough qualifications to go deep-sea diving.
   Brian has got .... few qualifications to go deep-sea diving.
4 This online game isn't simple enough to learn in an afternoon.
   This online game is .... to learn in an afternoon.
5 We only had one textbook between two of us.
   We didn't have .... for us each to have one.

GRAMMAR

6 Complete the sentences with the correct form of the verbs. Use the past simple, past continuous and past perfect.

1 The strong wind the day before .... (blow) all the leaves off the trees and they .... (look) very ugly.
2 Although I .... (hear) the news earlier, I still .... (not believe) it.
3 A man .... (stand) at the school gates for ages, but when I .... (look) again, he .... (disappear).
4 My younger sister .... (never visit) the mall before, so I .... (take) her there last Saturday.
5 When I was young, I never .... (leave) the table until everyone else .... (finish) eating.
6 I .... (decide) not to go on the evening river cruise, as I .... (not feel) well all day.

7 Complete the sentences with the future continuous form of the verbs in the box.

> enjoy   happen   study   travel   wait

1 This time next week we .... the sun in the south of Spain.
2 Next week, our class .... the fruit fly in biology.
3 Lots of free events .... when the music festival is on.
4 My dad .... for us outside the stadium.
5 Looking at the timetable for our trip, we .... mostly at night.

8 Rewrite the sentences to give advice. Use *don't have to*, *should* or *shouldn't*.

1 Make sure you get plenty of sleep. You …
2 It isn't necessary to book a tour in advance. You …
3 If I were you, I wouldn't spend so much money on sweets. You …
4 It isn't necessary to bring anything to eat. You …
5 It isn't sensible to walk home on your own at night. You …

9 Complete the conditional sentences with the correct form of the verbs.

1 If we .... (catch) the early bus, we'd get to school by 8.00.
2 If Sam .... (have) enough time, he'll bring that video game round later.
3 If Tom doesn't see anyone at the weekend, he always .... (get) really bored.
4 I'd make a cake if I .... (know) everyone was coming later.
5 We'll meet at the zoo tomorrow, unless you .... (suggest) somewhere else.

Corpus challenge

10 Tick the two sentences without mistakes. Correct the mistakes in the other sentences.

1 I bring the games and you bring some snacks.
2 I hope it would be sunny tomorrow.
3 Let me know if you're coming to visit this weekend.
4 I told him if he is tired, I'd take him home.
5 I came home and saw my sister made a cake.
6 It's going to be cold so if you come, I think you should bring a coat.
7 You haven't to bring any drinks, but you must bring some snacks.
8 When I woke up, I realised that I was sleeping.

11 ● Read the text below and choose the correct word for each space.

Water clocks

The oldest water clock is **(0)** .... 3,500 years old and was discovered in Egypt. The Ancient Greeks also used flowing water to show time **(1)** .... , and Chinese engineers developed many complicated **(2)** .... of water clock as well. Some of these **(3)** .... building towers nine metres high. In certain parts of the world, similar types of water clock were **(4)** .... in use right up until the last century. Now, in the 21st century, there is an attractive, environmentally-friendly **(5)** .... for keeping time, which is **(6)** .... as the Eco-friendly Water-powered Clock. It **(7)** .... uses water from a tap and natural lemon juice to create power for a simple battery. The water in the clock doesn't **(8)** .... to be replaced for at least six months, either. The clock has a digital display, is available in a choice of colours, and, **(9)** .... it is cheap to produce, sells for a **(10)** .... reasonable price.

0 (A) around	B besides	C during	D since
1 A moving	B setting	C passing	D going
2 A fashions	B designs	C methods	D details
3 A involved	B joined	C consisted	D contained
4 A yet	B still	C already	D ever
5 A experiment	B technology	C connection	D invention
6 A called	B agreed	C known	D said
7 A almost	B quite	C once	D just
8 A ought	B would	C have	D could
9 A because	B although	C while	D unless
10 A too	B very	C so	D enough

12 ● Here are some sentences about starting at a new school. Complete the second sentence so that it means the same as the first. Use no more than three words.

1 Ben is going to attend a new school next year.
   Ben .... attending a new school next year.
2 Ben's new school is a long way from his home.
   Ben's new school isn't .... his home.
3 It isn't necessary for Ben to cycle to school at the moment.
   Ben .... to cycle to school at the moment.
4 When Ben starts at the new school, he'll travel there by bike.
   Ben is .... travel to his new school by bike.
5 Ben wants to start at his new school very much.
   Ben is really looking .... at his new school.

VOCABULARY Photography and advertising

Your profile

Where and when do you take selfies (photos of yourself using a phone)? Describe your favourite one.

Do you ever use your computer to make changes to your photos? Why?

1 Look at these 'before and after' pictures, where digital changes were made to the original photos. What improvements do you notice in each one?

a

b

c

2 ▶1.35 Listen to a teenager. Which 'after' picture does she describe, b or d?

3 ▶1.35 Listen again and complete the sentences with the words in the box.

> advert   image   position   product
> purpose   result   software   techniques

1 My brother saw an .... on TV for some new photo editing ....
2 He wanted to try out a few digital ....
3 I know this kind of software can sometimes be used for the wrong ....
4 If a company wants to sell a .... , they can make it look better than it really is.
5 He downloaded another .... of the Oscars ceremony.
6 Unfortunately, he couldn't change the .... of the other people.
7 I really like the .... he's created.

4 Match the words you added in exercise 3 to the meanings.

1 programs used to make a computer do different things
2 a picture, especially in photography, or as seen in a mirror
3 something that happens because of a previous action
4 a picture or short film which encourages people to buy something
5 where something is in relation to other things
6 something that is made or grown to be sold
7 special ways of doing something
8 the reason why something exists or is done

5 Describe the changes that were made to the other 'after' photo in exercise 1. Use some of the words from exercise 3.

6 Discuss the questions.

1 Have you ever used photo editing software? How?
2 What images would you like to create with it?

ADEMY AWARD'   HE A A

READING

1 Look at the title and the photo. What do you think the article will discuss?

2 Read the article quickly to check your ideas.

CREATING THE *perfect* IMAGE

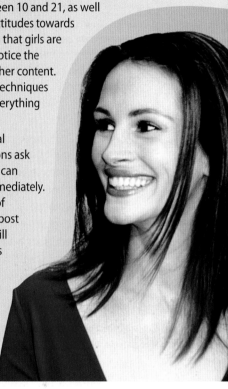

A The advertising industry's use of digital editing was back in the news recently, after complaints from politician, Jo Swinson, about two adverts for make-up products. In both cases, 'airbrushing' techniques were used to improve the images of actor, Julia Roberts, and supermodel, Christy Turlington. Swinson said that, as the images were changed, they didn't show the true results that could be achieved by using this make-up.

B The company producing the products admitted Turlington's image was improved digitally. This included making her skin lighter, reducing dark shadows around her eyes and giving her lips a more regular shape. They also agreed that changes were made to the image of Julia Roberts.

C Swinson's complaint was handled by the Advertising Standards Authority (ASA). They couldn't consider the digital effects in detail, as they weren't given the original photos, so, in the end, they decided that the adverts couldn't be shown. Jo Swinson had this to say: 'Both Christy Turlington and Julia Roberts are naturally beautiful women who don't need retouching to look great. The ASA's decision sends a powerful message to advertisers – let's get back to reality.'

D Are people actually worried by all this? A new report provides interesting information about attitudes to digitally improved photos in advertisements and magazines. According to the report, today's teenagers know that these 'perfect' images are false and many dislike them, realising that they were created for the purpose of selling a product. In fact, one 14-year-old American schoolgirl, Julia Bluhm, challenged the New York-based magazine *Seventeen* to reduce the number of false images it uses, saying that she wanted to see regular girls that looked like her in a magazine that was supposed to be for teenagers.

E The way an advertising image is seen by an audience depends on their age and how familiar they are with technology. So says Karen Fraser, who is currently studying the results of research she carried out in this area. She asked girls between 10 and 21, as well as their mothers, about their attitudes towards advertising messages. It seems that girls are quicker than their parents to notice the difference between ads and other content. 'They recognise that different techniques are used, but do not believe everything they see,' says Fraser.

F Having grown up with digital technology, younger generations ask more questions about ads and can recognise changed images immediately. Indeed, many change photos of themselves in a similar way to post online. However, Jo Swinson still believes that advertising of this kind may have a bad effect on teenagers, making them less confident and possibly putting their health in danger.

3 ● Read the article again and decide whether sentences 1–10 are correct (A) or incorrect (B).

1 Jo Swinson complained because the adverts gave a false idea of the make-up's benefits.

2 The company said that Christy Turlington's eyes were made lighter in colour.

3 The ASA's decision was the result of a lack of information about the images.

4 Jo Swinson described the two celebrities in a positive way.

5 The report suggests that teenagers realise why advertisers improve images digitally.

6 Julia Bluhm thinks *Seventeen* magazine contains enough pictures of girls who are similar to her.

7 Karen Fraser has completed all the work on her research project.

8 According to Karen Fraser, girls often have doubts about the truth of adverts.

9 Karen Fraser suggests that teenagers understand the digital techniques involved because of their personal experience.

10 Jo Swinson has proved that there is a link between certain adverts and teenage health problems.

4 Find phrases in the article to match the meanings.

1 considered to be an important story again (paragraph A)

2 finally (paragraph C)

3 a strong comment (paragraph C)

4 with the intention of (paragraph D)

5 change in a negative way (paragraph F)

EP Word profile *result*

The final images didn't show the true results that could be achieved.

Karen Fraser is currently studying the results of research she carried out.

I really like the result he's created.

page 135

Talking points

66 Should there be limits on how photos are changed in advertising? Why? / Why not?

Why do companies use celebrities to advertise their products? 99

▶ **Video extra**   Perfect or real?

GRAMMAR   The passive

1 Underline the passive forms in the examples. Which example tells us who performed the action of the verb?

1 *The images of both celebrities were changed.*
2 *Teenagers recognise that different techniques are used.*
3 *Swinson's complaint was handled by the Advertising Standards Authority.*

2 Complete the rules with the correct words.

> be   by   past   present
> subject   was   were

a We form the passive with the verb .... + past participle.
b For the .... simple passive, we use *is* or *are* + past participle.
c For the .... simple passive, we use .... or .... + past participle.
d We use the passive when:
   • we want something to become the .... of the sentence.
   • we don't know who performed the action.
   • it isn't important who performed the action.
e To say who performs the action in a passive sentence (the agent), we use .... + agent.

→ Grammar reference **page 157**

3 Complete the second sentence so that it means the same as the first, using the passive.

1 A talented artist drew these cartoons.
   These cartoons .... a talented artist.
2 A company chooses popular celebrities to support their products.
   Popular celebrities .... to support a company's products.
3 Lewis Hamilton drove the car in that advert.
   The car in that advert .... Lewis Hamilton.
4 This documentary didn't show us the full facts about airbrushing.
   We .... the full facts about airbrushing in this documentary.

Modal passives

4 Read the examples. Complete the rule about modal passives.

1 *It's amazing what **can be done** on a computer.*
2 *The images didn't show the true results that **could be achieved**.*
3 *The ASA decided the adverts **couldn't be shown** any longer.*

> Modal verbs are often used in passive structures. We use:
> modal verb + ... + ...

5 Complete the sentences with the correct modal passive forms. Sometimes a negative form is needed.

1 A lot of time .... (can / spend) in preparing adverts.
2 Mobile phones .... (must / use) during the performance.
3 A visa .... (may / require) for certain countries.
4 All project work .... (must / complete) by Friday.
5 People arriving late for the concert .... (may / allow) to enter.
6 You .... (might / give) a free ticket for the exhibition.

⊙ Corpus challenge

Find and correct the mistake in the student's sentence.

This game can be play online.

VOCABULARY   Phrases with *in*

1 Read the examples and match the bold phrases to two of the meanings a–f.

1 *They couldn't consider the digital effects **in detail**.*
2 ***In fact**, one 14-year-old schoolgirl challenged the magazine Seventeen.*

a usually, or in most situations
b giving more information, which is often surprising
c finally, after a lot of thought or discussion
d before a particular time or before doing something
e considering all the information about something
f especially

2 Choose four phrases from the box that match the remaining meanings in exercise 1. What does the extra phrase mean?

> in advance   in future   in general
> in particular   in the end

3 Complete the text. Use phrases from exercises 1 and 2.

> When I saw the advert, I couldn't believe my eyes – my favourite band was going to play in our town! There was a problem though, because it was on a school night. [1] .... , my parents don't let me stay out late during the week, but I had to persuade them this was special. So I told them about the concert two months [2] .... and after a huge amount of 'discussion', [3] .... they agreed I could go. My dad was great and offered to drive me there with a friend and pick us up afterwards. [4] .... , he even wanted to get a ticket for himself, but Mum persuaded him not to be so embarrassing! Anyway, it was a great concert and we liked all the songs, but the new songs [5] .... I'll never forget it.

WRITING An online review

1 What do you think these things can do? Which one would you like to try?

a **Ball camera**

b **Mini drum machine**

c **Action video camera**

2 Read the online review. Which product (a–c) is it describing? Does the review recommend the product?

This product is awesome. Its touch and slide technology is really easy to use. Another advantage is that it's small enough to fit in your pocket. You can achieve a huge amount with this tiny piece of electronic equipment! For a start, there are 150 different sounds to select, covering all kinds of dance music. The drum effects are very real, and you can overdub as much as you want. Plus you can create original soundtracks – a tiny microphone is built in, or you can plug in your own. I've been able to create some cool music for my personal videos, and I'm no musician! Amazingly, any 'wrong' notes you make are deleted, to produce the perfect final result. Definitely worth saving up for!

3 Read the *Prepare* box. Then complete the table with the highlighted words and phrases from the review.

Prepare to write – Writing an online review

In an online review:
- write in an informal style.
- use adjectives and adverbs to show how positive or negative you feel about the product.
- use phrases to join your ideas.
- end the review by saying whether or not you recommend the product.

Words and phrases for positive reviews		
Positive adjectives	Adverbs	Linking phrases
awesome	really	another advantage is that

4 Complete the sentences with the words and phrases for negative reviews.

Besides this problem	limited
One disadvantage	really disappointing
too expensive	

1 It's .... for most people to buy.
2 .... is its size – it can't be put in a pocket.
3 The choice of games is .... to very simple ones.
4 .... , there are bugs in the software.
5 In fact, this product is .... overall!

5 Tick the sentences that make a recommendation and put a cross beside ones that advise against a product.

1 If you can only buy one game this year, choose this!
2 This camera is just not worth the money.
3 Definitely something to put on your wish list!
4 You can't afford to miss this opportunity.
5 Don't even consider it!

6 You are going to write an online review. Choose one of the other products in exercise 1 and plan your review. Go online to find out more facts about the product if necessary.

7 Write your review.
- Use the tips in the *Prepare* box.
- Write about 100 words.
- Remember to check your spelling and grammar.

VOCABULARY Verbs for cooking

Your profile

Do you enjoy cooking, or do you prefer others to prepare food for you?

Describe your favourite meal. Why do you like it?

1 Look at the dishes. What ingredients do you recognise in each one? Do you know how to cook any of them?

2 ▶2.02 Listen to three young chefs, Adam, Melissa and Ravi, talking about the dishes in exercise 1. Match each chef to a dish.

3 ▶2.02 Read the extracts from three recipes and match them to the three chefs. Listen again and check.

1

Barbecue these pieces, or **roast** them in a hot oven for 40 minutes. Then **bite** into their delicious, spicy heat!

2

Fry the onion and garlic – don't let it **burn**! ... **Stir** the stew occasionally with a wooden spoon.

3

Cook this really slowly on the stove – it mustn't **boil** hard. **Taste** and add salt and pepper.

4 Match the **verbs** in the recipes in exercise 3 to the meanings.

1 spoil food by cooking it for too long or at too high a temperature
2 mix food or liquid with a spoon
3 cook food outside using charcoal
4 break up food with your teeth
5 cook food in very hot water
6 use an oven to cook meat or vegetables
7 put food in your mouth to discover what flavour it has
8 cook food in hot oil or fat

5 ▶2.02 Work in groups of three. Listen to the chefs again and each write down as many ingredients as possible for one recipe.

6 Tell each other as much as you can remember about your chef's recipe.

7 What dishes can you cook? Write a recipe for something tasty!

READING

1 Describe the photo below. What is the boy doing? Where is he? What other details can you see?

2 Read the beginning of the text and answer the questions.

1 When did Flynn McGarry begin to cook?
2 What nationality is he?

AMERICAN TEEN CHEF *Flynn McGarry*

Flynn McGarry's cooking career started when he was 11, partly thanks to his mother. "My mom didn't really like cooking, and when she did cook, I didn't really like her food. I was watching something on the Food Network channel and I thought, 'I could do this,' so I went to the bookstore and looked for the biggest cookbook I could find."

Within a year, he had produced most of its recipes and was ready for a bigger challenge. "I wanted to create my own dishes and I started to cook for more people than just my family too." His parents allowed him to build a test kitchen in his bedroom. "At first, they were fine with it, but then they asked, 'Do you want to be sleeping next to a stove?' Yes, I said! It started off as two tables with some gas burners, my desk and my bed, but then I needed more space for cooking, so I got rid of the desk and got a fold-away bed." Then Flynn's older sister, whose bedroom had more space, went off to college. He moved down to her room and fitted it with a large oven, four work stations and a long area for preparing the end results on plates.

McGarry and his mother set up Eureka, a supper club pop-up business that organizes monthly events inside his home. Flynn, who has also cooked in top-class restaurants around the US, says he's not doing it for the money, but because he loves cooking. "At the point in your life where you stop caring if you're going to be famous or do well, your dream will come to you. I did something with my talent and people recognized it. I hope to keep getting better and better."

3 🔴 Read the text again and answer the questions. You need to pay special attention to the parts of the text within speech marks (" ").

1 Flynn says he began to cook because
   A his mother never cooked at home.
   B he realised one day he might have the ability.
   C his mother suggested it as a future career.
   D he saw information about a cookbook on TV.

2 When Flynn suggested changing his bedroom into a test kitchen
   A he knew there would be no space for his desk.
   B his sister had already left home to go to college.
   C he had no doubts about his plans to cook there.
   D his parents refused because it was dangerous.

3 What does Flynn say is important for him?
   A to earn a lot of money
   B to become a celebrity chef
   C to care about the future
   D to improve a skill he enjoys

4 What would someone eating at the Eureka supper club say?

A My friends and I come here once a fortnight. Flynn's a fantastic cook and we always eat well here.	B Flynn gets everything ready in his sister's old bedroom – he even roasts food in there. Luckily, it's on the ground floor!
C We started coming here after I saw Flynn on the Food Network channel and bought his cookbook.	D It's too bad Flynn no longer does the cooking himself – I'd prefer to eat in a top-class restaurant.

EP Word profile *keep*

I hope to keep getting better and better.

I keep the spices in a special tin.

Can you keep a secret?

page 135

Talking points

❝ Why might working in a restaurant be stressful? What are the benefits of cooking your own food? ❞

GRAMMAR Non-defining relative clauses

1 Read the examples, then complete the rules with who, which and whose.

1 *Flynn, **who** has also cooked in top-class restaurants, says he's not doing it for the money.*

2 *Her favourites are green beans and aubergines, **which** I cut into slices.*

3 *Flynn's older sister, **whose** bedroom had more space, went off to college.*

We use a non-defining relative clause to give more information about the subject of a sentence.
We put commas around the clause because it contains extra information, which could be deleted.
We use the pronoun:

a .... to introduce more information about things.

b .... to introduce more information about people.

c .... to introduce something that belongs to a person, thing or place.

→ **Grammar reference page 158**

2 Complete the sentences with who, which or whose.

1 The pop-up café, ... serves Mexican street food, is very popular with students.

2 We stayed in the Malatya region of Turkey, ... is famous for its apricots.

3 My friend's brother, ... baking skills are amazing, made her a birthday cake.

4 Eighteen-year-old Claire Gourley, ... lives in New Zealand, has a website called 'It's my turn to cook tonight.'

5 The cookbook, ... recipes can all be completed within 20 minutes, has become a bestseller.

6 This spicy dish uses several Asian ingredients, ... you can buy in any supermarket.

3 Read the examples. Which has a defining relative clause? Which has a non-defining relative clause? Match the examples to the meanings.

1 *The recipes, which teenagers have created, will be posted on our website.*

2 *The recipes which teenagers have created will be posted on our website.*

a There are recipes from people of all ages, but only the ones from teenagers will be posted.

b The recipes are all by teenagers and they will all be posted.

4 Correct the mistakes in the sentences.

1 The amount of salt, which is in ready meals, could be reduced.

2 That loaf of bread who I bought isn't particularly fresh.

3 Sam whose birthday is on Friday is going to have a pizza party.

4 The boy which you met knows how to make fresh pasta.

5 Argentina whose beef is world famous is hoping to export more meat to Europe.

5 Rewrite the information in single sentences. Use non-defining relative clauses.

0 Thai food can be quite hot. (it uses chillies and other spices)
Thai food, which uses chillies and other spices, can be quite hot.

1 The waiter is very friendly. (he comes from Barcelona)

2 My mum's soup is delicious. (it is made from beans, garlic and tomatoes)

3 Kim will order my birthday cake. (her uncle is a baker)

4 This dessert is very rich. (it has 300 gm of chocolate in it)

5 The market sells fresh fish and vegetables. (its location is very central)

6 Johnny has definitely lost weight. (he has been on a diet recently)

Corpus challenge

Find and correct the mistake in the student's sentence.

Or we can visit São Paulo, that has lots of great restaurants.

VOCABULARY Nouns often in the plural

1 Complete the sentences with the words in the box. Are these nouns often used in the plural in your language?

arrangements   ingredients   initials   interests
memories   qualifications   tears

1 The writer used to end every email with 'J.H.S.', which were his ....

2 I have very clear .... of my grandmother's wonderful desserts.

3 Susie burst into .... because the biscuits she made tasted burnt.

4 What .... have you made for next week's concert?

5 My main .... are playing football, dancing and cooking.

6 This sauce is delicious – what are its .... besides cheese?

7 Does he have any other .... apart from his English certificate?

2 Discuss the questions.

1 Do you have good memories of your childhood?

2 What are your initials?

3 What are your main interests?

4 Have you made any arrangements for next weekend?

5 What qualifications would you like to get?

LISTENING

1 You will hear five people talking about choices or decisions. Read the questions and predict what the people might say.

2 ● ▶2.03 Listen to the recordings and choose A, B or C. Each recording is heard twice, so don't worry if you miss an answer.

1 Where do the friends decide to eat?

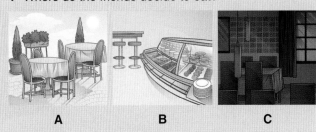

    A   B   C

2 What ingredients would the girl prefer to use in her cooking?

    A   B   C

3 Which product do they select for their art project?

    A   B   C

4 What does the boy choose for his dinner?

    A   B   C

5 Which cake do they agree to make for Sally?

    A   B   C

SPEAKING Discussing options (2)

1 Imagine you want to choose what food to cook for some friends. Which of these things would be the most important to consider? Why?

- cost of ingredients
- time needed to prepare the food
- OK for everyone, e.g. vegetarians?
- easy to eat inside/outside

2 ▶2.04 Look at the picture and listen to Laura and Ben making arrangements for a party outdoors. Which food do they decide would be best?

3 ▶2.04 Read the *Prepare* box. Then listen again. Which phrases do Ben and Laura use?

4 ● Turn to page 130.

Prepare to speak — Suggestions and decisions

Making suggestions	Considering options	Making a decision
Let's try your first idea.	If we … , it would be … .	It's time to decide!
How about …?	… might be a better choice?	Are you OK with that?
So, why not … then?	What if we …?	We'll go for that one, then.

Culture
Advertising and you!

1 How aware are you of advertising? Follow the instructions and discuss the questions.

1 Think about the five products in the box and write the name of the company that made the type you own or prefer.

> smartphone   mobile device, e.g. tablet, laptop
> trainers   jeans   chocolate bar

2 How do the companies advertise these products? Do you have a favourite advert? What do you like about it?

3 Do you think these adverts would work in other languages, or other countries? Why? / Why not?

2 Look at these photos. These products have been sold across the world, but sometimes their names, or the language used to advertise them, caused problems. Can you match the products to the problems?

1 The name means *illness* in another language.

2 The name was translated as *toilet water*.

3 The translation of the advertising slogan was *eat your fingers off*.

4 The name means *doesn't go* or *won't go* in some countries.

5 The name means *burnt farmer* in another language.

3 ▶2.05 Listen to a podcast from a TV show about amusing adverts and check your answers.

4 ▶2.05 Listen again and complete the table.

	Product	Country/countries with problem translation
1		
2		
3		
4		
5		

5 Look at the two photos on page 85. They are both adverts aimed at young people. What are they advertising?

6 Read the text quickly and check your answers. What is the purpose of the text? Choose the best description.

1 to sell some clothes to teenagers

2 to explain how to make a good advert for teenagers

3 to make teenagers think about the adverts they see

4 to describe some good adverts aimed at teenagers

7 Read the second paragraph of the text carefully. Choose the four reasons why advertisers try to sell to you.

1 It can be important to have the same kind of things as our friends.

2 We have a lot of money to spend.

3 We are often a bit unhappy about the way we look.

4 We can make independent decisions about what to buy.

5 We don't think carefully enough about what we buy.

6 We can spend our money on us – we don't have to buy for the family.

8 ▶2.06 Read the last part of the text about advertising techniques carefully. Listen to four conversations about new adverts. Match them to the techniques below.

a using 'star power'

b selling an image

c selling happy families

d using an 'easy-to-remember' tune

9 ▶2.06 Listen to the recordings again. What kind of product is each one advertising?

Be ad aware!

Look at these two photos. What do they show?
They are both adverts aimed at young people. What attracts you to the ads?

Well, the first advert is for a clothes company, and that shows happy, smiling young people – so perhaps you'll be happy if you buy these clothes? The second advert is for milk and it shows the Formula 1 driver, Jenson Button. He is obviously fit and healthy – because he drinks milk? Adverts like this are shown all over the world; the messages they contain are understood everywhere because advertising is now a worldwide industry with social media and international celebrities.

Before we look at how adverts like these work, let's look at why advertisers try to sell to young people. What does the teen audience have? First, money. You may not think you have much money, but you can spend it on what you like. Second, unlike children, you choose what to spend your money on, not your parents. Third, a lot of young people are quite anxious about certain things. You may not be happy with your body image, for example, or maybe your skin isn't perfect – this is really important to you and advertisers will use it. Finally, you're very aware of what your friends have and do, and no one wants to be different.

So how do ads work to persuade you to buy things and what should you be aware of? One of the adverts above uses 'star power' – this works by suggesting that if your favourite singer, actor or sports star uses the product, it must be good. But do they really use it? Does Jenson Button really drink milk? We don't know. Adverts often sell images, not products – another advert for milk showed Beyoncé in a beautiful golden dress, looking rich and happy. So maybe you'll be rich and happy if you drink milk? Well, the advert is trying to persuade you that you will be. Another way to sell to young people is by showing families having fun together. As a teenager, it's natural for you to argue with your parents sometimes. But maybe you'd really like to get on better, and the advert suggests that this will happen if you buy this product. Finally, advertisers often use music to appeal to teens. Cool music on an ad can often stay with you for a long time. You can't get the tune out of your head and this makes you think about the product, so maybe you'll buy it.

So, next time you see an ad that is aimed at you, stop and think about it. Don't be fooled!

Project

Work in pairs or groups to design an advert.

- Think of a product, or choose an existing product that you like. It must be suitable for teens.
- Decide how you are going to advertise it. Choose one or more techniques in exercise 8.
- Write the conversation for the advert, or a description of the action. Do you want music?
- Decide on the images – can you draw them roughly in a 'storyboard'?
- Work out how you could present your advert to the class – can you act it? Can you make a poster?

Present your advert to the class.

VOCABULARY City and natural world

Your profile

Do you live in a city, a small town or in the countryside? Would you like to live somewhere different? Where? Why?

1 What type of person are you? Do the quiz and find out!

City or *country*?

1 What is your perfect Saturday in summer?
  a waking up early to the sound of the **wildlife**, ready for an active day walking up the hill and down into the **valley**!
  b spending the morning with your friends at the shopping centre – there's **air conditioning**!
  c going to visit some **historic buildings** and learning something new.
  d inviting your friends round to play video games and then ordering a pizza.

2 Which would you like to do in your holidays?
  a Look at historic **monuments** and **ruins** – all your history lessons come alive!
  b Visit relatives who live in a small village. It's so quiet, and you can read your book!
  c Go on a camping trip away from all the **pollution** and **street lights**.
  d Admire **modern architecture** (probably a shopping centre!) and bright city lights.

3 Which would you love to have?
  a a horse
  b that bag you saw in your favourite shop
  c a new pair of trainers to go with your new jumper
  d a new bike or surfboard

4 Which is important to you in the place where you live?
  a peace and quiet, and **open spaces**
  b interesting things to see and do
  c people and shopping!
  d **facilities** such as sports centres, cinemas and **clinics**

5 Which is your favourite season?
  a I love all the **seasons** – I like seeing the differences in nature.
  b I love winter – clothes are so stylish!
  c I don't really like summer – too many bugs.
  d If the air conditioning or the central heating is working, it's all the same to me.

2 Turn to page 130 and add up your scores. Do you agree with the description of you?

3 ▶ 2.07 Listen to three teenagers talking about where they live. Match each speaker to a picture. What do they like about the place where they live?

4 Choose the correct words.
  1 Although it is an old town, there is quite a lot of *modern architecture / historic buildings*.
  2 The levels of *pollution / air conditioning* in our city have increased a lot because more people have cars.
  3 I love the countryside because of the *valley / wildlife* like small birds and animals.
  4 With all the *ruins / street lights* on at night, it's hard to see the stars.
  5 With the temperature going up to 40°C today, I'm glad we have *air conditioning / pollution*.
  6 Our city has excellent *seasons / facilities* where you can find most things you want.

5 What are the advantages and disadvantages of living in the places in the pictures? Use the words in the quiz to discuss each place.

6 Discuss the questions.
  1 What facilities would you like to have closer to your home? Why?
  2 How important is it to look after historic buildings? Why?
  3 How important is it to protect wildlife? Why?

READING

1 Check the meanings of the words in the box. Discuss the meanings with a partner.

> Aussie   beach   CBD (central business district)
> creek   kangaroo   outback   water hole

2 You are going to read about two Australian teens. Read the texts quickly. Where do they live? Do they like living there? Why? / Why not?

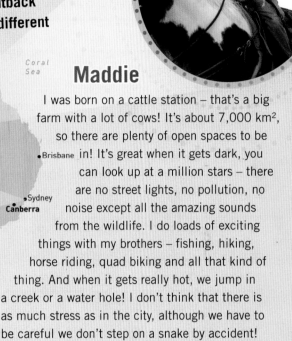

Teentalk ... down under

What is living in Australia really like? Can life in the outback be fun? We caught up with two Aussies who have very different experiences of life down under.

Map labels: Darwin • ; Indian Ocean; Coral Sea; • Alice Springs; AUSTRALIA; • Brisbane; Perth •; • Adelaide; • Sydney; Canberra •; Melbourne •

Harry

I live in a part of Sydney called Manly. It's incredibly beautiful and I'm really lucky to live here. In fact, tourists visit Manly all year round because of its amazing beaches. It's situated by the ocean – well, I guess most of Sydney is! In summer, there are almost more visitors than people who live here and I don't like that. I catch a ferry and then a bus to my school, which is near the CBD. One of my friends lives in the Blue Mountains and he visited me last holidays. I showed him around and we did loads of interesting things, including a trip to the zoo, and hanging out in my favourite mall. We hardly stayed in at all! But the best part was our surfing lessons on Bondi Beach! I think that being free in the ocean and seeing the tall buildings of the city at the same time is the best thing in the world. After all, it's the best of both worlds.

Maddie

I was born on a cattle station – that's a big farm with a lot of cows! It's about 7,000 km², so there are plenty of open spaces to be in! It's great when it gets dark, you can look up at a million stars – there are no street lights, no pollution, no noise except all the amazing sounds from the wildlife. I do loads of exciting things with my brothers – fishing, hiking, horse riding, quad biking and all that kind of thing. And when it gets really hot, we jump in a creek or a water hole! I don't think that there is as much stress as in the city, although we have to be careful we don't step on a snake by accident! For me, country living is certainly healthier living. Something else that is different – I didn't actually go to a school until I was 12. The nearest school was a six-hour drive away, so I attended the School of the Air. That meant I had classes at home and did school work over the internet. Most terms there was a camp where we all joined in loads of different activities. It was great fun and I met all my friends. Now I go to a boarding school in a city and I definitely miss the open spaces and my animals.

3 Read the texts again and answer the questions. Write M (Maddie), H (Harry) or B (both).

Who ...

1 mentions doing fun activities with a family member?
2 mentions visiting interesting places?
3 swims in natural places?
4 mentions that they used the internet a lot for school?
5 uses public transport daily?
6 is living away from home at the moment?
7 suggests that there are many things to do nearby?
8 loves seeing nature and modern things together?

Talking points

> Why do most young people prefer to live in cities?
> What things make a place enjoyable to live in?

EP Word profile *all*

> We **all** joined in loads of different activities.

> Tourists visit Manly **all** year round.

> After **all**, it's the best of both worlds!

page 136

GRAMMAR Articles: *a / an, the* and zero article

1 Match the examples to the rules.

1 *What is living in **Australia** really like?*
2 *I didn't actually go to **a school** until I was 12. **The nearest school** was a six-hour drive away.*
3 *It is the best thing in **the world**.*
4 *One of my friends lives in **the Blue Mountains**.*
5 *You can hear all **the sounds** from **the wildlife**.*
6 *Mum's **a writer**.*
7 *In fact, **tourists** visit my suburb all year round.*

> We use *a / an*
> **a** when we mention something for the first time.
> **b** to describe a person's job or what they do.
> We use *the*
> **c** when we mention something for the second time.
> **d** when we talk about particular people or things.
> **e** when there is only one of something.
> **f** in the names of groups of mountains, oceans, and states, and countries that are plural.
> We use zero article
> **g** to talk about plural or uncountable nouns when we are talking in general.
> **h** with the names of towns, countries and continents, and individual lakes and mountains.

→ Grammar reference **page 159**

2 Choose the correct words. Can you say why they are correct? Compare your answers with your partner.

1 My friend Jade has *a / the* holiday job.
2 She's teaching little kids to swim – she's *a / –* swimming instructor.
3 She works at *the / –* local swimming pool.
4 She teaches *the / –* children of all ages.
5 I'm going to buy *a / –* newspaper tomorrow.
6 Although I could just look on *the / –* internet now.

3 Complete the sentences with *a / an, the* or zero article.

1 The population of .... Australia is 21 million.
2 .... Mount Kosciuszko is the highest mountain in Australia.
3 .... Lake Eyre is often empty unless there is a lot of rain.
4 .... capital of .... Australia is .... Canberra.
5 .... Australia is .... island and .... continent.
6 .... Great Barrier Reef is made up of over 2,900 individual reefs and 900 islands.

⊙ Corpus challenge

Find and correct the mistake in the student's sentence.

It is beautiful city.

4 Add seven missing articles to the text.

> Tasmania is one of Australia's largest islands. It is island state and is part of Commonwealth of Australia. It is situated 240 km south of Australian continent and is separated by Bass Strait. It is surrounded by Indian and Pacific Oceans.
> In Tasmania you can find mountains, rainforests and beaches. The tallest mountain is Mount Ossa which is in national park. Capital of Tasmania is Hobart.

VOCABULARY Phrasal verbs

1 Read the examples. Underline the phrasal verbs.

I showed him around.
Some people think we stay in all the time.

2 Match the phrasal verbs in the box to the meanings.

> catch up with   end up   move in   move out
> show someone around   stay in

1 start living in a new home
2 go to a place with someone and show them different things
3 not leave your home
4 be in a particular place or situation after a series of events
5 meet someone after you have not seen them for a period of time, and talk about things you have done
6 stop living in a particular home

3 Complete the sentences with the correct form of the phrasal verbs in exercise 2.

1 My sister .... last year to go to college.
2 If it's raining, we usually .... and watch a movie.
3 When my friends came to visit, I took them to London and .... them ....
4 My cousin went on a train journey across Europe and .... in Turkey.
5 I can't talk now – let's .... each other later.
6 Our new neighbours .... about three weeks ago – they're still unpacking.

4 Tell your partner about:

1 a time when you showed someone around your school.
2 someone you want to catch up with soon.
3 things you enjoy doing when you stay in.

WRITING   An informal letter or email (2)

1 Where do you and your friends usually meet up? Compare your answers with your partner.

2 Read the task, then read Inês' letter. Does she answer all the questions in the task?

> This is part of a letter you receive from your English friend Jon.
>
> > I'm doing a project at school about where people live and I need some information. Please write to me and tell me about the places where teens meet where you live. Is the area where you live quiet or lively? Are there lots of things for teens to do?

Hi Jon,

Brussels is a really fun and lively city, despite the weather – that's awful! I usually catch up with my friends in a café near my house on Saturday afternoons. My street is really beautiful and it's often quite quiet. However, it sometimes gets busy in summer because there's a famous museum nearby. Actually, I'm going to visit the museum with my friends next week. There are loads of things to do here – cinemas, cafés, and shops, of course! Probably the best place for teens to hang out is the Central Café, in the city centre – lots of students go there, and it's really cool!

Finally, I have some great news – I got the highest mark in the class for maths last term! Whoo hoo! Very happy!!!

Write soon.

Inês

3 Read the *Prepare* box. Then look at the highlighted linking words in Inês' letter. Match them to their meanings 1–4.

Prepare to write — An informal letter or email (2)

In informal letters and emails:
- use linking words to link your ideas.
- use adjectives to make your writing interesting.
- remember to use informal language and short forms.

1 used to introduce something that is surprising
2 used to introduce a contrast, or an opposite point
3 used to introduce the last point you want to make
4 used when something is true, although something makes it unlikely

4 Complete the sentences with the highlighted words in Inês' letter.

1 I still went to Jamie's house after school, ... having lots of homework.
2 We wanted to play some online games. .... , the internet wasn't working properly.
3 Amsterdam is a lovely city. .... , my cousin lives there.
4 .... , I got home at about 7 pm after a six-hour journey!

5 What adjectives does Inês use to describe these things? What other adjectives could you use?

1 the city
2 her street
3 the museum
4 the Central Café

6 You are going to write a reply to Jon's letter. Read the task in exercise 2 again and plan your ideas. Remember to answer all the questions.

7 ⬤ Write your letter to Jon.
- Use the tips in the *Prepare* box.
- Remember to begin and end your letter correctly.
- Write about 100 words.
- Remember to check your spelling and grammar.

16 Let's film that!

VOCABULARY Film

Your profile

What was the last film you saw?
Have you ever made a film at school or on holiday?

1 Look at photos a–f. Answer the questions.

1 Which of the films have you seen? Which would you like to see?
2 Who is the person in picture f? What is his job?

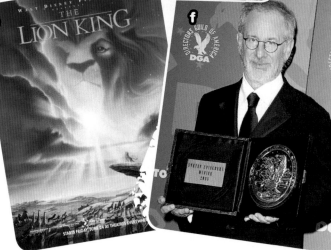

2 Match the sentences to the photos in exercise 1.

1 Adele's **performance** at the Oscars was fantastic. *Skyfall* was her first **recording** of a film title song.
2 George Lucas is a famous American **film-maker**. He **directed** the movie *Star Wars*.
3 The film of *The Lion King* has great **animations**. It's also a musical which you can see **live** at the theatre.
4 A lot of new films **come out** at special times of the year; for example, **animated** films are often around during school holidays.
5 Jennifer Lawrence had the lead **role** in *The Hunger Games* films. She has **acted** in several films.
6 Steven Spielberg is a very well-known film **director**. He has also **appeared in** some films, such as *Gremlins*.

3 Choose the correct words.

1 I'd love to *direct / act* in a film.
2 My best friend Ally and I want to see a new film that *comes out / acts* in December.
3 There's going to be a *live / animated* show of *Wicked* at the town theatre next week.
4 The *recording / role* of soundtracks for local films takes place near my house.
5 The *director / animation* tells the actors and actresses what to do.
6 I loved the main actor's *performance / animation* in the new Bond film.

4 ▶2.08 Listen. Match each speaker to the type of film that they want to see.

a an interesting animated film
b a film starring an actor who won a TV show
c a new film by a well-known director

5 ▶2.08 Listen again. Which film would you like to see? Why?

6 Complete the sentences with your own ideas. Then compare with a partner.

1 The most famous film director in my country is …
2 A live show that I would like to see is …
3 My favourite animated film is …
4 The film … is coming out in …
5 I loved …'s performance in the film …
6 I don't think … acts very well in … because …
7 The role of … in … was amazing because …
8 If I could appear in one film, it would be …

Marty's Blog:

Hi, I'm Marty. Technology is something that I love and in my free time I do things on my computer – especially games. By the way, I asked someone else to film me as well. Free time is screen time for me!

Hi guys. I'm Marty and I've made a short film about a treetop course I did at Larrumby Wildlife Park last weekend. It's near where I live and you can imagine the views from up there – amazing! Anyway, the film's called *Scary!* and I'm the director, the main cameraman and the leading actor. And I made it with my new video camera, which is awesome – it's really good quality and you just fasten it to your head and off you go. By the way, I asked someone else to film me as well. So that's me on the zip wire!

As soon as I got there, the guide directed us to a waiting room and announced that the instructor was going to be late. So I had the opportunity to ask my group some questions. I asked one girl if she was scared. She said she was terrified, but her brother had insisted that she should do the course. I talked to him too, but I hadn't remembered to turn the sound on, so you can't hear his interview.

Finally, the instructor, whose name was Phil, arrived and he asked the group some questions. He asked me if I had done this before and I told him that I hadn't. I don't think anyone had, actually. Phil said we would

enjoy it, and he told us to put on some special equipment and get ready. Then he gave us some important instructions for the course – like remembering to fasten the blue clips, called 'karabiners', for safety reasons. He really did stress that over and over again. I know being safe is VERY important, but as a film-maker I found it quite boring. I did film him saying all these things, but when I got home I decided to cut that part out.

So here we are! This is the Green course. Everyone has to do this course first to make sure that they are able to do the other courses, which are more challenging. Phil said that a young boy had found this bit quite difficult last week. I thought I could get some great scenes for the film here and I did! Just look at this! It was really high up! But I think it looks scarier than it actually was!

After the Green course we went straight onto the most challenging one – the Black course. I thought it was going to be easy to film, but you go down the Giant Flying Fox so fast you can't see or hear anything. But I put some funky music on and well, I think it's pretty cool. It was really scary though! Well, that's my first short film. Like I said, it was all done on my new camera, which worked like a dream. The best present ever! So, if you enjoyed this short film, hit that Like button. Watch this channel for my next short film: *Surfers' Delight!* Maybe one day I'll be a famous film-maker!

1 Read Marty's profile. How would you describe him?

2 Look at the photos and the introduction to the blog. Where did Marty go? What did he film?

3 Read Marty's blog quickly. Was Marty pleased with his film in general? Why? / Why not?

4 Read the blog again and answer the questions.
1 What three roles did Marty have in the film-making?
2 What question did Marty ask the girl?
3 Which was the most boring part of the course that Marty filmed?
4 Why was the Black course hard to film?
5 What does Marty ask people to do after watching the film?
6 What will Marty's next film be about?

5 Discuss the questions.
1 Do you enjoy watching short films made by other people online? Why? / Why not?
2 Have you ever put a film online? What was it about? Did people like it?
3 What would you most like to make a short film about? Why?

EP Word profile *direct*

There's a direct train from Central Station.

He directed the movie *Star Wars*.

The guide directed us to a waiting room.

 page 136

Talking points
66 Why do you think online video sites, such as YouTube, are so popular? 99

GRAMMAR Reported speech

1 Match the speech bubbles to the examples.

a I'm the director, the main cameraman and the leading actor.

b A young boy **found** this bit quite difficult last week.

c You'll enjoy it.

d No, I **haven't done** this before.

1 *Phil said that a young boy* **had found** *this bit quite difficult last week.*
2 *Marty said he* **was** *the director, the main cameraman and the leading actor.*
3 *Phil said we* **would enjoy** *it.*
4 *I told him that I* **hadn't done** *it before.*

2 Choose the correct words to complete the rules.

> We use reported speech to report what someone said in the past.
> **a** We usually ¹ *change / keep* the verb tense.
> **b** We generally move the verb one tense ² *back into the past / forward into the future.*
> **c** We sometimes need to change the ³ *pronouns / adjectives* in the sentence.
> **d** In reported speech, *will* becomes ⁴ *was / would* and *can* becomes *could*.

→ Grammar reference **page 160**

3 Complete the reported speech with the missing verbs.

1 'I like making films.' ⟶ He said he .... making films.
2 'I'm making a film.' ⟶ He said he .... a film.
3 'I've made a film.' ⟶ He said he .... a film.
4 'I made a film.' ⟶ He said he .... a film.
5 'I'll make another film.' ⟶ He said he .... another film.
6 'I can make good films.' ⟶ He said he .... make good films.

4 ▶ 2.09 Listen to Sally talking about her favourite thing. What is it?

5 ▶ 2.10 Complete the reported speech with the words in the box. Listen and check your answers.

> had already sent   her   couldn't
> had saved   was   loved

> Sally said it ¹ .... quite new. She said she had bought it last year. She said that ² .... mum had given her some money for it and that she ³ .... up the rest. She said she used it to text and to look things up on the internet. She said she ⁴ .... 30 texts. She said it was silver and she ⁵ .... it. She said she ⁶ .... imagine her life without it.

6 Rewrite the sentences using reported speech.

1 'I really enjoyed the performance,' my dad said.
2 'I'm making your favourite dinner,' said Anna's mum.
3 'My parents haven't visited England,' said Maria.
4 'It was my first trip on an aeroplane,' said Paul.
5 'I'll do my homework after dinner,' Tom said.
6 'I can ride my bike with no hands,' Jason told his friends.

7 Tell your partner about one of the things below. Talk for 30 seconds. Listen and make notes while your partner talks.

- Your computer
- Your favourite food
- Your favourite story
- Your weekend activities

8 Report what your partner said to the class.

Maria told me that she loved her tablet computer.

◎ Corpus challenge

Find and correct the mistake in the student's sentence.

I told him if he is late, I'd wait for him.

VOCABULARY Reporting verbs

1 Read the examples and notice how the reporting verbs are used.

1 *She* **said** *she was terrified.*
2 *I* **told** *him that I hadn't done it before.*
3 *He* **announced** *that the instructor was going to be late.*
4 *He had* **insisted** *that she should do the course.*

2 Choose the correct reporting verb for each sentence.

> ~~announce~~   demand   explain   insist   suggest

0 The train will arrive at platform 5 at 5.30 pm.
  announce
1 First you have to press this button and then you can choose the channel you want.
2 I really need to finish this homework before dinner.
3 Why don't we visit the exhibition together?
4 Give me that letter back!

3 Complete the sentences with the correct form of the verbs from exercise 2.

0 The guard ..*announced*.. that the train ..*would*.. arrive at 5.30 pm.
1 He .... that first you had to press the button and then you .... choose the channel you wanted.
2 He .... that he .... to finish his homework before dinner.
3 She .... that they .... the exhibition together.
4 Sue .... that I .... her the letter back.

LISTENING

1 Have you ever read a book and then seen a film of the same story? Which did you prefer? Why?

2 ▶2.11 You will hear a conversation between Aysha and Henry. Read the sentence and listen to the first part of the conversation. Is the sentence below correct or incorrect? How do you know?

1 Henry was disappointed with the action film they saw.

3 ● ▶2.12 Listen to the full conversation. Decide if each sentence is correct or incorrect. If it is correct, choose A for YES. If it is not correct, choose B for NO.

	A	B
2 Aysha and Henry both attended the film club last week.	☐	☐
3 Aysha believes that seeing a story's locations in a film is helpful.	☐	☐
4 Henry was pleased that the TV detective was how he imagined him.	☐	☐
5 They agree that directors should have experience of what they are filming.	☐	☐
6 Henry prefers watching horror films to anything else.	☐	☐

SPEAKING   Describing a picture (2)

1 Look at the photo. What can you say about it? Note down your ideas.

2 ▶2.13 Listen to Marcus talking about the photo. Did he have the same ideas as you?

3 ▶2.13 Read the *Prepare* box. Then listen again. Which phrases do you hear?

Prepare to speak — Describing what you can see

Describing what you can see
I can see …
In the background there is / are …
On the left / right there is / are …
In the middle is …

Making guesses
It looks like they are …
It might be …
I think the …

When you don't know the word
I don't know what it's called.

4 ● Work in pairs. Turn to page 131. Follow the instructions.

5 On page 90 you saw some people from the world of entertainment. You are going to talk to a partner about what forms of entertainment you like. Think of three questions to ask, and write them down.

6 ▶2.14 Listen to Marcus and Alex talking about entertainment. How many questions do they ask each other? Were any of their questions the same as yours?

7 ● Work with a partner. Talk together about the different forms of entertainment that you like and those that you don't like. Ask your questions, and the questions below.

1 Why do people like going to the cinema?
2 Why are programmes like *American Idol* and *The X Factor* so popular?
3 Many people nowadays want to be stars. Is this a good thing? Why? / Why not?

Language
Film reviews

1 Look at the photos, headings and names under the texts. Answer the questions.

1 What kind of texts are these?

2 Where might you see them?

3 Who wrote them?

4 Who is likely to read them?

2 Read the reviews quickly. Which type of film is each one about?

action/adventure   animation   comedy   crime   drama   horror   science fiction   thriller

3 Reviewers usually give films a number of stars (★) to say how good the film is. How many stars do you think each reviewer gave? (★ = very bad → ★★★★★ = excellent)

4 Read the three reviews again carefully. Underline any words or phrases that are connected with talking about films. The first few are done for you.

5 Which reviewer might give these opinions about the film he/she reviewed? Which parts of the reviews tell you?

1 It's not quite right for an older audience.

2 The main actors were amazing!

3 One part of the movie was alright, but the rest of it was not very good at all.

4 Sometimes these scenes seemed just a bit too good to be real.

5 In places, the film doesn't know whether it's an action film or a documentary commenting on society.

6 I think film-makers sometimes turn a film into a series just to make money and it isn't necessary.

6 Each film review has four paragraphs. Match the information below to the correct paragraph (1–4).

a description (of the story, action and maybe characters)

b advice (about whether to see the film or not)

c information (about the actors, director, type of film)

d opinions (about what is good or bad in the film)

7 ▶2.15 Listen to a class discussing how to write a review. Tick the things that they agree should be in a review.

Information
the actors
the story
the ending
the director
surprises in the story
opinions on everything
a recommendation

Language
contractions
phrasal verbs
trendy words
some informal words
questions
talking to the reader
bad language

8 Find examples of the things you ticked in exercise 7 in the three reviews on page 95.

9 Work in pairs. Choose a film to review and complete the information about it.

Film:

Audience (who is it for?):

Director:

Stars:

Story:

Characters:

Positive things:

Negative things:

Words and phrases to describe the film:

A PITCH PERFECT (2012)

This follows the success of TV super-hit *Glee*, with a similar <u>story</u> of musical competition set in a US college. The <u>director</u> is Jason Moore and this is his first film, although he has <u>directed</u> episodes from TV series such as *Dawson's Creek*. The <u>stars</u> are Anna Kendrick (*Twilight*) and Skylar Astin (*Taking Woodstock*).

At Barden University, all-boy group The Treblemakers and all-girl group The Bellas are both attempting to win a national singing competition. The boys' group is doing better than the girls' until talented Beca (Kendrick) appears on the scene, giving the girls a much better chance.

The best thing about the film is the script (written by Kay Cannon of *30 Rock*), which is fast and funny. The music's cool in places, but some of it's a bit too 1980s. The performances are great and the dancing is fantastic, though some people might think it's too perfect.

In general, I'd recommend this film. It's one of the most entertaining musical comedies I've seen in recent years!

Review by Ally, 15, Los Angeles

B DESPICABLE ME 2 (2013)

The second in the animated *Despicable Me* series (there are certainly going to be more), this is a bit disappointing. It's directed by Pierre Coffin and Chris Renaud again, and it stars the voices of Steve Carrell and Benjamin Bratt. The story starts a couple of years after the end of *Despicable Me*, when Gru had stopped his criminal activities and become a father. That was a great ending. Why start again!?

In *Despicable Me 2*, a secret laboratory disappears when it is attacked and 'stolen' by a new villain. This bad guy is trying to change sweet little animals into terrible killers and Gru is asked by Anti-villain League agent Lucy Wilde to find out who is behind the plan. However, romance comes on the scene and things get complicated when Gru's daughter falls for the bad guy's son.

There are good points about *Despicable Me 2* – some great moments in the story, and the music (by Pharrell Williams) in particular is awesome – but Gru's character is just not as much fun as it was in the original movie. It was fresh and new there, but now it's more of the same.

Would I recommend the film? Yes, I would, but I think you have to look at this as a completely different film from DM1. Then it's fun and a good laugh.

Review by Felipe, 14, São Paulo

C TARZAN (2014)

This big-budget CGI animated movie is the latest in a long list of films about Tarzan, and audiences will compare it with the others, especially the Disney movie of 1999. It's directed by film-maker Reinhard Klooss, using the 'motion capture' technique, which bases animations on real actors.

If you don't know the story of Tarzan, it's about a young boy who grows up in the African jungle, ending up living with the apes. In this film, the boy survives a helicopter crash, but his parents are both killed. He is happy enough until, as a teenager, he meets Jane Porter, visiting her explorer father. Fast forward a few years and Jane is back – and adult Tarzan meets her again.

The scenes when Tarzan is growing up, and some of the scenes with Jane, are enjoyable enough, but the story goes from OK to quite bad in the second half – it's all connected with environmental issues and the destruction of the dinosaurs, and it just doesn't work alongside the Tarzan story very well.

Tarzan is a fairly simple adventure story, and it might be worth seeing if you have nothing better to do, but in my view it's better for younger kids, and not really suitable for teens.

Review by Marcin, 15, Lublin

Project

Write a film review with your partner of the film you chose in exercise 9. Remember to:

- give basic information about the film.
- describe the story and characters.
- give your opinions of the good and bad things about the film.
- give your recommendation.

Collect your reviews together as a class. Make a class book of film reviews.

Review 4
Units 13–16

VOCABULARY

1 Find 12 nouns in the word search (→ and ↓) and match them to the definitions.

i	n	g	r	e	d	i	e	n	t	s	p	l	q
n	s	t	e	n	i	o	e	r	t	l	t	r	u
i	m	i	f	a	c	i	l	i	t	i	e	s	a
t	w	p	e	f	t	i	o	l	e	r	a	p	l
i	c	u	t	i	m	s	i	d	r	a	r	l	i
a	r	r	a	n	g	e	m	e	n	t	s	x	f
l	i	p	d	r	t	i	a	m	e	e	s	t	i
s	w	o	r	t	i	o	g	p	r	c	h	a	c
p	r	s	t	i	p	l	e	w	s	h	o	b	a
l	r	e	s	u	l	t	r	t	y	n	x	p	t
w	r	b	r	e	y	n	o	l	e	i	n	s	i
f	c	p	o	s	i	t	i	o	n	q	u	o	o
a	s	w	y	u	v	i	a	r	e	u	f	g	n
g	r	o	v	m	e	m	o	r	i	e	s	t	s

1 events you remember from the past
2 drops of water that come from your eyes when you cry
3 the score at the end of a competition
4 a picture used in advertising or on film
5 the first letters of your names
6 things that you get when you are successful in exams
7 the buildings, equipment and services at a place
8 the reason why you do something or why something exists
9 a particular way of doing something
10 all the different kinds of food you need for a recipe
11 the place where someone or something is
12 plans for how something will happen

2 Complete the sentences using a word from each box to make a phrase.

animated	air
historic	live
street	

buildings	conditioning
film	lights	performances

1 Taylor Swift gave two .... in London last night.
2 There are many .... in the town, some more than 500 years old.
3 Can you turn up the ....? It's very warm in here!
4 There were no .... in the town last night due to the power cut.
5 *The Simpsons Movie* is an example of an ....

3 Complete the questions with the phrasal verbs in the box. Then answer the questions.

catch up with	end up	move in
move out	show around	stay in

1 Are you going out tonight, or are you going to .... ?
2 Who would you like to .... your town? Where would you take them?
3 Why might you .... missing the last bus home?
4 If you could .... an old friend, what would you talk to them about?
5 If you could .... somewhere new, where would you choose to live?
6 What would make you .... of your home?

4 Complete the sentences by forming a suitable phrase with *in* and the words in the box.

advance	case	detail
future	general	particular

1 I haven't looked at the information .... yet.
2 Why not take a magazine .... you get bored?
3 I love that director's movies, ... his most recent one.
4 .... , men are taller than women.
5 You've broken another glass! Could you be more careful .... ?
6 Train tickets are cheaper if you book them ....

GRAMMAR

5 Rewrite the sentences in the passive. Use *by* + agent if necessary.

1 A top advertising company created the adverts.
   The adverts ....
2 You can use different ingredients in this recipe.
   Different ingredients ....
3 Danish architect Bjarke Ingels will design these New York apartments.
   These New York apartments ....
4 You couldn't see anything from the tower because of the fog.
   Nothing ....
5 They didn't show me how to edit video clips on the course.
   On the course, I ....
6 People might forget traditional techniques of bread-making.
   Traditional techniques of ....

6 Complete this text with the missing articles. Sometimes no article is needed in the space.

Canada is [1]............ second largest country in [2]............ world by area after [3]............ Russia. It is located in [4]............ northern part of [5]............ North America. [6]............ west coast of Canada faces [7]............ Pacific Ocean, [8]............ east coast faces [9]............ Atlantic Ocean, and the country is also surrounded by [10]............ Arctic Ocean to [11]............ north. Canada is [12]............ rich nation, and is [13]............ member of various international trade organisations, such as [14]............ G8. Canadians believe their quality of [15]............ life is very good, and they enjoy [16]............ very high standard of living in a beautiful natural landscape.

7 Report the questions and sentences.

1 'Did you buy anything in town, Ben?'
   Jo asked Ben ....

2 'I'm planning to play tennis later, Sally.'
   Sally's brother told ....

3 'I didn't go surfing after all.'
   James said ....

4 'We won't have time for a coffee unless we leave at 5.30.'
   Louise insisted ....

5 'Can I join the film-making course?'
   Matt asked ....

6 'You didn't have your phone on, Harry.'
   Freddy complained ....

Corpus challenge

8 Tick the two sentences without mistakes. Correct the mistakes in the other sentences.

1 Well, my dad called David.
2 Football can be play on the beach.
3 It will be in the stadium wich is near the bus station.
4 It's about a boy whose dog is lost.
5 I had a lot of fun last weekend.
6 It is beautiful country.
7 She say she was Spanish.
8 He answer that he like this game too.

9 Read the text below and choose the correct word for each space.

Chilli peppers

Chilli peppers have probably been eaten by humans **(0)** .... almost 10,000 years. Experts in early history **(1)** .... they were grown in Ecuador over 6,000 years ago and they were also one of the first **(2)** .... grown in Mexico.

The explorer Christopher Columbus ate chillies in the Caribbean and a doctor **(3)** .... board his second voyage brought the first ones back to Spain in 1494. Portuguese traders then took chillies to Asia, **(4)** .... they continue to be an important ingredient in Indian and South-East Asian **(5)** ....

Today, chillies are produced in large **(6)** .... all over the world. As well as **(7)** .... flavour to meals, they **(8)** .... healthy vitamins. Some of the hottest varieties are the Scotch Bonnet and Habanero, **(9)** .... bright red and orange colours give some warning of their heat. Most green and yellow chillies are less likely to **(10)** .... your mouth!

0	**A** for	**B** by	**C** since	**D** with
1	**A** imagine	**B** hope	**C** believe	**D** tell
2	**A** products	**B** crops	**C** choices	**D** goods
3	**A** in	**B** at	**C** to	**D** on
4	**A** where	**B** when	**C** why	**D** how
5	**A** bowls	**B** dishes	**C** ovens	**D** plates
6	**A** sums	**B** parts	**C** quantities	**D** figures
7	**A** adding	**B** joining	**C** mixing	**D** putting
8	**A** consist	**B** handle	**C** contain	**D** replace
9	**A** that	**B** whose	**C** which	**D** who
10	**A** boil	**B** grill	**C** roast	**D** burn

10 Here are some sentences about a holiday in the countryside. Complete the second sentence so that it means the same as the first. Use no more than three words.

1 Natalia spent last summer in the countryside with her grandparents, who have a farm.
   Natalia, ... have a farm, spent last summer in the countryside.

2 Natalia learned how to ride a horse there.
   Natalia was .... how to ride a horse there.

3 Natalia's grandfather said he would show her where to find wild strawberries.
   Natalia's grandfather said '............ show you where to find wild strawberries.'

4 Natalia used to feed the chickens every morning.
   Every morning, the chickens .... by Natalia.

5 'It has been the best summer ever,' said Natalia.
   Natalia said that .... the best summer ever.

17 Getting the message

VOCABULARY   Verbs of communication

1 Read the paragraph in the questionnaire. Match the words to situations 1–8.

1 You don't think the same way about something as your friend.
2 You want someone to realise they might be in danger.
3 You think your friend has forgotten to return something of yours.
4 You need to comment on the poor quality of goods you bought online.
5 You want to say sorry for a mistake you have made.
6 You aren't being serious about something.
7 You want to tell your friend that you will definitely do something for her.
8 You are unsure about something and are thinking about it as a result.

Texting **is quick and easy**, but if you want to **apologise** for a mistake or **complain** about a problem, isn't it better to speak on the phone or communicate your message face to face? Texts are useful to **remind** someone where to meet or to **warn** them you'll be late – or to **joke** about something funny – but we **wonder** whether texts can be used in more serious situations? You might **disagree** with us – so why not do this questionnaire and send us your answers? We **promise** to publish the results soon.

1. Tick the things you have done in the last 24 hours.

visited a social networking site ☐
posted your status online ☐
tweeted something ☐
used a video chat ☐
chatted in an online game ☐
commented on a blog ☐

2. Tick the things you do at least once a day.

send a text or photo from your phone ☐
use email ☐
visit a virtual world ☐
use Instant Messaging or a similar service ☐

3. Do you agree? Social networking:

helps me keep in touch with friends. ☐
helps me get to know other students at my school. ☐
allows me to connect with people who share my interests. ☐
is totally safe. ☐

4. How do you usually communicate with friends?

through a social networking site ☐
via email ☐
face to face ☐
on the phone ☐
by texting ☐

2 Complete the questionnaire. Then compare your answers and discuss your reasons.

3 ▶2.16 Listen to part of a radio show. Were any of your ideas mentioned?

4 ▶2.16 Choose the correct words. Then listen again and check.

1 We *promised* / *complained* to give you the results of our questionnaire.
2 We *warned* / *wondered* whether teenagers often used email.
3 A lot of teenagers *remind* / *disagree* that social networking is completely safe.
4 Their parents and teachers have *warned* / *promised* them about the dangers.
5 It's easier to laugh and *complain* / *joke* about things face to face.
6 They can easily send a text to *apologise* / *remind* a friend that they're meeting up.
7 They also find it easier to *disagree* / *apologise* for something in a text.
8 They *complain* / *promise* that phoning is too expensive.

5 Discuss the questions.

1 What things have you promised to do recently?
2 What was the last thing you apologised for?
3 How often do you disagree with your friends? Do you think it matters?

READING

1 Look at the photo. If you sent a message in a bottle, what would you write?

2 Read the article and answer the questions.

MESSAGE IN A BOTTLE

Canadian Steve Thurber was walking along the beach one morning when he noticed an old green bottle lying in the sand. There was a note inside signed by Earl Willard and dated September 29th, 1906. Earl was on board a ship that was sailing north along the west coast of the USA and 'posted' his note during the voyage, by throwing the bottle into the sea.

If it turns out to be genuine, this message in a bottle will be the oldest ever found. However, the content of the message remains unknown, as Steve Thurber has refused to open the bottle and find out exactly what Earl wrote. There were a lot of angry comments online about this. Many people wanted to know why Steve wouldn't open the bottle and solve the mystery.

1 Who sent the message?
2 What was unusual about it?
3 What do you think the message said?
4 Why do you think Steve wouldn't open the bottle?

3 People write a lot of messages in daily life. Look at messages 1–5 and match each one to its writer, a–e.

1 Hi, I'm wondering whether you'll be in the café later – I need to borrow your notes from yesterday's geography lesson before next week to see what I missed. Max

2
To Giulia From Martha

Haven't heard from you for ages! I want to know whether you could suggest a good hotel for my dad. He's visiting your city for work in July. Email me soon!

3 Your laptop is fixed and ready for collection, or we can send it to your home for a small charge. Please confirm your choice. Dolores Winter, CC Computers

4 Good morning Ben! Kelly's party was fun – why didn't you come? Mum's left your dinner money on her desk. I'm at college all day, as you know. See you tonight. Anna

5 I'm grateful to everyone involved in last night's school concert – you should be very proud of yourselves! Please sign below if you'd like a recording of the performance. Mrs Harris

....

a a teacher
b a local friend
c a family member
d a penfriend
e a shop assistant

4 ● Read each message in exercise 3 carefully. What does it say? Read each question and choose A, B or C.

1 Why has Max sent this text?
  A to offer to do someone a favour
  B to arrange a meeting for next week
  C to request some help with class work

2 A Martha would like Giulia to recommend something locally.
  B Martha is keen for her father and Giulia to meet.
  C Martha wants to ask whether she can stay with Giulia in July.

3 Dolores Winter says that
  A a new laptop model is available at CC Computers.
  B a delivery of the repaired laptop can be arranged.
  C a payment must be made before the laptop is collected.

4 In this note, Anna mentions
  A who she met at Kelly's party last night.
  B when their mother will be back from work.
  C where Ben will find something important.

5 A Mrs Harris is thanking the performers and offering them a souvenir of the event.
  B Mrs Harris is hoping that everyone will be involved in the next school concert.
  C Mrs Harris is asking whether any student in the audience filmed the performance.

EP Word profile *know*

I'm at college all day, as you know.

I can get to know other students.

Do you know the whole of this poem by heart?

page 136

Talking points

" Will we still be writing messages like these in the future? Why? / Why not?
What other methods have people used in the past to communicate? "

GRAMMAR Reported questions

1 Read the examples of reported questions and match them to the direct questions a–d. What do you notice about the tenses used in 1–4?

1 *Many people wanted to know why Steve wouldn't open the bottle.*
2 *We asked teens which activities they had done in the last 24 hours.*
3 *We wondered whether teens often used email.*
4 *We asked them if they agreed with the comments.*

> **a** Do you often use email?

> **b** Why won't you open the bottle?

> **c** Do you agree with the comments?

> **d** Which activities have you done in the last 24 hours?

2 Complete the rules with the words in the box.

> ask   never   statements
> whether   which   wonder

When we report questions:
a we can use .... , *want to know* or .... to introduce the reported question.
b we use the same word order as in ....
c we start reported *yes / no* questions with *if* or ....
d we .... use the auxiliary verb *do* in reported *yes / no* questions.
e we start reported *wh*-questions with a *wh*-question word, such as .... or *why*.

→ Grammar reference **page 161**

3 Read the online questions about Steve's message in a bottle and complete the reported questions.

0 Does anyone really care what Steve does?
> Nancy wondered whether anyone really ..cared.. what Steve .did..

1 Is the bottle worth more money unopened?
> Holly wanted to know whether the bottle .... worth more money unopened.

2 How long will a metal bottle top last in sea water?
> Kevin asked how long a metal bottle top .... last in sea water.

3 Why doesn't Steve want to open the bottle?
> Dan wondered why Steve .... want to open the bottle.

4 Are people sure the message is genuine?
> Jimmy asked if people .... sure the message .... genuine.

4 Complete the reported questions. Make the necessary changes to pronouns, possessive adjectives and tenses.

0 'Do you miss your aunt in Canada?'
Rob asked
..me if I missed my aunt in Canada..

1 'Will there be any food at the party?'
Rob wondered .... any food at the party.

2 'Have you ever lost your phone before?'
Sally asked .... phone before.

3 'Why haven't you bought yourself a new phone?'
Sally wondered .... a new phone.

4 'When did you last see your cousin?'
Rob asked .... cousin.

5 'How many songs have you downloaded for your trip?'
Sally asked .... trip.

⊙ Corpus challenge

Find and correct the mistake in the student's sentence.
I asked him how did he come here.

5 Work in groups of three. Turn to page 131.

VOCABULARY Adverbs of degree: *fairly, pretty, quite, reasonably*

1 Read the examples and answer the questions.

1 *Do you keep your bedroom **reasonably** tidy?*
2 *Are you **fairly** reliable as a person?*
3 *I'm **pretty** good at table tennis.*
4 *The old door opened **quite** easily.*
5 *We're working **reasonably** hard at the moment.*

a Do the bold adverbs mean 'very'?
b How is the meaning similar or different?
c What parts of speech follow the adverbs?

2 Complete the description. Combine adverbs from exercise 1 with words from the box.

> confident   happily   large   typical   well-behaved

I'd say I'm a ¹ .... person who doesn't mind performing in front of a ² .... audience. I can ³ .... do a long solo on my guitar, for example. It doesn't bother me. At school, I'm a ⁴ .... student – I do most of my homework on time and I'm ⁵ .... in class!

3 Complete the sentences about you. Use *fairly, pretty, quite, reasonably* and *very*, and suitable adjectives and adverbs.

1 I'd describe myself as … .
2 My friends would say that I'm … .
3 My bedroom is always … .
4 I usually do … in exams.

WRITING   A short message (2)

1 Read the three emails A–C and match them to the tasks 1–3. Does each email cover the three points in the task?

A

Hi! Guess what? A friend of mine introduced me to a great band the other day, The Red Stars. Check them out on YouTube – you'll love them because they have an awesome guitarist. What bands are you into now? Tell me in your next email, OK? Bye,

B

Hello! I'm emailing you about next Saturday – don't forget! How about trying that new pizza place at lunchtime? I've heard it's quite good. By the way, could you bring my games with you? Thanks! See you soon.

C

Hi! I'm so sorry, I completely forgot about your birthday last week! I hope you had fun – did you have a party? Anyway, I've decided to send you something traditional from my country – it's a pretty cool ring. Hope you like it. Love,

1

You have forgotten your penfriend's birthday. Write an email to your penfriend, Sam.
In your email, you should
* apologise to Sam
* ask whether Sam had a party
* say what present you are sending Sam.

2

You have just discovered a new band. Write an email to your American friend, Bobbie.
In your email, you should
* tell Bobbie how you found out about the band
* explain why you think Bobbie would enjoy their music
* ask which bands Bobbie likes at the moment.

3

You are meeting your English-speaking friend Alex next Saturday. Write an email to Alex.
In your email, you should
* remind Alex where you are meeting
* suggest what you could do for lunch
* ask Alex to return something of yours.

2 Find an example of 1–5 in the emails in exercise 1.
1 apologising
2 asking for information
3 explaining something
4 reminding someone
5 suggesting something

3 Read the *Prepare* box, then read the task. Which phrases from the *Prepare* box can you use in this task?

Prepare to write – Phrases for short messages

You can use these phrases when you write a short message:
* Apologising: *Sorry I couldn't … ; I'm really sorry …*
* Reminding someone: *Don't forget; Remember to …*
* Suggesting something: *Why don't we … ? How about … ?*
* Closing the message: *Take care, Bye.*

You arranged to play tennis with your Scottish friend Andy on Saturday, but now you aren't free. Write an email to Andy.
In your email, you should
* apologise to Andy
* explain why you can't play tennis on Saturday
* suggest another arrangement.

4 ◖◗ Write your answer to the task in exercise 3.
* Cover all three points in the task.
* Write in an informal style.
* Use phrases from the *Prepare* box.
* Write 35–45 words. Don't write more than 50 words.
* Remember to check your spelling and grammar.

18 We love the celebs!

VOCABULARY Feelings and qualities

Your profile

Who is your favourite celebrity? Why?
Do you enjoy reading about the lives of the
celebrities? Why? / Why not?

1 ▶2.17 **Listen to five people talking about
celebrities. Match four of the speakers to the
sentences.**

1 This speaker isn't really interested in the lives of the
celebrities.
2 This speaker thinks that celebrities should be
careful about what they do because fans do the
same.
3 This speaker felt sad about what the celebrities did.
4 This speaker was surprised by the celebrity.

2 ▶2.17 **Listen again and complete the sentences
with the words in the box.**

> annoyed charming curious delighted
> lonely mad (about) nasty professional
> rude shy stressful unexpected

1 **Joanne** is .... about celebs – she wants to
know all about their lives.
2 **Phil** sometimes gets .... about the celebs.
3 He thinks that people who are crazy about the
celebs might be a bit ....
4 **Nicole** says that she was too .... to ask a
famous person for their autograph.
5 When the celeb had gone, she found an ....
souvenir.
6 **Andy** thinks that having your photo taken all the
time must be ....
7 But he thinks that they shouldn't behave badly, or
be .... to their fans.
8 He says that most celebs are polite, or ....
9 Often fans copy the celebs and so this is a good
reason for the celebs to be .... at all times.
10 **Maggie** was .... that her favourite band had a
tour date in her town.
11 She was upset that the band didn't interact with the
audience. She thought they were ....
12 Some fans were .... because they couldn't hear
the band.

3 Which of the speakers do you agree with the
most? Why?

4 Look at the words in exercise 2 again. Are they
generally positive or negative? Compare your
answers with your partner.

5 Look at the photos and answer the questions.
Use words from exercise 2.

What is happening in each picture?
How do you think the people are feeling? Why?
What do you think of their behaviour?

READING

1 Which of these things do you think a celebrity might do for you?

- visit you if you are not well
- phone you
- hang out with you
- send you a signed photo
- be your Facebook friend
- let you take your photo with them
- give you their autograph
- come to your wedding

2 Read the article quickly. Which ideas from exercise 1 are mentioned?

WHAT ARE STARS WITHOUT THEIR FANS?

The charming American singer-songwriter, **Taylor Swift**, once spent two hours having lunch with a fan who was unwell. She had just broken up with **Harry Styles** of One Direction. What a great way to get over your boyfriend! Instead of sitting at home feeling sorry for herself, she did something useful! She spent some quality time with a person who needed it.

Talking of **Harry Styles**, he has no problems with fans, but he's fed up with photographers following him everywhere – in fact, he went to court to stop them doing it! We agree with Harry – we think celebs should be able to do their shopping, or go to the gym, without a whole pack of photographers chasing them! Give a celeb some space!

Now what about the footballer, **Cristiano Ronaldo**? He's been in the news for football, girlfriends and … helping a young boy? Well, yes! A young fan with a chronic illness was delighted when he watched Ronaldo play a game and dedicate a goal to him. But that's not the end of the story. The boy is now having his medical treatment paid for by Ronaldo. What a great thing to do!

Selena Gomez usually takes the time to stop and have a chat with her fans. And we heard that once, because of a huge number of crazy reporters and photographers, she invited some excited fans into her car! And she has used social media to stop bad behaviour. She wants her fans just to be themselves. Go Selena! People notice things like that!

But what about when your favourite singer laughs at you? Nasty, but did it really happen? Well, the fan says that's exactly what **Joe Jonas** did. But the singer, his dad (!) and lots of other fans said that definitely didn't happen. If it did, that's just rude.

And what about if you love your celebrity as much as your future husband? Australian fan Branda Delic opened a Facebook page called 'Bon Jovi, Walk Me Down the Aisle?' She got 1,793 likes and 80s rock star, **Bon Jovi**, walked her down the aisle in the church when she got married.

What are fans without their stars?
But what do we fans really expect of our celebs? Well, we can respect them for their talent, or the way they look. We like reading about them in magazines (like this one!). We enjoy watching their movies and we buy their music, their clothing label or their perfume. But remember, show them respect and give them space. Like you, they want a decent quality of life.

3 Read the article and answer the questions.

1 How did Taylor Swift help a fan?
2 What is referred to in 'We agree with Harry'?
3 What good thing did a football player do?
4 Why did Selena Gomez invite fans into her car?
5 What does Joe Jonas say he didn't do?
6 How did Branda get Bon Jovi to her wedding?
7 What does the author think it is OK for fans to do?
8 What does the author say fans should remember to do?

4 Match the highlighted words in the article to the meanings.

1 see something
2 very serious
3 an ability to do something very well
4 take place
5 polite behaviour towards someone
6 a place where people can exercise

EP Word profile *quality*

She spent some quality time with him.

Like you, they want a decent quality of life.

Some have a lot of good qualities.

▶ page 136

Talking points

❝ Why are many people so interested in the lives of celebrities?

In what ways do celebrities affect the way that young people behave? ❞

GRAMMAR _have something done_

1 Read the examples and choose the correct words to complete the rule.

1 _My best friend and I even **had** our hair **cut** in the same style._

2 _She **has** her car **washed** at a garage._

> We can use _have something done_ to talk about something that _we do ourselves / someone else does for us._

→ **Grammar reference page 162**

2 Match the sentence halves.

1 She has her nails
2 She has her clothes
3 She has her hair
4 She has her emails
5 She has her food
6 She has fresh flowers

a done by a hairdresser every day.
b delivered every day.
c read to her every 10 minutes.
d cooked for her by a chef.
e painted twice a week.
f chosen for her by a personal shopper.

3 What have the people had done? Put the words in the right order.

1 their / have had / cleaned / windows / Phil and Emma

2 computer / her / has had / town / fixed / in / Monica

3 his / has had / repaired / Andy / watch

4 her / photo / Rita / taken / has had

5 some / has had / delivered / Fred / pizzas

6 tree / Mike / planted / has had / a

4 Tell your partner about five things that you have had done or would like to have done.

I had my face painted once when I was younger.
I'd love to have my toenails painted!

Corpus challenge

Find and correct the mistake in the student's sentence.

I'm going to the dentist's to checking in my teeth.

VOCABULARY Prepositions

1 Read the examples and match the bold prepositions to the meanings.

1 _**According to** everything you read in magazines, the life of a celebrity must be really hard._

2 _And we heard that **because of** a huge number of crazy reporters and photographers, she invited some fans into her car!_

3 _Do you think the celebs are interested in anything else **besides** their appearance and clothes?_

4 _**Despite** adding them to Facebook, they aren't 'real' friends!_

5 _Some celebs look for the photographers **instead of** avoiding them._

6 _The famous woman met with her agent **regarding** the photo shoot on the beach._

a in place of
b as said by someone or shown by something
c although
d as a result of
e about
f in addition to

2 Complete the sentences with the prepositions in the box.

> according to   because of   besides
> despite   instead of   regarding

1 Mike and Andrea went to buy ice cream .... buying sweets.

2 .... the news, my favourite tennis player has just lost an important match.

3 Jane cycled to school .... the awful weather.

4 Is that boy interested in anything .... his computer and his phone?

5 Our teacher is in a meeting .... our school trip.

6 Arabella wasn't at school today .... her cold.

3 Complete the text with the prepositions from exercise 2.

SO YOU WANT TO BECOME ONE OF THE RICH AND FAMOUS?

(1) .... Jacob Blacksmith, of London's model agency 'Spot', there are lots of things you can do to get seen. He says that if you are walking down the street, make sure you are wearing something bright **(2)** .... a boring pair of jeans. We asked him if there is anything else **(3)** .... appearance that want-to-be models should do? He told us that you have to think that every time you step outside your door, the cameras might be there. So **(4)** .... that, you should always think about how you look and who you are with. Ashlee from London sent us her story in an email. She said that **(5)** .... doing everything that fashion agencies advise you to do, some people simply won't get seen. But don't give up! There are even courses giving helpful advice **(6)** .... careers in fashion houses.

Contact spotmenow@spot.co.uk for more info.

LISTENING

1 Imagine that you want to find out information about how celebrities live.
Look at the pictures and discuss the advantages and disadvantages of these ideas.

2 You will hear part of an interview with the journalist Terry Peters, author of the book *Celebrity Lives*. Before you listen, read the questions and possible answers. Can you guess any of the answers?

1 What did Terry especially want his book to show?
   A what celebrities are like as employers
   B where celebrities go during the day
   C how celebrities behave as people

2 Why did he move to Hollywood?
   A He wanted to hold celebrity parties.
   B He had a celebrity friend who invited him.
   C He wanted to become friends with the celebrities.

3 What did he do to really find out about the celebrities?
   A He looked through their bins.
   B He asked them interesting questions.
   C He tried to copy their behaviour.

4 How did he feel about the methods he used?
   A He felt he didn't have a choice.
   B He wasn't proud of his behaviour.
   C He says that anyone would have done the same.

5 How did the celebrities act towards Terry?
   A Some of them invited him to the gym.
   B They wanted to know more about him.
   C Most of them were too busy to take any notice of him.

6 How far has Terry changed his views on the celebrities?
   A He feels the same as when he began the book.
   B He now understands why they need a private life.
   C He says that really they are no different to any other human.

3 ▶2.18 Listen. For each question, choose the correct answer, A, B or C.

4 What do you think of Terry's methods?
Give your reasons.

SPEAKING Discussing a topic (2)

1 Read these questions from a discussion about celebrities. Decide how you might answer them.

1 Can anyone famous really have a private life?
2 Do you agree that journalists should leave celebrities alone?
3 But what about the children of famous people?

2 ▶2.19 Listen to two people discussing the questions. Did they mention any of your ideas?

3 ▶2.19 Listen again. Does one speaker say more than the other? How does each speaker involve the other in the discussion?

4 ▶2.19 Read the *Prepare* box. Then listen again. Which phrases do the speakers use to keep the conversation going?

Prepare to speak — Keeping the conversation going

What do you think?	That's an interesting point.
Why do you say that?	I suppose so, although …
But what about …?	It depends, doesn't it?
Do you agree that …?	I'm not sure, because …

5 ● Read the questions and add two of your own. Then discuss them with a partner. Use phrases from the *Prepare* box to keep the conversation going.

1 How much do you know about your favourite celebrity?
2 What would you like to find out about your favourite film star?
3 Would you like to be famous? Why? / Why not?
4 How would your life change if you were famous?

Culture
Fan culture and social media

1 How many celebrities can you name in two minutes? Think about the ideas in the box.

> sports stars   film stars   TV actors   musicians

2 Discuss the questions.

1 Which celebrities are you a fan of? Why?

2 What does it mean to be a fan?

3 Are fans important to celebrities? Why? / Why not?

3 Look at the title of the text and the photos on page 107.

1 What do you think the text is going to be about?

2 Who or what is in each photo? Do you recognise them?

3 Are you a fan of the people/show/book in the photos?

4 Read the text. Which teen might say these things? There may be more than one answer.

1 Social media makes the world smaller.

2 It's no good recording it if you want to discuss it with your friends.

3 The use of social media brings celebrities and fans much closer.

4 You never know what is going to happen in it.

5 I gave my choice and, you know, I felt accepted, as it was the right one.

6 It just shows that we have a voice and people listen to us!

5 Do you follow football, or another sport? Answer the questions.

1 Which sport are you most interested in?

2 Who is your favourite player? (If you aren't interested in sport, think about film or music.)

3 Is your favourite celebrity the same nationality as you?

4 If not, how do you follow him/her?

6 ▶2.20 Listen to Jihoon, a South Korean sports fan, talking about his favourites. Does he follow them in the same way as you?

7 ▶2.20 Listen again. Are these statements true (T) or false (F)?

1 Jihoon isn't interested in Korean football at all.

2 He wasn't a fan of South Korea in the World Cup.

3 Jihoon thinks Özil is a very good player.

4 Jihoon watches live football when he has school the next day.

5 He and his friends discuss the matches in online forums.

6 Jihoon thinks that it's difficult to follow your favourite footballer nowadays.

FAN POWER

There have always been celebrities and there have always been fans. Film stars in the early years of cinema had huge fan followings, and pop stars in the mid-twentieth century had fans who used to follow them everywhere and who were mad about them. Fans usually joined 'fan clubs', where they could buy posters, get cheaper tickets for concerts and films and even write to their heroes. So, what's different today? Is social media bringing celebrities and their fans closer together and is technology in general allowing fans from everywhere to join in and communicate?

We asked several teens what they felt was different about being a fan today.

Johanna, 17, from Austria, is a huge fan of Rihanna, the pop singer from Barbados. Johanna takes up the story: 'Rihanna is great; I've been following her for years, and she really connects with her fans, especially on Twitter. You know, when she was recording one mix of her song *The Only Girl in the World*, she actually tweeted her fans and asked us who we thought she should sing with on it. Amazing! And she accepted the fans' choice.'

Pop stars have had devoted fans ever since pop music came about in the 1960s. A newer type of fan following is the huge audience that some TV programmes get. **Arvin**, 15, from South Africa, is a fan of the British TV series *Doctor Who*. 'I know that *Doctor Who* has been around for a long time, but I've only been following it for a few years. It's great – such good quality TV and the ideas in it are so, well, so unexpected. You know, all my friends are mad about it, and we loved Matt Smith – he's just the coolest actor – but we like Peter Capaldi too. We always watch it live. I mean, we obviously want to talk about each episode as soon as we've seen it. We text and tweet each other, and send photos of us watching it, and it doesn't matter that we're in different parts of the country.'

It doesn't stop at TV programmes. Books have fans too. The American teen bestseller *The Fault in Our Stars* has a huge fan base all over the world. **Amy**, 14, from England loved the book. 'It's the best book I've ever read. I've been on quite a few forums about it now and have discussed it with teens from everywhere – the States, Japan, Spain, Turkey … It's awesome! What's really great is that there are so many fans that our opinions are listened to. This has meant that we're going to get some special showings of the movie a month before it comes out. We've got three here in England.'

Project

Work in pairs or groups to write a questionnaire about fan culture in your country.

- Decide on what you want to ask about: music, film, TV, sport.
- Write questions to ask about the following:
  - favourite stars, groups or programmes
  - when people watch or follow them
  - how people watch or follow them
  - how important technology and social media are in following them.
- Ask several people your questions: other students in your class or in other classes, your family, friends outside school.
- Put your results together, in a chart or table if possible.
- Give a presentation to the class about your results.

19 The world of work

VOCABULARY Work tasks

Your profile

What kind of job would you like in the future? Why?
Which jobs would you **not** want to do? Why not?

1 Look at the photos of teenagers doing work experience. What kind of work do you think they are doing?

2 ▶2.21 Listen to four teenagers. Match each speaker to a photo.

3 ▶2.21 Complete the sentences with the correct form of the verbs. Listen again and check.

arrange	calculate	deal with	deliver
develop	handle	install	manage
organise	produce	run	update

Connie
1 Our careers officer hadn't .... a place for me.
2 They .... the wooden doors for new houses.
3 I spent some time .... figures in the manager's office.

Vera
4 We planted the 147 trees that .... to local parks.
5 We weren't sure we could .... the work.
6 They .... our programme really well.

Ali
7 My dad .... a TV production company.
8 The man who was .... the project was very encouraging.
9 I even helped to .... ideas for costumes.

Gordon
10 She .... the problem immediately.
11 I saw how to .... new software.
12 I also .... the information about the store.

4 What kind of work experience would you enjoy? Why?

READING

1 You are going to read descriptions of eight places offering work experience to teenagers. Look at the eight titles in A–H. Answer the questions.

1 Which ones probably include some work outside?
2 What might teens be asked to do in each place?

2 Read the descriptions of the eight places quickly to check your ideas.

3 ● Read about five teenagers who are looking for work experience. Decide which place (A–H) would be the most suitable for each teenager.

1 Leila hopes to become a vet and wants to gain some useful experience. She would like to spend most of her time outdoors, but she also wants to try some office work.

2 Ben would like to avoid any kind of work where he would be sitting at a desk. He has good local knowledge and is reasonably strong for his age.

3 Helen loves using computers and wants further experience in this. She wants to join a team of experts in order to see how they handle big challenges. She's also interested in cultural activities.

4 Marco would like to experience the kind of work involved in the tourism industry. He enjoys researching topics online and is good at communicating with younger children.

5 Jade has above average ability in maths and wants to be able to use this skill in the area of leisure and entertainment. She would like to find a company with easy access to the city centre.

WORK EXPERIENCE
TASTER FORTNIGHTS WITH LOCAL BUSINESSES

A DELIVERY COMPANY

If you know the area around the city quite well and enjoy travelling around, come and help us. Our vans provide a fast delivery service for online orders and we also transfer goods for other companies. You'll sometimes have to help the driver lift heavy boxes and parcels.

B CRUISE SHIP

Our company is important for tourism because it provides cruises worldwide. When ships are in port, we get them cleaned and make sure cabins are ready for new passengers. You will spend 40% of your time on board helping our staff with cleaning and general repairs, and also work in the office on a busy customer service desk.

C RIDING SCHOOL

You'll look after one particular horse while you're here, dealing with everything from its food to its appearance and daily exercise routine. Although your work will be mostly in the fresh air, you'll be at a desk for brief periods, in order to answer phones and arrange customers' lessons.

D FESTIVAL OFFICE

This city's cultural festival is world-famous and our small out-of-town office is open all year round, booking next year's performers. Join our friendly team, helping with general enquiries, printing and design of our advertising. You will find out a lot about the entertainment industry.

E FOOTBALL CLUB

Every year, students on work experience get the chance to meet players at our club, which is located close to the heart of the city. Last year's students worked outside on the training ground, whereas this time you'll be in our financial department, learning about costs and earnings from top accountants.

F TELEVISION STUDIO

We make many popular comedy shows, drama and wildlife programmes, some here in the building and others on location outdoors. Our busy IT department welcomes students with some knowledge of this fast-moving area. You will stay with a single project group, learning from experienced people and developing new skills, including how to install systems software.

G PRIMARY SCHOOL

We encourage secondary school students to work in our classes, reading to the youngest children and helping older ones with maths problems. If you are good at sport, why not help to teach our junior football team what you know? As the school is in the north of the city, it takes about an hour from the centre by bus.

H CITY MUSEUM

While you don't have to know about local history, we do expect you to put your internet skills to good use! Find out interesting facts about the objects on display, which you can then pass on to kids and their parents as you guide them around the building. Many of these visitors come from other countries.

EP **Word profile** *order*

She wants to join a team of experts in order to see how they handle big challenges.

Our vans provide a fast delivery service for online orders.

The drinks machine is out of order.

page 137

Talking points

66
Do you think it is useful to gain some experience of work as a teenager? Why? / Why not?

What are the advantages and disadvantages of working outdoors?

Are some jobs more important than others? Which ones and why?
99

The world of work 109

GRAMMAR Different types of clause

1 Read the examples and match the bold clauses to the types of clause (a–c) in the rules.

1 *You'll have to be strong, <u>so that</u> you can lift the heavy boxes and parcels.*

2 *Last year's students worked outside, <u>whereas</u> this time you'll be in our financial department.*

3 *<u>As the school is in the north of the city</u>, it takes about an hour from the centre by bus.*

> We use linking words to join clauses.
>
> **a** Contrast clauses
>
>   To add different or surprising information in the same sentence, we can use the linking words .... , ... and ....
>
> **b** Purpose clauses
>
>   To explain the purpose of something in the same sentence, we can use the linking words .... and ....
>
> **c** Reason clauses
>
>   To explain the reason for something in the same sentence, we can use the linking words .... and ....

→ **Grammar reference** page 163

2 Complete the rules with the linking words in the box. Check your answers in the examples above and texts on page 109.

> although   as   because   in order to
> so that   whereas   while

3 Choose the correct linking words.

1 I'll be late home *as / so* I've got football practice.

2 *Although / Because* I arrived very late, my friends had waited for me.

3 You need to place your order one week in advance *while / so that* it can be delivered on time.

4 Why don't you arrange an appointment with the careers officer *whereas / in order to* discuss your future plans?

5 The report states that there was no damage to the environment, *because / whereas* actually, local wildlife suffered greatly.

6 I'd quite like to work outside in the fresh air, *as / although* not in the winter!

4 Match the sentence halves and join them with a suitable linking word.

1 People who work at a desk are often unhealthy

2 Farmers need to listen to weather forecasts

3 Accountants normally have a degree in maths

4 Some of our greatest performers have no drama training

a company directors sometimes lack financial skills.

b they admit that their acting has improved with experience.

c they don't get any exercise during the day.

d they know when to bring young animals inside.

Corpus challenge

Find and correct the mistake in the student's sentence.

I have to go I promised to help my father.

5 Complete the sentences so they are true for you. Use linking words from exercise 2.

1 I hope to / don't want to earn a lot of money …

2 I'm learning English …

3 I really like / dislike science …

VOCABULARY *as* and *like*

1 Read the examples. Which preposition, *as* or *like*, introduces an example?

1 *One guy in my group thinks he might do it **as** a job.*

2 *I did jobs **like** printing and photocopying.*

2 Read the text. Match the bold examples of *as* and *like* to the uses a–d below. There are two examples of one use.

> Although we were only on work experience, my friend and I were just ¹ **like** any other employee in the company – we had the same coffee breaks and were able to buy cheap meals in the canteen. Most mornings, I was working ² **as** a receptionist on the front desk, so I had to wear smart clothes, but my friend was outside helping the gardeners, so she was able to wear things ³ **like** jeans and t-shirts. We got to know quite a few of the staff and were known ⁴ **as** the Terrible Twins, because we look so similar. When we left, they gave us a big bag of souvenirs, ⁵ **like** coffee mugs with their company name on, mint chocolates and special pens.

a used to introduce an example

b used to mean 'similar to'

c used with a verb to talk about a job

d used with a verb to mean 'called'

3 Complete the text beside each picture with *as* or *like*.

1 When Luke worked .... a waiter, he had to balance several things on his tray at the same time, ... dirty plates and glasses.

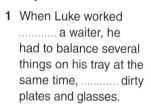

2 Maria went to the fancy dress party .... a mouse, but forgot she had to get there on public transport.

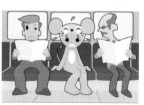

3 The group of swimmers looked just .... a flower floating in the water.

WRITING An informal letter or email (3)

Hi Jo

That's awesome news. You're lucky to have such a nice aunt! If I were you, I'd go for the restaurant because gardening can be really hard work. Also, you don't have any experience of that, do you? Working in a restaurant could be good fun, although the hours are usually quite long, of course. Good luck, and don't forget to tell me at the end of the summer what you've learnt. Make sure you keep in touch. I guess you'll get to try some delicious dishes there!
Bye,

1 Read the task. Then tick the three things that Jo wants you to write about.

- Read part of a letter from your penfriend Jo.

> My aunt has offered me some work experience this summer, either as a waiter in her busy restaurant or working outside in her garden, where she grows all the vegetables for the restaurant. Which of the two jobs should I take? What could I learn by doing this job? Which parts of it might be difficult for me, do you think?

- Write a reply, answering all Jo's questions.

1 Suggest what Jo might find hard about the job.
2 Say which job you would prefer to do.
3 Advise Jo which job to choose.
4 Explain what benefits Jo might gain from the work.
5 Give Jo some information about both jobs.

2 Read the *Prepare* box. Then read the reply to Jo's letter. Which of Jo's questions has the writer failed to answer properly? What information should you add?

Prepare to write — An informal letter or email (3)

When you are replying to a friend's letter or email:
- make sure you answer all the questions the friend asks.
- organise your ideas, so that the letter reads clearly.
- include some longer sentences with linking words.
- remember to use short forms and informal language, such as phrasal verbs.
- remember to use an informal phrase to begin and end your email or letter.

3 Read the reply in exercise 2 again. The ideas are well organised, but one sentence is in the wrong place. Which sentence is it? Where should it go?

4 Look at the highlighted linking words in the reply. Complete the sentences below with *although* or *because*.

1 You'll enjoy this job .... you enjoy working with animals.
2 It's fun working outside, ... it's sometimes cold and wet in the winter.
3 Babysitting is fun, ... young children can be difficult sometimes.
4 I'd love to work for a TV company .... I might meet some famous people!

5 Find these things in the reply in exercise 2:

1 a phrasal verb meaning 'choose'
2 two more examples of informal language

6 Read the task below and plan your answer. Remember to plan answers to all the questions.

- Read part of a letter from your English-speaking friend, Nik.

> In class today, we were discussing possible jobs we might do in the future. What would be your perfect job? Why would you like to do it? How could you find out more about this type of work? Tell me what you think!

- Write a reply, answering all Nik's questions.

7 ⬤ **Write your reply to Nik's letter.**
- Use the tips in the *Prepare* box.
- Write about 100 words.
- Remember to check your spelling and grammar.

VOCABULARY Hopes and dreams

Your profile

In what situations do you make plans?
What are your plans and hopes for the future?

1 Look at the photos. Describe them to your partner.

2 ▶ 2.22 Listen to three teenagers talking about their plans and hopes for the future. Match the speakers to three of the photos.

3 ▶ 2.22 Answer the questions. Then listen again and check.

1 What did speaker 1 always dream of doing?
2 What did his mother encourage him to do?
3 Who has speaker 2 always admired?
4 What does he imagine himself doing before a game?
5 Where does speaker 3 aim to study?
6 What advice does she give to other young people?

4 Complete the sentences with the correct form of the words in the box.

achieve   admire   aim   choose   dream
encourage   go for   imagine   keep on
try your best

1 When he was younger, my dad .... of being an astronaut.
2 I can't .... what it's like to work all day.
3 Max .... to study French and Spanish when he was 14.
4 Jane .... reading her book hours after midnight. It was such a good story.
5 I really .... sports stars who practise for hours.
6 Mum .... me to take up dance classes.
7 Nelson Mandela .... many great things in his life.
8 Jenny .... to go running every day before school, but she found it really hard.
9 This year Milan .... the position of school captain. He'll definitely get my vote!
10 Don't be sad. You .... and no one can ask more.

5 Discuss the questions.

1 What would you like to achieve in the next five years?
2 Who do you admire most? Why?
3 What subjects do you think you will choose to study when you're older?
4 Do you dream of having 15 minutes of fame?
5 What or who encourages you most when you have to study?
6 In what situations do you try your best?

READING

1 Read Bonnie's profile. How would you describe her?

2 Look at the photo and the newspaper headline. What do you think Bonnie's story is? Read the article quickly and check your answers.

Hi, I'm Bonnie! I'm from Australia and I live in the Snowy Mountains. My passion is snowboarding, but I also enjoy surfing in summer.

TEEN ENJOYS SNOWBOARD SUCCESS

Local teenager Bonnie Williams has just become the champion of the Perisher snowboarding competition, which takes place every year in August. Bonnie, who has been a member of the Snowy Mountain Snow Club for the last two years, took part in the national event at just 14 years and three months. She was competing against much older girls, who are among the best in the country.

But this isn't all that this young girl has achieved. At the age of ten, she was signed up by the sportswear designer label, *Booyong*. 'That was really important,' she says. 'After that, I was certain that I could be really good because people outside my family believed in me. It was fantastic.' Her parents, Johnny and Kath, who live in the Snowy Mountains, own a shop that sells snow sports equipment. Bonnie started snowboarding at the young age of four, after her father gave her a snowboard.

'I let her watch her older brother, who never took snowboarding very seriously! Bonnie knew just what to do. She had real talent from the start!' her proud father Johnny told the *Snowy Gazette*. But Bonnie has worked hard. She began with lessons from local snowboard instructor, Jim Higgins. Then, two years ago, international coach Millie Furilly started working with Bonnie and was much more demanding of her, both in the amount of training they did and in improving her technique. 'There were days when it was so hard to keep going, you know, I was so tired and so cold. But I'm so grateful to Millie!'

Bonnie has also competed in the USA, including in a competition in Copper Mountain, Colorado where she finished in first place. We asked her how she managed that, because there is a lot of strong competition in the States. 'I know, there are a lot of really good boarders out there. I don't know how I did it. I just always try my best!' she told us.

Bonnie attends her local school, but aims to get a grant to go to the Australian Institute of Sport. 'I dream of going to the Winter Olympics and the X-trail Jam, an Asian competition held in Japan. It's really hard, but I believe that if you want something like that then you've got to go for it. I can definitely see myself as a champion!' We think she already is a champion. Well done, Bonnie!

3 Read the article again and choose the correct answers.

1 What has happened to Bonnie recently?
   A She has won a snowboarding competition.
   B She has joined a new snowboarding club.
   C She has celebrated her 14th birthday.

2 What does Bonnie say about the agreement with *Booyong*?
   A She is involved in their design decisions.
   B Her parents sell these clothes in their shop.
   C It has proved her snowboarding ability to herself.

3 Bonnie became interested in snowboarding when
   A she joined a class with a local instructor.
   B she received a present from her father.
   C she supported her brother in a competition.

4 What is Bonnie's opinion of Millie Furilly's coaching now?
   A Millie spent too little time on technique.
   B Millie was right to insist on the extra training.
   C Millie didn't help her to improve enough.

5 What does Bonnie say about winning the Copper Mountain competition?
   A She always felt that she was the best boarder out there.
   B The competition wasn't particularly strong this year.
   C She isn't sure why she was so successful.

6 What are Bonnie's hopes for the future?
   A She wants to attend a special sports school.
   B She aims to find some training in Japan.
   C She dreams of winning an Olympic event.

EP Word profile *place*

She finished in first place.

The competition takes place every year in August.

If I pick one place, then maybe …

page 137

Talking points

❝ What qualities do you need to be successful in a sport?
How important is luck in achieving your aims? ❞

GRAMMAR Verbs with two objects

1 **Read the two examples. Which verb has two objects? Which is the direct object?**

1 He **gave** his daughter a snowboard.
2 Their shop **sells** snow sports equipment.

2 **Read the examples. Then choose the correct words to complete the rules.**

1 My friend **sent** me this photograph.
2 My friend **sent** this photograph to me.

> Some verbs can be followed by two objects, a direct object and an indirect object.
>
> **a** The direct object is usually a *person / thing*.
> **b** The indirect object is usually a *person / thing*.
> **c** If the *direct / indirect* object comes first, we use *to* or *for* before the indirect object.
> **d** If the *direct / indirect* object comes first, we don't use *to* or *for*.

→ Grammar reference **page 164**

3 **Underline the direct object and circle the indirect object in each sentence.**

1 She gave him some flowers.
2 He took his dad a present.
3 The girl sent her mother a photo.
4 My best friend told me a secret.
5 I was sick and Mum brought me a glass of juice in bed.
6 The girls showed each other their phones.

4 **Put the words in order to make sentences.**

0 some flowers / for / they / brought / me
   They brought some flowers for me.
1 his / Jack / friend / an / wrote / email / to
2 gave / she / some flowers / boy / the / to
3 her / showed / a / to / photo / friends / she
4 book / I / for / a / bought / brother / my
5 story / to / she / her / class / told / the

5 **Rewrite the sentences in exercise 4 with the indirect object first.**

0 They brought me some flowers.

6 **Answer the questions with your partner.**

1 Who did you send your last text message to?
2 What presents did people give you for your last birthday?
3 Has anyone promised you anything recently? What was it?
4 Who do you usually show your homework to?

Corpus challenge

Find and correct the mistake in the student's sentence.
She asked the time to him.

VOCABULARY Phrasal verbs

1 **Read the examples and underline the phrasal verbs.**

1 We always believed in you.
2 People tell me to just go for it.

2 **Read the sentences and match the bold verbs to the meanings.**

1 Bonnie's father **believed in** her ability as a snowboarder.
2 Her advice for people who want to do competitions is to **go for** it.
3 The school office **deals with** all enquiries about after-school activities.
4 My friend Janey **got into** the national team. She was so pleased.
5 I think it's important to **join in** group activities.
6 Her success **depends on** her ability to practise every day.

a believe that someone can succeed
b be influenced by something
c become a member of a team or group
d try your hardest to achieve something
e take part in something with other people
f take action to solve a problem

3 **Discuss the questions.**

1 What activities do you join in at school?
2 Do you think success depends on ability, hard work or both?
3 How do you deal with problems at school?
4 Do you have a talent? Are you going to go for it and try to be successful? Why? / Why not?

LISTENING

1 ▶ 2.23 Listen to Marty, Bonnie, Allan, Eva and Elena talking about their year. Write down their main achievements.

	Achievement
Bonnie	
Allan	
Elena	
Eva	
Marty	

2 ▶ 2.23 Listen again and answer the questions.

1 Why does Bonnie describe her schedule as 'crazy'?
2 What does Allan say was the best part of his course?
3 What does Elena say about London?
4 Which was the best topic on Eva's class blog, in her opinion? Why?
5 What part of video making is Marty interested in?

SPEAKING Discussing options (3)

1 Look at the pictures of activities on a summer activity course. Which activities would you like to do on holiday? Why?

A boy is going to do a **summer activity course** during his holidays. Here are the different things that he could do. Talk to each other about the **benefits** of these different activities and then decide which would be best.

2 ▶ 2.24 Read the task in exercise 1. Then listen to three people discussing the different activities. Decide if the sentences are true or false.

1 Sophie thinks that sleeping all summer holiday would be boring.
2 Ana thinks it's nice to learn something new in the holidays.
3 Jon thinks that team activities are better than individual activities.
4 Jon doesn't think that rock climbing is a team sport.
5 The three people agree that rock climbing and painting are the best activities.

3 ▶ 2.24 Read the *Prepare* box, then listen again. Which phrases do you hear?

4 ● Turn to page 131.

Prepare to speak—Agreeing and disagreeing

Agreeing
I completely agree with you.
That's (very) true.
That's an excellent idea!
I agree with you

Disagreeing
I don't agree with you because …
That's quite a good idea, although …
Yes, but at the same time …

Asking for agreement
Do you agree with me?
Do you think the same?
Is that how you feel?
What do you think?

ICT
Internet safety

1 Answer the questions. Then compare your answers.

1 How many hours do you spend on the internet on a typical day?
a) less than 1
b) 1 to 2
c) 3 to 4
d) more than 4

2 What electronic device do you use most often for going online?
a) smartphone
b) tablet
c) laptop computer
d) desktop computer

3 How much do you think you know about internet safety?
a) nothing
b) a bit
c) quite a lot
d) a lot

2 Read the text. Match photos (a–d) to a rule. How well do you follow these rules?

STAY SAFE ONLINE!

The internet can be a lot of fun, as long as people use it safely and responsibly. Here are some basic rules that you should follow.

1 Protect information like your real name, address, phone number and date of birth. This information is too personal to share.

2 Don't accept friend or chat requests from strangers. Your online contacts should be people that you know well.

3 Be careful with websites and apps that tell people your location. You don't want strangers to know when you aren't home!

4 If you really want to meet a new online friend for the first time, always tell your parents first. They may want to go with you.

5 Think before you share personal photos or videos. Stop and ask yourself, "Do I want everyone in the world to see this?"

6 Don't share photos or videos of other people without their permission. Be polite and respect other people's privacy.

7 Keep your passwords secret, so strangers can't use your email or other accounts. And don't choose an easy password like 123456!

8 Don't write nasty comments about people. Respect their feelings. You wouldn't want someone to say things like that about you!

9 If you have problems online, ask an adult for help. It's better to talk with someone as soon as possible. Don't keep it a secret!

CAN WE MEET?

3 **Answer the questions. Use ideas from the text.**

1 What type of information should you keep personal?
2 What must you do if you want to meet a new online friend?
3 What can happen if you share a silly photo of yourself?
4 When can you safely accept online friend requests?
5 Why shouldn't you write nasty comments about people?

4 **Read the comments. Are these people using the internet safely? Why? / Why not? Discuss your opinions.**

Comments

Travis says
posted 2h ago
I use the same password for all my online accounts. It's much easier for me to remember that way.

Angela says
posted 2h ago
I love posting photos of my friends online. Sometimes they get angry with me, but I think it's funny.

Daniel says
posted 1h ago
I don't like it when strangers send me friend requests. I never answer, and I block them when I can.

Kelly says
posted 40min ago
I use a phone app that shows people where I am, but only my parents can see that information.

Samuel says
posted 1min ago
When people insult me online, I always insult them back. Sometimes it gets really nasty.

5 ▶2.25 **Listen to Melissa, Justin, Laura and David. Choose the correct answers.**

1 A boy posted comments about *Justin / David* on a social network.
2 A boy was writing nasty comments about *Melissa / Laura* last year.
3 Girls were making fun of *Laura / Melissa* because she looks different.
4 *David / Justin* always receives lots of emails from strangers.

6 ▶2.25 **Listen again and write the correct names: Justin, David, Laura or Melissa.**

1 .... got a new phone. Now she blocks messages from strangers.
2 .... changed the privacy settings on his profile.
3 .... has closed his email account five times already.
4 .... didn't tell her parents about the cyberbullying.

Project

Make an information poster about cyberbullying. Include practical tips for your classmates.
1 What types of things do cyberbullies do?
2 Why shouldn't they do these things?
3 What should victims of cyberbullying do?
4 Why is it important to talk about this problem?
5 Where can teens find more information about cyberbullying?
Display your poster at school.

Review 5
Units 17-20

VOCABULARY

1 Unscramble the verbs in the box and use them to complete the sentences.

> anrw   diernm   edegaisr
> noewrd   spagoolie   sporime

1 I'm definitely going to do my homework after dinner – I ....!
2 I'm really sorry I didn't text you earlier. I .... for the confusion.
3 I don't want to forget about my appointment. Can you .... me?
4 I don't have the same opinion as you – I .... with you.
5 Mum and Dad will be asking themselves where you are – they will .... where you are.
6 The police will .... us if there is any danger of flooding.

2 Write the adjective to describe each person.

1 I want to know all about kangaroos and other animals from Australia. c _ _ _ _ _ _
2 Argh! The internet isn't working, so I can't chat to my friends! a _ _ _ _ _ _
3 I'm really happy with my grade for my project! d _ _ _ _ _ _ _ _
4 I don't know anyone at this school. I miss my old school. l _ _ _ _ _
5 I don't want to talk to anyone. I feel silly. s _ _
6 Sometimes he doesn't even say hello to me when he sees me! r _ _ _

3 Complete the sentences with the verbs in the box.

> arrange   calculate   develop
> handle   run   update

1 We want to .... a better design, which won't have so many problems.
2 It's a difficult situation and I'm not sure how to .... it.
3 I'd like to .... an appointment to see the doctor.
4 She loves cooking and she'd love to .... her own restaurant one day.
5 We .... the website with new information every day.
6 I've got all the figures, so I can .... the total.

4 Choose the correct words.

1 If you want to do something, you should *go for / go at / try to* it.
2 I can't study any more – I have *tried the best / tried my best / done the best*.
3 I really *admire / imagine / dream* people who have more than one job – they're amazing!
4 Jacki *chose / encouraged / achieved* to visit her best friend after school.
5 I *aim / encourage / dream* of being a famous sports star.
6 I *keep on / aim / imagine* to be rich by the time I am 20.

GRAMMAR

5 Complete the reported questions.

1 How many celebs actually enjoy their status?
  I wondered ....
2 Did you all enjoy the film?
  Mr Hamilton wanted to know ....
3 Did you finish the maths homework?
  Margit asked me ....
4 Can you speak more than one foreign language?
  I asked my uncle ....
5 Have you seen the new James Bond movie?
  Julia wanted to know ....
6 Where is Stefan going on Saturday?
  George wondered ....

6 Fill in the missing words to rewrite the sentences.

1 The woman painted my nails.
  I .... my nails ....
2 She brushed my hair.
  I .... my hair ....
3 She took my photo.
  I .... my photo ....
4 She did the shopping.
  I .... my shopping ....
5 She brought my dinner to my room.
  I .... my dinner .... to my room.

7 Choose the correct linking words.

1 I went to the shop *because* / *although* we didn't have any bread.
2 My favourite colour is red, *whereas* / *as* my best friend's is blue.
3 *As* / *Although* we have to get up early tomorrow, I'm going to bed now.
4 We're going to check in online *in order to* / *because* get the best seats.
5 I like most kinds of rice dishes *although* / *because* I don't really like fried rice.

8 Put the words in order to make sentences.

1 dad / my / a / me / new / Christmas / for / gave / bike
2 them / email / an / explaining / Susan / wrote / everything
3 showed / her / Jessica / photos / holiday / us
4 bunch / took / flowers / aunt / a / I / of / my
5 teacher / our / us / told / biology / our / grades
6 grandmother / sent / my / me / a / gift

Corpus challenge

9 Tick the two sentences without mistakes. Correct the mistakes in the other sentences.

1 She ask me to tell her about my holiday.
2 He started to tell me about where did he come from.
3 She's having her car washed at the garage.
4 We asked if we could have taken a photo with him.
5 I like the summer althought it can be too hot sometimes.
6 We play video games together. Because we both enjoy this.
7 Before I left, my parents gave me a car as a gift and wished me good luck.
8 My parent gave me some presents.

10 Read the text below and choose the correct word for each space.

Do you work?

Many young people **(0)** .... the world have weekend jobs. These jobs might be serving customers in a shop, or looking after children. **(1)** .... most teens don't need the jobs, they gain useful **(2)** .... from these jobs for later. Part-time jobs can teach you practical **(3)** .... , such as how to give the exact change to customers. You can also learn how to **(4)** .... difficult situations and manage your own time. While working, you have to communicate with many different members of **(5)** .... Having a weekend job **(6)** .... be seen as an opportunity to learn how to behave with adults. Most of us don't realise how much we have to learn as we **(7)** .... the adult world.
(8) .... , employers prefer people to have **(9)** .... knowledge of the world of work and at least one qualification. And you will love **(10)** .... (and spending!) your own money.

0	**A** around	**B** from	**C** on	**D** through
1	**A** Although	**B** Whereas	**C** Because	**D** As
2	**A** advice	**B** research	**C** experience	**D** opinions
3	**A** experiences	**B** manners	**C** skills	**D** ways
4	**A** support	**B** handle	**C** deal	**D** advise
5	**A** culture	**B** population	**C** society	**D** life
6	**A** ought	**B** should	**C** has	**D** would
7	**A** enter	**B** arrive	**C** land	**D** move
8	**A** Rarely	**B** Never	**C** Ever	**D** Generally
9	**A** both	**B** each	**C** some	**D** another
10	**A** creating	**B** paying	**C** earning	**D** winning

(0 A around is circled)

11 Here are some sentences about a boy who likes singing. For each question, complete the second sentence so that it means the same as the first. Use no more than three words.

1 Steve's new singing teacher is much better than his previous one.
Steve's old singing teacher wasn't .... **his new one.**
2 Steve asked his teacher, 'Can I enter a singing competition?'
Steve asked his teacher .... **enter a singing competition.**
3 Steve's teacher wondered whether he had enough time to practise.
Steve's teacher asked him, ' .... **enough time to practise?'**
4 Steve sang brilliantly, so he won the competition.
Steve won the competition .... **brilliantly.**
5 Nowadays, a hairdresser does Steve's hair before he goes on stage.
Nowadays, Steve has .... **by a hairdresser before he goes on stage.**

Exam profile 1

Reading Part 5 Multiple-choice cloze

What is Part 5?
- One short text with ten spaces
- Ten four-option questions testing vocabulary and grammar

1 Read the text quickly for general meaning. Then look at the first sentence and the example (0). The answer is A. A–D are all prepositions.

2 Now look at the highlighted answers in the text and the options A–D for questions 1–4. What type of word is in each set? Choose four types from the box.

> adjectives   adverbs   modal verbs   nouns   pronouns   verbs

3 Why are the other three options wrong? Look at the words around each space.

Example

0 A in   **B** on   **C** at   **D** of

Answer: 0 <u>A</u> B C D

The value of friendship

Friendship is important **(0)** .... our lives. Many experts **(1)** say that it is good to have different kinds of people within a friendship group.

Someone reliable will always help you with a problem or keep a special **(2)** secret. However, you **(3)** might never go dancing with that person and you would probably ask someone else to explain your homework, **(4)** especially if he or she knows more than you do about a subject.

Occasionally, it can **(5)** .... be helpful to have someone to go to **(6)** .... is completely separate from your **(7)** .... group of friends. This person can be honest about a difficult **(8)** .... and help you to solve it.

Even with only a small **(9)** .... of close friends, we need to **(10)** .... for sure that they will each be there to support us when we need them.

1	**A** tell	**B** say	**C** speak	**D** talk
2	**A** idea	**B** advice	**C** plan	**D** secret
3	**A** ought	**B** must	**C** can	**D** might
4	**A** extremely	**B** absolutely	**C** especially	**D** really
5	**A** also	**B** enough	**C** too	**D** very
6	**A** what	**B** who	**C** which	**D** whose
7	**A** average	**B** whole	**C** normal	**D** various
8	**A** situation	**B** opinion	**C** explanation	**D** conclusion
9	**A** figure	**B** total	**C** number	**D** sum
10	**A** imagine	**B** hope	**C** think	**D** know

> **Now you try Reading Part 5**
> - Decide what type of word is needed in each space.
> - Look at the words near each space – do they go with your chosen answer?

4 Now complete questions 5–10.

Writing Part 2 Short communicative message

What is a Part 2 message?
- 35–45 words long
- An email, note or postcard covering three content points

1 Read the exam task and match the sentences to each content point. Which sentence should start the email?

> You have been to a new café and want to tell your Canadian friend Dani about it.
>
> Write an email to Dani. In your email, you should:
> - tell Dani where the café is
> - explain why you like it
> - offer to take Dani there.
>
> Write your email in **35–45 words**.

1 *We could go together on Saturday afternoon if you like.*
2 *It's in that narrow street behind the cinema.*
3 *They serve fantastic fresh juice there and it's a really cool place.*
4 *I went to a great café that opened this week.*

> **Now you try Writing Part 2**
> - Make sure you include all three points.
> - Remember to use informal language.

2 Put the sentences in exercise 1 in the best order and write the email to Dani.

Listening Part 2 Multiple choice

What is Part 2?
- Usually an interview with one main speaker, which is heard twice
- Six three-option multiple-choice questions

1 Read the instructions and question 1. What words do you think you might hear in the recording?

You will hear part of an interview with a girl called Ruth Leyton, who plays tennis.
1 Who suggested that Ruth should try playing tennis?
   A one of her parents   **B** her brother   **C** a coach

2 ▶2.26 Listen to the recording and read the recording script for question 1. Notice where the answer comes.

Interviewer I'm here at Ruth Leyton's local tennis club, to ask her about her chosen sport. Ruth, who was it that suggested you should start playing tennis?

Girl Well, my mum used to bring me along with my older brother – he had lessons with the club coach, Pat Edwards, and I had to sit and watch. Ballet was my after-school activity then, and Mum wasn't keen for me to take up anything else, but one day Pat noticed how bored I looked – and asked if I would like to hit some balls. I loved it immediately. My brother found this a bit annoying!

> **Now you try Listening Part 2**
> - Read each question and options carefully before the recording starts.
> - Check your answers during the second listening.

3 ▶2.27 Now read question 2 and think about what you might hear. Then listen and choose the correct answer.

2 Before she was 11, Ruth
   A attended training at the national centre.
   B did well in several tennis competitions.
   C had tennis lessons with her brother.

121

Exam profile 2

Reading Part 2 Matching people to short texts

What is Part 2?
- Five descriptions of what people want or need
- Eight short texts – select five to match to the people

1 Read the description and underline the three things George is looking for in a music website.

George wants to watch band members from the past talking about their work and get albums that are difficult to find. He also wants to read reliable reviews by experts.

2 Read texts A–D. Use the questions below to help you decide on the right answer for George.
1 Text C talks about bands from the past. Why isn't it suitable for George?
2 Texts A, B and D all mention reviews but only one is right for George. Which one and why?

Music websites

A The scene

This website provides advance information on various festivals and free concerts. There's also an opportunity to win a prize every month by uploading your own album reviews. And interesting interviews with the most famous performers of today are available to download to your phone as podcasts.

B Sound buzz

Although it isn't always reliable in its reviews of live performances, this website has an amazing amount of unusual music to listen to, from electronic sounds to folk songs. It also provides downloadable advice from experts on how to produce demo tracks without access to a studio or a sound technician.

C Hot stuff

Set up by a well-known DJ, this site offers brilliant suggestions for what to include in playlists for an event at home and has some free dance music downloads. There's also a photo gallery where you'll find your favourite bands from the past, but the site has no video clips, unfortunately.

D Music freaks

Some of the best music journalists write reviews for this website, which also has a good collection of video interviews with musicians who were performing twenty years ago. You won't find up-to-date news, or photos of today's celebrities – it's serious stuff! But there are links to online music stores, where you can buy rare CDs.

> **Now you try Reading Part 2**
> - Read the description and highlight important words.
> - Choose the text that includes everything the person wants.

3 Now read Ella's description and choose a website for her.

Ella likes writing about her favourite music and posting it online. She wants to find out about future live events and be able to download interviews with celebrities she can listen to later.

Writing Part 1 Completing sentences with similar meaning

What is Part 1?
- Five sentence transformations, all on the same topic
- Between one and three words are needed to complete each sentence

1 **Look at question 1. What information is already given in the second sentence? What is missing? Think of an adjective that is related to the noun 'importance'.**

Here are some sentences about staying healthy.

1 Taking exercise and having a healthy diet are of equal importance.

   Taking exercise is just .... as having a healthy diet.

Now you try Writing Part 1
- Make sure the second sentence means the same as the first one.
- Use no more than three words in the space.

---

2 **Now do questions 2–5 in exercise 1.**

2 My sister suggested joining her gym.

   My sister said, " .... you join my gym?"

3 To lose weight, you should reduce the amount of sugar in your diet.

   To lose weight, your diet should contain .... amount of sugar.

4 If you want good skin, you shouldn't eat lots of chips.

   If you want good skin, you .... not to eat lots of chips.

5 You'll feel tired if you get too little sleep.

   You'll feel tired if you don't get .... sleep.

Listening Part 1 Short extracts

What is Part 1?
- Seven questions, with three-option multiple choice pictures
- Short recordings with either one or two speakers

1 ▶2.28 **Look at the three pictures in question 1 and read the question. Predict what you might hear, then listen and check.**

1 How has the girl changed the appearance of her jeans?

   A   B   C

2 **Now look at the recording script. Match each highlighted part to one of the pictures. What is the correct answer?**

Boy   Hi Suzy, great jeans! Have you just bought them?

Girl   No, they're my oldest pair, actually. Mum wanted to throw them away because of the holes, but I decided to fix that by putting some material behind them.

Boy   Cool. The stripes look great – you could have the same stuff round the bottom of each leg.

Girl   Do you think so? Well, maybe. I wondered about a big pocket on each leg as well, but I haven't got any material left and I bought it ages ago.

3 ▶2.29 **Listen and answer questions 2 and 3.**

Now you try Listening Part 1
- Think about what the three pictures show.
- Check your choice of answer at the second listening.

---

2 Which concert is the boy talking about?

   A   B   C

3 What happened to the girl during her hockey match?

   A   B   C

Exam profile 3

Reading Part 4 Multiple choice

What is Part 4?
- A text with five four-option multiple-choice questions
- Tests opinion and detailed meaning, as well as writer purpose and global meaning

1 Read the text quickly for general meaning. Does the writer enjoy backpacking?

TRAVELLING WITH A BACKPACK
BY ANDY ROBINSON

Why is it that the people you meet when backpacking seem to be more interesting and easygoing than your friends at home? That's my experience, anyway. Occasionally you may be unlucky, put in a hostel room with someone you have nothing in common with, but more often than not, you'll meet people that are fun to visit the local sights with and who are worth getting to know. I've spent time with many nationalities and have found out some fascinating things about their cultures, although I'm sometimes embarrassed at how little I know about certain parts of the world.

It's generally very easy to make new friends while you're travelling, and you'll be able to hang around with them for a few days, until you or they leave for the next destination. Relationships of this kind are shorter but can be just as strong as friendships back home, because you do so much together in that short time. I often find I'm willing to admit things about myself that I'd never say to my close friends, safe in the knowledge that we probably won't meet again, except online.

2 Read the first paragraph and then look at the multiple-choice question below. The highlighted parts in the text show you where the answer comes – what is it? Why are the other options wrong?

1 What does the writer say about the people he meets backpacking?
- **A** They generally come from one or two countries only.
- **B** He finds it difficult to share accommodation with them.
- **C** They often know more about the sights than he does.
- **D** He learns valuable information by talking to them.

> **Now you try Reading Part 4**
> - Highlight the parts of the text that give you the answer.
> - Check that the other three options are definitely wrong.

3 Read the second paragraph and answer the next question.

2 According to the writer, friendships made with other backpackers
- **A** are less serious than those with his friends at home.
- **B** never last beyond the short time they spend together.
- **C** allow him to share personal thoughts in a surprising way.
- **D** often have an effect on the selection of future destinations.

Writing Part 3 Story

What is a Part 3 story?
- About 100 words long
- Starts from a sentence or title that is on the question paper

1 Read these exam tasks and then answer questions 1–4 for each task.

- Your English teacher has asked you to write a story.
- Your story must begin with this sentence:
  Alex read the text message and felt very happy.

- Your English teacher has asked you to write a story.
- Your story must have this title:
  My first day at a new school

1 What pronoun will you use in the story – *I, he* or *she*?
2 Which tenses will you need?
3 How will your story begin and end?
4 What good language can you use to show your ability?

Now you try Writing Part 3
- Plan your story so that it has a beginning, middle and end.
- Make sure your story is clear and interesting for the reader.

2 Choose one of the stories in exercise 1 and write it in about 100 words.

Listening Part 3 Note completion

What is Part 3?
- A recording giving information, with one speaker
- Six spaces to complete with one or two words, or a number

1 You will hear a radio announcement about an animal park. Read the notes. What kind of information is missing?

APPLETON ANIMAL PARK

Open every day from 9.30 a.m.
Closing time in summer: **(1)** .... p.m.
Most popular animal in the park: **(2)** ....
Location of Green Café: **(3)** ....

2 ▶ 2.30 Listen to the recording for question 1. You will hear several times mentioned. Which one is correct? Why?

Now you try Listening Part 3
- Read the notes and decide what kind of information is missing.
- Be careful with spelling when you complete the answer sheet.

3 ▶ 2.31 Now listen and answer questions 2 and 3.

Exam profile 4

Reading Part 3 True/false

What is Part 3?
- Ten sentences about a text, which are either correct or incorrect
- Tests understanding of facts and information in a longer text

1 Read sentences 1 and 2 below and think about the highlighted parts. How could you say these phrases differently? For example, what is another way of saying 'more than once'?

1 Emily used to watch certain films more than once.
2 Peter Jackson told Emily to contact him again about film-making.

2 Read the first paragraph of the text. Then look at the highlighted parts that match the highlighted words in exercise 1. Why is sentence 1 in exercise 1 correct? Why is sentence 2 incorrect?

Emily Hagins: teen film-maker

American teenager Emily Hagins showed a strong interest in films and film-making at a young age, and often happily sat through some movies several times at her local movie theatre in Austin, Texas. She once wrote a letter to Peter Jackson, the director of her favourite series of films *The Lord of the Rings*. In his reply, he suggested a useful contact for Emily, who she later got in touch with.

Emily started by producing several short films and a documentary. Her father was helpful early on, having spent time with directors on film sets due to his job in advertising. However, although he guided her through what needed to be done, he made sure he left all the directing up to Emily.

This keen young film-maker then went on to write the story for a full-length movie, and the filming of this happened in her home town when she was just 12. Emily could only do this work at weekends and during school holidays, but somehow everything got done. Her efforts at directing this film won Emily a grant from the Austin Film Society, which made it possible for her to turn the results into a finished 68-minute movie.

Since this early success, Emily has made more films and is definitely a name to look out for in the future.

Now you try Reading Part 3
- Read the sentences before you read the text and highlight important words and phrases.
- Concentrate on the parts of the text that deal with the information in the sentences.

---

3 Now read the rest of the text and answer questions 3–6. If the sentence is correct, write A. If it is incorrect, write B.

3 Emily's father had some experience as a film director.
4 Emily set her first full-length film in Austin, Texas.
5 Emily was given time off school to complete her filming.
6 The Austin Film Society gave Emily some financial help.

Writing Part 3 Letter

What is a Part 3 letter?
- About 100 words long
- A reply to a letter from a friend

1 Read this exam task. Which two questions should you answer?

> - This is part of a letter you receive from an English friend.
>
> > For a piece of homework, I have to find out about a capital city in another country. What tourist attractions does your capital city offer? What can you tell me about the city's history? Write and tell me soon!
>
> - Now write a letter, answering your friend's questions.
> - Write your letter in about **100 words**.

2 Decide which question each phrase (b–g) is answering. Then use some of the ideas to write a letter about your own capital city.

	Attractions	History
a built by the Romans		✓
b wonderful street markets		
c fantastic sports facilities		
d became the capital in the 18th century		
e river cruises during the summer		
f population grew due to industry		
g beautiful parks		

> **Now you try Writing Part 3**
> - Make sure your letter answers the friend's questions fully.
> - Use informal language and show a range of structures and vocabulary.

Listening Part 4 True/false

What is Part 4?
- A conversation including attitude and opinion
- Six sentences that are either correct or incorrect

1 You will hear a conversation about cooking. Read sentences 1 and 2 before you listen to the first part. What words might you hear in the recording about these sentences?

	YES	NO
1 Julia thought there was a lack of variety on her cooking course.	A	B
2 Ben and Julia agree about the disadvantages of becoming a chef.	A	B

2 ▶2.32 Now listen to the recording. Which sentence is correct (A) and which is incorrect (B)? Listen again to check.

> **Now you try Listening Part 4**
> - Underline the verbs used in the sentences before you listen.
> - Use the second listening to check your answers.

3 ▶2.33 Read sentences 3 and 4, then listen to the next part of the recording and decide if they are correct or incorrect.

	YES	NO
3 Julia prefers cooking desserts to other dishes.	A	B
4 Julia suggests that Ben could improve his skills online.	A	B

127

Exam profile 5

Reading Part 1 Notices and messages

What is Part 1?
- Five very short texts, a mix of public notices and personal messages
- Tests understanding of the main content or purpose

1 Look at texts 1 and 2. What is the purpose of each one?

1

Jenny
Hope you haven't forgotten about our tennis match this afternoon? I'll see you at the courts just before 3 pm, as arranged. Bring your own water bottle this time!
Max

2

SALE ENDS FRIDAY
All boots half price
30% off other goods
(except designer bags)

2 Now choose the correct letter A, B or C.

1 Why has Max sent this text message?
   A to ask Jenny to bring water for him
   B to make a new arrangement with Jenny
   C to remind Jenny about their plans

2 A The shop is offering discounts for a limited period.
   B Everything in this shop is selling at half price until Friday.
   C Customers buying designer bags will pay less this week.

> **Now you try Reading Part 1**
> - Think about the purpose and meaning of the text.
> - Check that the answer you choose matches the text.

3 Look at the text in each question. What does it say?

3

PHOTO COMPETITION
Subject: families
Email entries to school secretary
Prize for each year group!

This competition will only
A have one winner in the school.
B accept printed photographs.
C be on a single topic.

4

From Anna
To Jess
As you've finished your geography homework, could I borrow your textbook overnight? Mine's disappeared! I can collect it now if you're at home? Promise I'll return it tomorrow!

A Anna wonders whether Jess could bring the textbook tomorrow.
B Anna wants Jess to lend her the textbook because hers is lost.
C Anna suggests doing their homework together at Jess's home.

Speaking Parts 2, 3 and 4

What is Part 2?
- A shared task using a picture with different ideas on it
- Making suggestions, discussing them and agreeing on a choice

1 **Look at the picture and read the task instructions.**

Some teenagers are writing to a group of **penfriends** in Canada for the first time and they are deciding what **subject** to write to them about. Talk together about the **different** subjects they could write about and then decide which would be **best**.

2 ▶2.34 **Now listen to two students doing the task in exercise 1. Which subject do they think it would be best to write about? Why?**

> **Now you try Speaking Part 2**
> - Talk about all the ideas and agree on the best one.
> - Think of different ways to make suggestions.

What are Parts 3 and 4?
- Part 3 – an individual task describing a photo for one minute
- Part 4 – a discussion on the same topic as Part 3

1 **Look at the pictures and read the task instructions.**

I'm going to give each of you a photograph of people **doing sport**. Please tell us what you can see in your photograph.

2 ▶2.35 **Listen to the first student talking. Which picture is she describing? Can you add anything to what she says?**

> **Now you try Speaking Parts 3 and 4**
> - Say as much as you can about the photo in Part 3.
> - Give your partner time to speak in the Part 4 discussion.

3 Now describe the second picture yourself. Talk for about a minute.

4 ▶2.36 Read the task instructions for Part 4. Then listen to the discussion. What sports do they mention?

Your photographs showed people **doing sport**. Now I'd like you to talk together about the different sports you enjoy playing or watching, and suggest a sport that you'd like to try in the future.

Pairwork

UNIT 6 PAGE 39   Speaking

1 Read the instructions for the task below.
Think about each party idea and make notes.
Compare your notes with a partner.

A young boy is having a party for his sister because
she is coming home from hospital. Talk together about
the **different** party ideas that he has and then decide
which one would be the **best**.

2 ⬤ Discuss your ideas with your partner.
Talk about all the ideas and agree on which
is best. Use phrases from the *Prepare* box
on page 39.

UNIT 8 PAGE 49   Speaking

1 Look at the picture. What interesting adjectives
can you use to describe it?

2 ⬤ Describe the picture to your partner.
Use interesting adjectives, and use phrases
from the *Prepare* box on page 49 if you don't
know the right words.

UNIT 14 PAGE 83   Speaking

⬤ Work in pairs. Look at the picture and read
the instructions. Then talk together. Use phrases
from the *Prepare* box on page 83.

Some teenagers are planning to attend a one-day
cooking course. They are trying to decide what type
of **food** to learn how to make. Talk together about the
different courses and decide which one would be
best.

UNIT 15 PAGE 86

Key for quiz

Add up your scores.

1	a1 b4 c2 d3	4	a1 b2 c4 d4
2	a2 b1 c 1 d4	5	a1 b4 c2 d3
3	a1 b4 c3 d2		

What your score says about you

Low score (5–9)
You love nature and being outdoors. You especially
love animals and know when they are unhappy.
You like walking home and being in open spaces.
You're an awesome country teen!

Medium score (10–14)
You are a bit of both. You like the excitement of
the city but not the pollution and crime. As for the
country, well, that's just a bit too quiet for you. You
like your facilities, and you're interested in history, too.
So you are a town teen! All the good things of the city
without the bad things! Rock it down, town teen!

High score (15–19)
You love the street lights, the sounds, and the smell
of the city! It's just so exciting! You like surprises in
the city but not in the countryside. All those animals?
Not you at all! You are a city teen – go city you!

UNIT 16 PAGE 93 Speaking

> ● Student A: Look at this photograph and describe what you can see in it. Talk for about one minute.

> ● Student B: Look at this photograph and describe what you can see in it. Talk for about one minute.

UNIT 17 PAGE 100 Grammar

1 Work in groups of three. Follow the instructions.

Student A: Choose three questions to ask Student B.
Student B: Answer Student A's questions.
Student C: Report Student A's questions and Student B's answers.

> **Are you fairly reliable as a person?**
> How much time do you spend online each day?
> **Have you ever chatted with someone in another country online?**
> Are your grandparents on Facebook?
> **How many friends do you have on Facebook?**
> What is the most recent photo you have taken on your phone?
> **What is the most interesting fact you have found out online?**
> Which music website can you recommend?
> **What is your biggest fault?**
> What is the strangest thing you've ever done?
> **Do you prefer oranges or lemons?**
> Which films have made you laugh?
> **Which films have made you cry?**
> Do you keep your bedroom reasonably tidy?

2 Swap roles and practise again.

UNIT 20 PAGE 115 Speaking

1 ● **Look at the pictures and read the task below. Which ideas do you think are best? Why? Plan your ideas.**

A boy wants to do something **different** during his summer holidays. His friends and family have found the following **ideas**. Talk together about the different holiday ideas that he could do and then decide which would be **best**.

Here is a picture with some ideas to help you.

2 ● **Discuss your ideas with your partner. Talk about all the ideas and agree on which is best. Use phrases from the *Prepare* box on page 115.**

Word profiles

UNIT 1
WORD PROFILE: *thing* /θɪŋ/

that kind of thing	I like pasta, pizza – *that kind of thing.*
the best thing ever	His latest song is *the best thing ever!*
the same thing	Mum offered me her old phone but it isn't *the same thing.*
things like that	I love swimming, surfing and *things like that.*
the thing	*The thing* I love about that film is the music.

1 Match the sentence halves.

1 I love all outdoor activities
2 The thing I love about holidays
3 I think skiing is
4 We have to write about where we live,
5 Takeaway pizza is not

a our best friend, that kind of thing.
b and things like that.
c the best thing ever
d is going to the beach.
e the same thing as my mum's.

UNIT 2
WORD PROFILE: *close* /kləʊs, kləʊz/

PUBLIC PLACE	The bank *closes* at 4 pm.
FRIENDLY	Angela and I are really *close.* We tell each other everything.
RELATIVE	I think Jane and Rachel are *close* relatives, like cousins?
NEAR	The library is *close* to the swimming pool.

1 Match the bold words in the questions to the meanings in the *Word profile* box. Then answer the questions about yourself.

1 Who is your **closest** friend?
2 Which classmate lives **closest** to you?
3 What time does your school **close**?
4 How many **close** relatives were at your last family party?

UNIT 3
WORD PROFILE: *give* /ɡɪv/

ALLOW TIME	*Give* me another day and then it'll be ready.
CAUSE	What you said just now has *given* me an idea.
ALLOW	Joining a library *gives* you the opportunity to borrow lots of books.
give in	I have no idea how to do this – I *give in.*
give in sth / give sth in	Have you *given* your English homework *in* yet?

1 Complete the sentences with the correct form of *give* and any other words that are necessary.

1 I don't know what you're thinking – I .... ! Tell me!
2 The tennis association .... hundreds of children the .... to play for free each year.
3 Can you .... me ten more minutes?
4 The moon last night .... me an idea for a painting.
5 I finished the work and .... it .... to the teacher.
6 Can you .... me another week to finish this?
7 Josie's parents finally .... and she got the latest mobile phone for her birthday.
8 We .... our project work last week.
9 My parents .... me the .... to go to Australia last year.
10 The contents of the letter .... Mr Peters quite a shock.

UNIT 4
WORD PROFILE: *case* /keɪs/

in this case	There have been other winter storms, but *in this case*, the wind speed was much higher than forecast.
in each case	Several houses were damaged and *in each case*, there were broken windows.
cases of	The number of new *cases of* this rare disease has risen.
(just) in case	Take my umbrella *in case* it starts raining.
in case of	*In case of* fire, leave the building immediately by the nearest exit.

1 **Complete the sentences using the correct phrase with *case*.**

1 We received more than 100 applications for this job and .... , we sent a personal email in reply.
2 Sports practice will take place in the gym .... rain.
3 Have there been any .... flu at your school?
4 Remember to bring a map .... you get lost!
5 You shouldn't really take this book out of the library, but .... , I'll allow it.
6 .... fire, use the emergency exits.

UNIT 5
WORD PROFILE: *look* /lʊk/

SEARCH	I've *looked* everywhere for the book you wanted.
look nice/strange, etc.	That skirt *looks* really good.
look forward to sth / doing sth	I'm really *looking forward to* the summer holidays.
look like	The building *looks like* a piece of glass.
it looks like / as if	It *looks like* it'll be sunny all day today.

1 **Complete the second sentence so that it means the same as the first. Use the correct form of *look* and any other words that are necessary.**

1 I'm taking my umbrella because it might rain later.
It .... it might rain later.
2 That dress really suits you.
That dress .... on you.
3 I have checked my bag, but I can't find my pen.
I've .... for my pen in my bag, but I can't find it.
4 I can't wait until Friday night when Dad gets home from the USA.
I'm .... to Friday night when Dad gets home from the USA.
5 I thought she was a nurse because of her blue dress.
She .... a nurse in that blue dress.

UNIT 6
WORD PROFILE: *only* /ˈəʊnli/

RECENTLY	He *only* arrived 20 minutes ago.
NOWHERE ELSE	You can *only* find kangaroos in Australia.
NOT MORE	There are *only* six people in my class.
NOT IMPORTANT	It was *only* a joke!
if only	*If only* my parents would listen!

1 **Match the pairs of sentences.**

1 Why isn't that boy talking to anyone?
2 I've got so many people to get presents for this year.
3 I woke up suddenly and I was crying.
4 My friend has an annoying habit of talking loudly.
5 Has anyone seen my mobile phone?

a Fortunately it was only a bad dream.
b If only she would stop doing that.
c He only joined the class yesterday.
d It must be in your room – that's the only place you leave it!
e Lucky you! I've only got my mum and my sister.

UNIT 7
WORD PROFILE: *just* /dʒʌst/

RECENTLY	I've *just* heard your news – congratulations!
EMPHASIS	I *just* don't understand.
ONLY	It was *just* a dream.
ALMOST NOT	We caught the train *just* in time.
EXACTLY	The film of the book was *just* as I thought it would be.
just about	I can *just about* see the bird in the tree.

1 **Complete the sentences using *just* and any other words that are necessary.**

1 We played really well and won the match – .... I thought!
2 Let's meet at 1pm .... for lunch.
3 I can .... read this writing, but it's not very clear.
4 Can you stop talking and .... listen, please?
5 I'm sorry you didn't find it funny; it was .... a joke!
6 We've only .... got home. The bus was really late.

UNIT 8
WORD PROFILE: *last* /lɑːst/

FINAL (adj)	It's the *last* programme of the series.
MOST RECENT (adj)	What was the *last* film you saw?
ONE BEFORE PRESENT (adj)	I liked her *last* film, but I'm not very keen on her latest one.
REMAINING (adj)	Who wants the *last* piece of cake?
MOST RECENT (adv)	When did you hear from her *last*?
CONTINUE (verb)	The batteries only *last* about five hours.

1 Match the sentence halves.

1 At my last school we didn't
2 When I get a sore throat
3 The band had a different singer
4 Fiona was feeling much better
5 That's the last time I'll
6 You won't find any beads because I

a when we last met her.
b it usually lasts a couple of days.
c hang around waiting for you!
d have to wear a uniform.
e bought the last ones they had.
f the last time I saw them play.

2 Complete the sentences so they are true for you.

1 The last party I went to was …
2 Our summer holiday lasted …
3 I last had my hair cut …

UNIT 9
WORD PROFILE: *actually* /ˈæktʃuəli/

TRUTH	So what *actually* happened?
SURPRISE	Don't tell me he *actually* gave you a present?
OPPOSITE	*Actually*, we met on Tuesday, not Wednesday.

1 Put *actually* in the right place in these sentences. There may be more than one possible answer.

1 Well, you're a very nice person!
2 We didn't think our team could win.
3 Do you mean you paid money for this?
4 It wasn't Simon you met but his brother.
5 By the way, did you try the other café?

UNIT 10
WORD PROFILE: *besides* /bɪˈsaɪdz/

EXTRA REASON	She won't mind if you're late – *besides*, it wouldn't be your fault.
IN ADDITION TO	*Besides* studying hard, she's working in a café on Saturdays.
APART FROM (preposition)	Do you play any other sports *besides* football and basketball?

1 Complete these sentences with your own ideas.

1 I don't do much at the weekend besides .... and ....
2 Besides .... , I can't think of another singer from Britain.
3 If you could go anywhere besides .... , where would you choose?
4 It doesn't matter if we miss the film – besides, ...

UNIT 11
WORD PROFILE: *by* /baɪ/

NEAR	Let's meet *by* the Café Capelli at four o'clock.
by itself	Suddenly the door opened *by itself*!
by hand	These jumpers are all made *by hand*.
by mistake/accident	I walked into the wrong room *by mistake/accident*.
by heart	I learnt all my French verbs *by heart*.

1 Complete the sentences.

1 She gave me a jumper that had to be washed ....
2 He left the milk in the supermarket ....
3 Maisy saw Frank .... the swimming pool.
4 Sophie didn't need to read the words because she knew the song ....
5 The dog got out of the house ....

2 Answer the questions.

1 Have you ever seen anything move by itself?
2 Do you like clothes that are made by hand?
3 Have you ever said something by mistake?
4 What have you learnt by heart?
5 Who is sitting by the door at the moment?

UNIT 12
WORD PROFILE: *check* /tʃek/

FIND OUT	*I checked the weather online before we left.*
EXAMINATION	*They do security checks before you go into the exam hall.*
check in	*We usually check in online these days.*
check-in (desk)	*I'll meet you at the check-in desk.*
check out	*The Jones family checked out at noon.*

1 Rewrite the sentences using the correct form of *check* and any other words that are necessary.

1 There was a long queue to check in our bags.
  There was a long queue at the ....
2 Do you know all the ingredients for the cake?
  Have you .... the ingredients for the cake?
3 As usual, Mum made sure that we had everything before we left.
  Mum did her usual .... of everything before we left.
4 We left the hotel after lunch.
  We .... of the hotel after lunch.
5 When you arrive at the hotel, you should register and get your key.
  When you arrive at the hotel, you should .... and get your key.

UNIT 13
WORD PROFILE: *result* /rɪˈzʌlt/

HAPPEN	*The fire was the result of an electrical fault.*
INFORMATION	*Have you had your maths results yet?*
COMPETITION	*The final result in the show surprised everyone.*
as a result	*I didn't get much sleep and as a result I'm tired.*

1 Match the sentence halves.

1 The only result of the meeting
2 Your good results this term
3 The losing team decided to
4 It's quite easy to achieve
5 They have just confirmed

a are due to hard work.
b the election results on TV.
c delicious results in baking.
d was a decision on advertising.
e organise extra practice as a result.

UNIT 14
WORD PROFILE: *keep* /kiːp/

HAVE	*Do you want your book back or can I keep it?*
STAY	*Why can't you keep quiet – I'm trying to read!*
keep (on) doing something	*I kept telling you not to believe him.*
keep a secret	*Alex couldn't keep a secret for very long.*
keep in touch	*We keep in touch with each other by email.*

1 Complete the sentences with the correct form of *keep*.

1 If we .... practising, we'd improve.
2 Is schoolwork .... you busy at the moment?
3 James .... in touch with his family once a week.
4 It's hard to .... a secret from your closest friends.
5 Coffee beans that are .... in the fridge last longer.

2 Discuss the questions.

1 Do things ever keep you awake at night?
2 How do you keep in touch with people in other places?
3 What things do you keep in your bag?
4 Why do you keep on learning English?

UNIT 15
WORD PROFILE: all /ɔːl/

EVERYONE OR EVERYTHING	Jake was happy because all his friends visited him last week.
WHOLE TIME	She spent all week in bed with flu.
at all	Do you want any help at all?
above all	I love my sister and above all, she's my best friend.
after all	It's a long way to go; after all, it's a 24-hour flight.
and all that	Mike hates shopping for clothes, jewellery and all that.
all is well	All's well with Grandma now she's out of hospital.

1 Complete the sentences with *all* and any other words that are necessary.

1 You can borrow an umbrella. .... , it's raining, so you will need it.
2 I'm pleased with my result and .... with the teacher's comment: 'excellent'.
3 I love swimming, surfing, beach games ....
4 I didn't understand the maths homework ....
5 .... my friends have the latest phone.
6 I haven't heard from my great aunt in a long time – I hope .... , and she isn't ill.
7 I need a break. I've been on my computer .... day.

UNIT 16
WORD PROFILE: direct /daɪˈrekt/

STRAIGHT	There is a direct flight from London to Lisbon every day.
FILM/PLAY	Titanic was directed by James Cameron.
ROUTE	We arrived early and they directed us to our seats.
NOTHING BETWEEN	He got into the football team as a direct result of his hard work.

1 Complete the sentences with the correct form of *direct*.

1 You don't have change planes because it's a .... flight.
2 Many actors want to .... films as well as act in them.
3 That man over there may be able to .... us to the town library.
4 There aren't any .... trains from here to York.
5 I asked a teacher, and he .... me to the head's office.
6 Joyce .... the play and also played the leading role.
7 Michael says that his grades are a .... result of his study.

UNIT 17
WORD PROFILE: know /nəʊ/

BE FAMILIAR WITH	I lived in Nice for a year so I know it well.
get to know	I'd really like to get to know their music.
as you know	As you know, it isn't possible to change sale items.
you know	You could ask me for help at any time, you know.
I know	What shall we do? I know, let's go to the mall.

1 Match meanings 1–5 to the meanings and examples in the *Word profile* box.

1 used when you have an idea
2 spend time on something so that you learn more about it
3 used to make what you say stronger
4 have personal experience of something
5 used when you are saying something that is already known

UNIT 18
WORD PROFILE: quality /ˈkwɒləti/

VERY GOOD (adj)	The picture on that TV is high quality.
GOOD OR BAD (noun)	The quality of these clothes is excellent.
CHARACTER	That singer has some great personal qualities.
quality time	It's important to spend quality time with your parents.

1 Complete the sentences with the correct form of *quality* and any other words that are necessary.

1 The air .... here is very poor because of all the traffic.
2 We went to a café and just spent some .... together.
3 This is a .... machine and will last for a long time.
4 I'm not surprised it broke – it wasn't good ....
5 I admire all Jessica's leadership ....

UNIT 19
WORD PROFILE: *order* /ˈɔːdə/

REQUEST (noun)	*I'd like to place an order for some dictionaries.*
REQUEST (verb)	*We ordered three different pizzas.*
ARRANGEMENT (noun)	*I've put the books in alphabetical order.*
in order to	*Beth worked all summer in order to save money.*
out of order	*We had to walk upstairs as the lift was out of order.*

1 **Complete the sentences with the correct form of *order* and any other words that are necessary.**

1 Our fridge is .... and we can't keep anything cold.
2 For the class photo we had to stand in rows in .... of height.
3 I'm going to Sam's flat .... meet his sister.
4 We had to wait ages to .... our food.
5 My last internet .... was delivered within two days.

UNIT 20
WORD PROFILE: *place* /pleɪs/

SOMEWHERE	*This looks like a nice place for a picnic.*
SEAT	*Jake's saved Margie a place on the bus.*
OPPORTUNITY	*They've offered Max a place on the football team.*
take place	*Our English class takes place on Mondays at five o'clock.*
in first/second/third, etc. place	*Trudie finished the race in first place.*

1 **Complete the second sentence using *place* and any other words that are necessary.**

1 Our seats are in row D.
   Our .... in row D.
2 Millie has the chance to study law in London next year.
   Millie has .... on a law course in London next year.
3 The match was played at the San Siro stadium.
   The match .... at the San Siro stadium.
4 Everyone was disappointed that Jack came in last.
   Everyone was disappointed that Jack finished ....
5 I think Bologna is a wonderful city to live in.
   I think Bologna is a wonderful .... to live.

adj = adjective   *adv* = adverb   *n* = noun   *v* = verb
pv = phrasal verb   *prep* = preposition   *phr* = phrase

UNIT 1

change /tʃeɪndʒ/ *v* IN SHOP to take something you have bought back to a shop and exchange it for something else

charge /tʃɑːdʒ/ *v* MONEY to ask an amount of money for something, especially a service or activity

charge /tʃɑːdʒ/ *n* MONEY the amount of money that you have to pay for something, especially for an activity or service

discount /'dɪskaʊnt/ *n* a reduction in price

online shopping /'ɒnlaɪn 'ʃɒpɪŋ/ *n* the activity of buying things on the internet

receipt /rɪ'siːt/ *n* PIECE OF PAPER a piece of paper that proves that you have received goods or money

refund /'riːfʌnd/ *n* an amount of money that is given back to you, especially because you are not happy with something you have bought

send sth back /send bæk/ *pv* to return something to the person who sent it to you, especially because it is damaged or not suitable

serve /sɜːv/ *v* SHOP to help customers and sell things to them in a shop

shop /ʃɒp/ *v* to buy things in shops

spend /spend/ *v* MONEY to use money to buy or pay for something

UNIT 2

annoying /ə'nɔɪɪŋ/ *adj* making you feel annoyed

anxious /'æŋkʃəs/ *adj* WORRIED worried and nervous

appear /ə'pɪə/ *v* BE SEEN to start to be seen

confident /'kɒnfɪdənt/ *adj* ABILITY certain about your ability to do things well

cruel /'kruːəl/ *adj* extremely unkind and unpleasant and causing pain to people or animals intentionally

disagree /dɪsə'griː/ *v* to have a different opinion from someone else about something

disappear /dɪsə'pɪə/ *v* to become impossible to see or find

dislike /dɪs'laɪk/ *v* to not like someone or something

easygoing /iːzɪ'gəʊɪŋ/ *adj* usually relaxed and calm, not worried or upset

honest /'ɒnɪst/ *adj* NOT CHEAT not likely to lie, cheat or steal

intelligent /ɪn'telɪdʒənt/ *adj* showing intelligence, or able to learn and understand things easily

reliable /rɪ'laɪəbl/ *adj* able to be trusted or believed

sensible /'sensɪbl/ *adj* showing good judgment

silly /'sɪli/ *adj* not taking things seriously

sociable /'səʊʃəbl/ *adj* Someone who is sociable enjoys being with people and meeting new people.

talented /'tæləntɪd/ *adj* having a natural ability to do something well

uninteresting /ʌn'ɪntrəstɪŋ/ *adj* not interesting

unkind /ʌn'kaɪnd/ *adj* slightly cruel

unpleasant /ʌn'plezənt/ *adj* not enjoyable or pleasant

unlucky /ʌn'lʌki/ *adj* having or causing bad luck

UNIT 3

absolutely /'æbsəluːtli/ *adv* COMPLETELY completely

ancient /'eɪntʃənt/ *adj* very old

beat /biːt/ *v* DEFEAT to defeat or do better than

enormous /ɪ'nɔːməs/ *adj* extremely large

enter /'entə/ *v* COMPETITION to take part in a competition, race or examination

exhausted /ɪg'zɔːstɪd/ *adj* extremely tired

extremely /ɪk'striːmli/ *adv* very, or much more than usual

freezing /'friːzɪŋ/ *adj* extremely cold

give /gɪv/ *v* PROVIDE to provide someone with something

have a go at sth /hæv ə gəʊ ət/ *phr* to try something you have not done before

incredibly /ɪn'kredəbli/ *adv* EXTREMELY extremely

join /dʒɔɪn/ *v* BECOME A MEMBER to become a member of a club, group, or organisation

lose /luːz/ *v* NOT WIN to fail to succeed in a game, competition, etc.

miss an opportunity /mɪs ən ɒpə'tjuːnəti/ *phr* to not use an opportunity to do something

score /skɔː/ *v* to get points in a game or test

terrible /'terəbl/ *adj* very bad, of low quality, or unpleasant

win /wɪn/ *v* COMPETITION to get the most points, or to get a prize, in a competition or game

UNIT 4

blow (sth) away /bləʊ əˈweɪ/ *pv* to move and make currents of air, or to be moved or make something move on a current of air

burn (sth) down /bɜːn daʊn/ *pv* to destroy something, especially a building, by fire, or to be destroyed by fire

come out /kʌm aʊt/ *pv* SUN When the sun, the moon, or a star comes out, it appears in the sky.

flood /flʌd/ *n* WATER a large amount of water covering an area that is usually dry

flow /fləʊ/ *v* If something such as a liquid flows, it moves somewhere in a smooth, continuous way.

forecast /ˈfɔːkɑːst/ *n* a report saying what the weather is likely to be like

hang out /hæŋ aʊt/ *pv* to spend a lot of time in a place with someone

lightning /ˈlaɪtnɪŋ/ *n* a sudden flash of light in the sky during a storm

pour /pɔː/ *v* RAIN to rain a lot

power /paʊə/ *n* ELECTRICITY energy, usually electricity, that is used to provide light, heat, etc.

put sth out /pʊt aʊt/ *pv* to make something that is burning stop burning

rise /raɪz/ *n* INCREASE an increase in the level of something

split (sth) up /splɪt ʌp/ *pv* to divide into smaller parts or groups, or to divide something into smaller parts or groups

tornado /tɔːˈneɪdəʊ/ *n* an extremely strong and dangerous wind that blows in a circle and destroys buildings as it moves along

UNIT 5

create /kriˈeɪt/ *v* to make something happen or exist

customise /ˈkʌstəmaɪz/ *v* to change something to make it suitable for a particular person or purpose

decorate /ˈdekəreɪt/ *v* MAKE ATTRACTIVE to add attractive things to an object or place

design /dɪˈzaɪn/ *n* PLANNING the way in which something is planned and made

finally /ˈfaɪnəli/ *adv* LAST POINT used especially at the beginning of a sentence to introduce the last point or idea

fix /fɪks/ *v* REPAIR to repair something or to make a bad situation better

invent /ɪnˈvent/ *v* NEW DESIGN to design or create something which has never existed before

mend /mend/ *v* to repair something that is broken, torn, or not working correctly

rebuild /riːˈbɪld/ *v* BUILD AGAIN to build something again that has been damaged or destroyed

recycle /riːˈsaɪkl/ *v* to collect used paper, glass, plastic, etc., and put if through a process so that it can be used again

sew /səʊ/ *v* to make or repair clothes by joining pieces of cloth using a needle and thread

suddenly /ˈsʌdənli/ *adv* quickly and unexpectedly

stick /stɪk/ *v* FIX to become joined to something else or to make something become joined to something else, usually with a substance like glue

UNIT 6

avoid (doing sth) /əˈvɔɪd/ *v* to intentionally not do something

bleed /bliːd/ *v* to lose blood

complain of sth /kəmˈpleɪn əv/ *v* to tell other people that something is making you feel ill

follow /ˈfɒləʊ/ *v* OBEY to do what someone or something says you should do

injure /ˈɪndʒə/ *v* to hurt a person, animal or part of your body

operate /ˈɒpəreɪt/ *v* TREATMENT to treat an illness or injury by cutting someone's body and removing or repairing part of it

prevent /prɪˈvent/ *v* to stop something from happening or someone from doing something

reduce /rɪˈdjuːs/ *v* to make something less

suffer from /ˈsʌfə frəm/ *v* to have an illness or other health problem

wrap /ræp/ *v* COVER to cover or surround something with paper, cloth or other material

UNIT 7

achieve /əˈtʃiːv/ *v* to succeed in doing something good, usually by working hard

achievement /əˈtʃiːvmənt/ *n* something very good and difficult that you succeeded in doing

advert /ˈædvɜːt/ *n* an advertisement

advertise /ˈædvətaɪz/ *v* to tell people about a product or service in newspapers, on television, on the internet, etc.

celebrity /sɪˈlebrɪti/ *n* someone who is famous, especially in the entertainment business

channel /ˈtʃænəl/ *n* TV a television station

concert hall /ˈkɒnsət hɔːl/ *n* a large building in which concerts are performed

DJ /ˈdiːdʒeɪ/ *n* someone who plays records on the radio or at live events

entertain /entəˈteɪn/ *v* to keep a group of people interested or enjoying themselves

entertainer /entəˈteɪnə/ *n* someone whose job is to entertain people by singing, telling jokes, etc.

entertaining /entəˈteɪnɪŋ/ *adj* funny and enjoyable

entertainment /entə'teɪnmənt/ *n* shows, movies, television, or other performances or activities that entertain people

festival /'festɪvəl/ *n* PERFORMANCES a series of special events, performances, etc. that often takes place over several days

guitarist /gɪ'tɑːrɪst/ *n* someone who plays the guitar, especially as their job

live /laɪv/ *adj* A live radio or television programme is seen or heard as it happens.

musician /mjuː'zɪʃən/ *n* someone who plays a musical instrument, often as a job

perform /pə'fɔːm/ *v* ENTERTAIN to entertain people by acting, dancng, singing, playing music, etc.

performer /pə'fɔːmə/ *n* someone who entertains people by acting, dancng, singing, playing music

sound production /saʊnd prə'dʌkʃən/ *n* FILM/MUSIC when someone controls how a sound recording is made

sound technician /saʊnd tek'nɪʃən/ *n* someone who works with the technical equipment in a recording studio

studio /'stjuːdiəʊ/ *n* TV/RADIO/MUSIC a room where television/radio programmes or music recordings are made

video clip /'vɪdiəʊ klɪp/ *n* a short video recording that you can see on a website

UNIT 8

brand new /brænd 'njuː/ *adj* completely new

classic /'klæsɪk/ *adj* TYPICAL A classic example of something has all the features or qualities that you expect

cosy /'kəʊzi/ *adj* comfortable and warm

fresh /freʃ/ *adj* DIFFERENT new and different and therefore interesting or exciting

historic /hɪ'stɒrɪk/ *adj* important or likely to be important in history

modern /'mɒdən/ *adj* NEW using the newest ideas, design, technology, etc. and not traditional

original /ə'rɪdʒɪnəl/ *adj* MADE FIRST existing since the beginning, or being the earliest form of something

recent /'riːsənt/ *adj* happening or starting from a short time ago

spectacular /spek'tækjʊlə/ *adj* extremely good, exciting, or surprising

traditional /trə'dɪʃənəl/ *adj* following the customs or ways of behaving that have continued in a group of people or society for a long time

unusual /ʌn'juːʒuəl/ *adj* different and not ordinary, often in a way that is interesting or exciting

UNIT 9

access /'ækses/ *n* the right or opportunity to use or look at something

battery /'bætəri/ *n* a device that produces electricity to provide power for mobile phones, laptop computers, radios, cars, etc.

connection /kə'nekʃən/ *n* JOINING THINGS something that joins things together

experiment /ɪk'sperɪmənt/ *n* a test, especially a scientific one, that you do in order to learn something or to discover whether something is true

fuel /fjʊəl/ *n* a substance that is burned to provide heat or power

invention /ɪn'venʃən/ *n* something which has been designed or created for the first time, or the act of creating or designing something

power /paʊə/ *n* energy in the form of light, heat, etc.

pump /pʌmp/ *n* a piece of equipment which is used to cause liquid, air or gas to move from one place to another

satellite /'sætəlaɪt/ *n* a piece of equipment which is sent into space around the Earth to receive and send signals or to collect information

torch /tɔːtʃ/ *n* a small electric light that you hold in your hand

UNIT 10

at all /ət ɔːl/ *phr* used for emphasis in questions or negative statements, to mean in any way or of any type

at first /ət fɜːst/ *phr* at the beginning of a situation or period of time

at its best /ət ɪts best/ *phr* at the highest level of achievement or quality

at least /ət liːst/ *phr* something you say when you are telling someone about an advantage in a bad situation

at (long) last /ət lɒŋ lɑːst/ *phr* finally

at once /ət wʌnts/ *phr* immediately

at present /ət 'prezənt/ *phr* now

creature /'kriːtʃə/ *n* anything that lives but is not a plant

crop /krɒp/ *n* a plant such as a grain, fruit or vegetable that is grown in large amounts, or the amount of plants of a particular type that are produced at one time

environment /ɪn'vaɪrənmənt/ *n* the air, land and water where people, animals and plants live

human /'hjuːmən/ *n* a man, woman or child

jungle /'dʒʌŋgl/ *n* a tropical forest in which trees and plants grow very closely together

landscape /ˈlændskeɪp/ n a large area of countryside, especially in relation to its appearance

population /pɒpjʊˈleɪʃən/ n PEOPLE all the people living in a particular area, or all the people or animals of a particular type

rainforest /ˈreɪnfɒrɪst/ n a forest in a tropical area which receives a lot of rain

UNIT 11

attend /əˈtend/ v BE PRESENT to go offically and usually regularly to a place

break up /breɪk ˈʌp/ pv END CLASSES When schools or colleges break up, the classes end and the holidays begin.

degree /dɪˈgriː/ n QUALIFICATION a qualification given for completing a university course

do badly /duː ˈbædli/ phr to be unsuccessful

do well /duː wel/ phr to be successful

education /edjʊˈkeɪʃən/ n the process of teaching or learning in a school or college, or the knowledge that you get from this

firework /ˈfaɪəwɜːk/ n a small object which explodes in the sky and produces bright lights

grade /greɪd/ n SCHOOL a school class or group of classes in which all the children are of a similar age

headteacher /hedˈtiːtʃə/ n the person in charge of a school

primary /ˈpraɪməri/ adj EDUCATION of or for the teaching of young children, especially those between five and eleven years old

qualification /kwɒlɪfɪˈkeɪʃən/ n STUDY something that you get when you are successful in an exam or course of study

secondary /ˈsekəndri/ adj EDUCATION relating to the education of children approximately between the ages of 11 and 18 years old

skateboard /ˈskeɪtbɔːd/ n a board with wheels on the bottom, that you stand on and move forward by pushing one foot on the ground

sunflower /ˈsʌnflaʊə/ n a large yellow flower

UNIT 12

abroad /əˈbrɔːd/ adv in or to a foreign country

cruise ship /ˈkruːz ʃɪp/ n a large ship like a hotel, which people travel on for pleasure

ferry /ˈferi/ n a boat that regularly carries passengers and often vehicles across an area of water

go away /gəʊ əˈweɪ/ pv HOLIDAY to leave your home in order to spend time in a different place

harbour /ˈhɑːbə/ n an area of water next to the coast, often protected from the sea by a thick wall, where ships and boats can shelter

land /lænd/ v ARRIVE to arrive at a place in a plane or a boat, or to make a plane or a boat reach the land

on board /ɒn bɔːd/ phr on a boat, train, aircraft, etc.

on display /ɒn dɪˈspleɪ/ phr If something is on display, it is there for people to look at

on foot /ɒn fʊt/ phr walking

on purpose /ɒn ˈpɜːpəs/ phr intentionally

on sale /ɒn seɪl/ phr available to buy in a shop, on the internet, etc.

on time /ɒn taɪm/ phr not early or late

public transport /ˈpʌblɪk ˈtrænspɔːt/ n a system of vehicles such as buses and trains which operate at regular times on fixed routes and are used by the public

sail /seɪl/ v TRAVEL ON BOAT to travel somewhere on a boat or a ship

set out /set aʊt/ pv JOURNEY to start a journey

timetable /ˈtaɪmteɪbl/ n TRAVEL a list of times when buses, trains, etc. arrive and leave

tourism /ˈtʊərɪzəm/ n the business of providing services for tourists, including organising their travel, hotels, entertainment, etc.

UNIT 13

advert /ˈædvɜːt/ n an advertisement

image /ˈɪmɪdʒ/ n PICTURE a picture, especially on film or television or in a mirror

in advance /ɪn ədˈvɑːnts/ phr before a particular time, or before doing a particular thing

in detail /ɪn ˈdiːteɪl/ phr including or considering all the information about something or every part of something

in fact /ɪn fækt/ phr giving more information which is often surprising

in future /ɪn ˈfjuːtʃə/ phr beginning from now

in general /ɪn ˈdʒenərəl/ phr usually, or in most situations

in particular /ɪn pəˈtɪkjʊlə/ phr especially

in the end /ɪn ðiː end/ phr finally, after something has been thought about or discussed a lot

position /pəˈzɪʃən/ n SITTING/STANDING the way someone is sitting, standing or lying

product /ˈprɒdʌkt/ n something that is made or grown to be sold

purpose /ˈpɜːpəs/ n REASON why you do something or why something exists

result /rɪˈzʌlt/ n something that you get at the end of an activity or process

software /ˈsɒftweə/ n programs that you use to make a computer do different things

technique /tekˈniːk/ n a particular or special way of doing something

UNIT 14

barbecue /ˈbɑːbɪkjuː/ v to cook food on a barbecue

arrangement /əˈreɪndʒmənt/ n PLANS plan for how something will happen

bite /baɪt/ v to cut something using your teeth

boil /bɔɪl/ v HEAT LIQUID If a liquid boils, or if you boil it, it reaches the temperature where bubbles rise up in it and it produces steam.

burn /bɜːn/ v COOK TOO LONG If you burn something that you are cooking, you cook it too much and if something you are cooking burns, it cooks too much.

fry /fraɪ/ v to cook food in hot oil or fat, or to be cooked in hot oil or fat

ingredient /ɪnˈgriːdiənt/ n FOOD a food that is used with other foods in the preparation of a particular dish

initial /ɪˈnɪʃəl/ n the first letter of a name, especially when used to represent a name

interest /ˈɪntrəst/ n ACTIVITY something that you enjoy doing, studying or experiencing

memory /ˈmeməri/ n EVENT REMEMBERED something that you remember from the past

qualification /kwɒlɪfəˈkeɪʃən/ n STUDY something that you get when you are successful in an exam or course of study

roast /rəʊst/ v If you roast food, you cook it in an oven or over a fire, and if food roasts, it is cooked in an oven or over a fire.

stir /stɜː/ v MIX to mix food or liquid by moving a spoon round and round in it

taste /teɪst/ v FOOD/DRINK to put food or drink in your mouth to find out what flavour it has

tear /tɪə/ n CRYING a drop of water that comes from your eye when you cry

UNIT 15

air conditioning /ˈeə kəndɪʃənɪŋ/ n the system used for keeping the air in a building or vehicle cool

architecture /ˈɑːkɪtektʃə/ n STYLE the design and style of buildings

catch up with sb /kætʃ ʌp wɪθ/ pv MEET to meet someone you know after not seeing them for a period of time and talk about things you have done

clinic /ˈklɪnɪk/ n a building, often part of a hospital, where people go for medical treatment or advice

end up /end ʌp/ pv be in a particular place or situation after a series of events

facilities /fəˈsɪlətiz/ n the buildings, equipment and services provided for a particular purpose

historic building /hɪˈstɒrɪk ˈbɪldɪŋ/ n an old building that is likely to be important in history

modern /ˈmɒdən/ n NEW using the newest ideas, design, technology, etc. and not traditional

monument /ˈmɒnjʊmənt/ n BUILDING/PLACE an old building or place that is important in history

move in /muːv ɪn/ pv to begin living in a new home

move out /muːv aʊt/ pv to stop living in a particular home

open space /ˈəʊpən speɪs/ n WITHOUT BUILDING an open area of land which has no buildings on it or near it

pollution /pəˈluːʃən/ n damage caused to water, air, etc. by harmful substances or waste

ruin /ˈruːɪn/ n OLD PARTS the broken parts that are left from an old building after it has been destroyed

season /ˈsiːzən/ n PART OF YEAR one of the four periods of the year: spring, summer, autumn or winter

show (sb) around /ʃəʊ əˈraʊnd/ pv to go to a place with someone and show them different things

stay in /steɪ ɪn/ pv to not leave your home

street light /ˈstriːt laɪt/ n a light on a tall post next to a street

valley /ˈvæli/ n an area of low land between hills or mountains, often with a river running through it

wildlife /ˈwaɪldlaɪf/ n animals and plants that grow independently of people in their natural environment

UNIT 16

act /ækt/ v PERFORM to perform in a film, play, etc.

animated /ˈænɪmeɪtɪd/ adj FILM An animated film is one in which drawings and models seem to move.

animation /ænɪˈmeɪʃən/ n an animated film, or an animated scene from a film or the process of making animated films

announce /əˈnaʊnts/ v to tell someone about something officially or with force or confidence

appear in /əˈpɪər ɪn/ v PERFORM to perform in a film, play, etc.

come out /kʌm aʊt/ pv BECOME AVAILABLE If a book, record, film, etc. comes out, it becomes available for people to buy or see.

demand /dɪˈmɑːnd/ v REQUEST to ask for something in a way that shows you do not expect to be refused

direct /daɪˈrekt/ v FILM/PLAY to tell the actors in a film or play what to do

director /daɪˈrektə/ *n* FILM/PLAY someone who tells the actors in a film or play what to do

explain /ɪkˈspleɪn/ *v* to make something easy to undertand by giving reasons for it or details about it

film-maker /ˈfɪlmmeɪkə/ *n* a film director, especially an independent one who has control over how the film is made

insist /ɪnˈsɪst/ *v* to say firmly, especially when others disagree with what you say or want you to do something different

live /laɪv/ *adj* A live radio or television programme is seen or heard as it happens.

performance /pəˈfɔːməns/ *n* ENTERTAINMENT acting, dancing, singing, or playing music to entertain people

recording /rɪˈkɔːdɪŋ/ *n* MUSIC/SPEECH a piece of music or a speech which has been recorded onto a disc, tape, etc.

role /rəʊl/ *n* ACTING an actor's part in a film or play

suggest /səˈdʒest/ *v* IDEA to express an idea or plan for someone to consider

UNIT 17

apologise /əˈpɒlədʒaɪz/ *v* to tell someone that you are sorry about something you have done

complain /kəmˈpleɪn/ *v* to say that something is wrong or that you are annoyed about something

disagree /dɪsəˈgriː/ *v* to have a different opinion from someone else about something

fairly /ˈfeəli/ *adv* QUITE more than average, but less than very

joke /dʒəʊk/ *v* NOT SERIOUS to say funny things, or not be serious

pretty /ˈprɪti/ *adv* QUITE quite, but not extremely or completely

promise /ˈprɒmɪs/ *v* SAY to say that you will certainly do something or that something will certainly happen

quite /kwaɪt/ *adv* COMPLETELY completely

reasonably (good/hard, etc.) /ˈriːzənəbli/ *adv* good/hard, etc. enough, but not very good or very hard, etc.

remind /rɪˈmaɪnd/ *v* to make someone remember something, or remember to do something

warn /wɔːn/ *v* to make someone realise a possible danger or problem, especially one in the future

wonder /ˈwʌndə/ *v* QUESTION to ask yourself questions or express a wish to know about something

UNIT 18

according to /əˈkɔːdɪŋ tuː/ *prep* OPINION as said by someone or shown by something

annoyed /əˈnɔɪd/ *adj* angry

because of /bɪˈkɒz əv/ *prep* as a result of

besides /bɪˈsaɪdz/ *prep* in addition to something or someone

charming /ˈtʃɑːmɪŋ/ *adj* pleasant and attractive

curious /ˈkjʊəriəs/ *adj* wanting to know or learn about something

delighted /dɪˈlaɪtɪd/ *adj* very pleased

despite /dɪˈspaɪt/ *prep* without taking any notice of, or being influenced by; not prevented by

instead of /ɪnˈsted əv/ *prep* in place of someone or something

lonely /ˈləʊnli/ *adj* PERSON unhappy because you are not with other people

be mad about sb/sth /bi: mæd əˈbaʊt/ *phr* to love someone or something

nasty /ˈnɑːsti/ *adj* UNKIND unkind

professional /prəˈfeʃənəl/ *adj* behaving in way which is suitable for their job

regarding /rɪˈgɑːdɪŋ/ *prep* about

rude /ruːd/ *adj* NOT POLITE behaving in a way which is not polite and upsets other people

shy /ʃaɪ/ *adj* not confident, especially about meeting or talking to new people

stressful /ˈstresfəl/ *adj* making you feel worried and not able to relax

unexpected /ˌʌnɪkˈspektɪd/ *adj* not expected

UNIT 19

arrange /əˈreɪndʒ/ *v* PLAN to make the necessary plans and preparations for something to happen

calculate /ˈkælkjʊleɪt/ *v* MATHS to discover an amount or number using mathematics

deal with /dɪəl wɪð/ *pv* to take action in order to achieve something or in order to solve a problem

deliver /dɪˈlɪvə/ *v* TAKE to take things such as goods, letters and parcels to people's houses or places of work

develop /dɪˈveləp/ *v* MAKE to make or invent something new such as a product or an idea

handle /ˈhændəl/ *v* DEAL WITH to deal with something

install /ɪnˈstɔːl/ v COMPUTER to put a computer program onto a computer so that the computer can use it

manage /ˈmænɪdʒ/ v CONTROL to be in control of an office, shop, team, etc.

organise /ˈɔːgənaɪz/ v PLAN to plan or arrange something

produce /prəˈdjuːs/ v MAKE to make or grow something

run /rʌn/ v ORGANISE to organise or control something

update /ʌpˈdeɪt/ v ADD INFORMATION to add new information

UNIT 20

achieve /əˈtʃiːv/ v to succeed in doing something good, usually by working hard

admire /ədˈmaɪə/ v RESPECT to respect or approve of someone or something

aim (to do sth) /eɪm/ v to intend to achieve something

believe in (sb / in sb's ability) /bɪˈliːv ɪn/ pv to believe that someone can succeed or do something well

choose (to do sth) /tʃuːz/ v to decide to do something

deal with sth /dɪəl wɪθ/ pv to take action in order to achieve something or in order to solve a problem

depend on sb/sth /dɪˈpend ɒn/ pv BE INFLUENCED BY If something depends on someone or something, it is influenced by them, or changes because of them.

dream /driːm/ v IMAGINE to imagine something that you would like to happen

encourage /ɪnˈkʌrɪdʒ/ v MAKE MORE LIKELY to make someone more likely to do something, or to make something more likely to happen

get into sth /get ɪntuː/ pv BE CHOSEN to succeed in being chosen to become a member of a team or group

go for /gəʊ fɔː/ pv TRY TO GET to try to get or achieve something, or to try your hardest to achieve something

imagine /ɪˈmædʒɪn/ v UNDERSTAND to have an idea of what something is like or might be like

join in sth /dʒɔɪn ɪn/ pv to take part in something with other people

keep on (doing sth) /kiːp ɒn/ pv to continue to do something, or to do something over and over again

try your best /traɪ jɔː best/ phr to make the greatest effort possible

Grammar reference

UNIT 1

COUNTABLE AND UNCOUNTABLE NOUNS; DETERMINERS

Countable and uncountable nouns

- Countable nouns can be singular or plural.
  card → cards   phone → phones
- A few countable nouns have irregular plurals.
  *child → **children**   woman → **women***
  *person → **people***
- Uncountable nouns are always singular.
  bread, information, news, homework, money, water
- We use other words to count these nouns.
  a slice of *bread*
  a piece of *information/news/homework*
  a great deal of *money*
  two glasses of *water*
- Some nouns can be both countable and uncountable.
  *There's **a strange noise** coming from that box.*
  *I don't like **noise** when I'm working.*
  *There's **a hair** in my soup!*
  *I've got long **hair**.*
  *Do you want **a coffee**?*
  ***Coffee** is my favourite drink.*

Determiners: *some, (not) any, no, (not) many, (not) much, plenty of, (not) a lot of, several*

- We use **some**, **any**, **no**, **plenty of**, **(not) a lot of** with plural countable nouns and uncountable nouns.
  *I've got **some biscuits** and **some cheese**.*
  *We haven't got **any apples** or **any milk**.*
  *There are **no oranges** and the shop has **no fruit juice**.*
  *I've bought **plenty of vegetables** and **plenty of cheese**.*
  *There are **a lot of people** here today but there is**n't a lot of food**.*
- We use **any** in questions and negatives.
  *Is there **any cake**?*
  *I don't need **any help**.*
- We sometimes use **some** in questions, when we offer something and if we expect the answer *Yes*.
  *Would you like **some tea**?*
- We use **(not) many** with countable nouns, in positive and negative sentences and questions.
  ***Many students** enjoy meeting in this café.*
  *We don't have **many places** to meet our friends.*
  *Do you go to **many parties** during the holidays?*
- We use **(not) much** with uncountable nouns in negative sentences and questions.
  *My brother is**n't much help** around the house.*
  *Do you watch **much sport** on television?*
- We use **several** with plural countable nouns, usually in positive sentences.
  *I've got **several** friends in the States.*

Practice

1 Choose the correct word(s) in each sentence.

1 How **much / many** teenagers came to the party?
2 Toby has been to that club **many / any** times.
3 I haven't got **a lot of / several** homework tonight so I can watch a film when I finish it.
4 I went out twice at the weekend so I've got **no / any** money to spend today.
5 Sassy goes to France quite often, I think she has **several / much** friends there.
6 I can't find **any / many** information about the times of the trains.
7 We haven't got **no / much** bread, but there's **several / plenty of** cake.
8 Do you know what's happening at the school? Have you heard **many / any** news today?

2 Six of the sentences are incorrect. Rewrite them in the correct form.

1 Angela has coloured her hairs pink. It's great.
2 Do you prefer coffee or fruit juice?
3 We had several fun when we went to the beach.
4 Did you get much help with your homework?
5 I put any sugar in my tea, but it tastes sweet.
6 Don't make a lot of noises when you come in late.
7 There's no any place for children to play here.
8 We had much trouble with our car on holiday.

....
....
....
....
....
....

3 Fill the spaces with the words from the box.

> a lot of   any   much   no
> several   some x3

Katie: Dad, I haven't got **(1)** .... money. Can you lend me **(2)** .... ?

Dad: Haven't you got **(3)** .... money from your birthday? **(4)** .... people gave you money, I know.

Katie: I had to spend **(5)** .... it on things for school at the beginning of term, and I bought Mum **(6)** .... perfume last week, so I've got **(7)** .... money left now. It isn't **(8)** .... fun going out when you can't even buy an ice cream.

Dad: OK, here you are.

Katie: Thanks, Dad, you're a star.

UNIT 2

THE -ING FORM

- The -ing form (**being, knowing, seeing, having, running,** etc.) is sometimes called the present participle or the gerund. It does not change form.
- We use the -ing form:
  - after verbs which mean *like* and *don't like*: **like, love, enjoy, dislike, hate, not mind, can't stand.**
    I love going out with my friends.
    We all hate revising for a test.
    Marie doesn't mind helping other students with maths.
    My dad hates being late for work.
    My mum can't stand doing housework.
  - after some adjective + preposition phrases which say how well people do things or how they feel about doing them: **good at, bad at, keen on, interested in, crazy about, afraid of, tired of.** These adjectives follow the verb **be.**
    My brother's good at singing.
    My sisters are crazy about dancing.
    My mum was interested in learning languages.
    Our cats were afraid of getting wet.

Practice

1 Complete the text with the *-ing* form of a verb from the box.

> annoy   eat   give   grow
> listen   see   sit   tell

I stayed with my cousins last weekend. I enjoyed
(1) .... them all, except my cousin Arash.
He knows I can't stand **(2)** .... to stupid
jokes but he likes **(3)** .... them and he
enjoys **(4)** .... me.
I helped my aunt make lunch. I don't mind
(5) .... her some help because she's
very kind. She's a good cook, so everyone loves
(6) .... her food.
After lunch we watched an old film. My uncle doesn't
like **(7)** .... inside in the afternoon, so he
went into his garden. He loves **(8)** .... fruit
and he brought us some apples to eat. They were
really good.

2 Complete the sentences with the correct preposition.

1 All the students in my class were crazy ....
playing tennis last term, but most of them are tired
.... doing that now.
2 Are you good .... keeping secrets?
3 I cycle home through the city centre because
I'm afraid .... going through the park after dark.
4 We're not really interested .... learning about
politics.
5 I'm quite keen .... understanding how machines
work so I'm not bad .... mending things.

3 Complete the second sentence so that it means the same as the first. Use *is* or *was* and the words in brackets + the *-ing* form of a verb and any other words you need.

0 James makes friends easily. (good at)
James *is good at making friends.*
1 Lisa got up early because she was worried she'd
miss her bus. (afraid of)
Lisa got up early because she ....
....
2 Nick went home because he didn't want to play
football any longer. (tired of)
Nick went home because he ....
....
3 Keira plays video games all the time. (crazy about)
Keira ....
4 Rupert wanted to go to Africa. (keen on)
Rupert ....
5 Michelle finds it difficult to remember new
vocabulary. (bad at)
Michelle ....
6 Paolo would like to learn Chinese. (interested in)
Paolo is ....

UNIT 3

PRESENT SIMPLE AND CONTINUOUS

Present simple

Positive	I, you, we, they **play / study**	he, she, it **plays / studies**
Negative	I, you, we, they **don't play / study**	he, she, it **doesn't play / study**
Questions	**Do** I, you, we, they **play / study**?	**Does** he, she, it **play / study**?

- We use the **present simple**:
  - for things we do regularly.
    *Most evenings, we **play** video games after dinner.*
    *My sister **doesn't get** home from school till four o'clock.*
    *What time **do** you **start** school?*
  - for things that normally happen in the same way.
    *Our teacher usually **helps** us with grammar.*
    *We **don't** always **get** all the answers right.*
  - for facts and things which are generally true.
    *My brother **doesn't live** near us.*
    *Swimming **helps** you keep fit.*
  - for most verbs which describe what we think and feel (these are called **state verbs** and are not normally used in a continuous tense).
    believe, dislike, hate, know, like, love, prefer, remember, think, understand, want, wish
    *Sam **thinks** this is the best café in town.*
    *Jonah **doesn't know** where his phone is.*
    *We **remember** the holiday we had with you.*
    ***Do** you **understand** what this word means?*
    ***Does** the cat **want** to go out?*

Present continuous

Positive	I'**m (am) watching / running** you, we, they'**re (are) watching / running** he, she, it'**s (is) watching / running**
Negative	I'**m not (am not) watching / running** you, we, they **aren't ('re not / are not) watching / running** he, she, it **isn't ('s not / is not) watching / running**
Questions	**Am** I **watching / running**? **Are** you, we, they **watching / running**? **Is** he, she, it **watching / running**?

- We use the **present continuous**:
  - for things happening now.
    *We'**re sitting** on the train.* (= we're sitting on the train now)
  - for definite future plans.
    *We'**re meeting** some friends after school.* (= we already have a plan to meet our friends)

Practice

1 **Choose the correct form of the verbs.**

1 My brother **runs / is running** for the school bus every morning because he **doesn't wake up / isn't waking up** in time.

2 I **think / I'm thinking** some video games are good for your brain, but **I don't play / I'm not playing** them very often.

3 **Do you believe / Are you believing** all the stories in the news?

4 **I have / I'm having** my break now. Our teacher **always gives / is always giving** us a break between lessons.

5 My parents **visit / are visiting** some friends this weekend so **I stay / I'm staying** with my grandma.

6 **I want / I'm wanting** some new trainers so **I go / I'm going** to the mall tomorrow.

2 **Make questions in the present simple or continuous, using the words given.**

1 what time / you / have lunch on Sundays?
....

2 what / that man / say / to your friend?
....

3 your sister / prefer / coffee or tea?
....

4 which game / your brother / play / now?
....

5 why / you / not / want / to come to the cinema with us?
....

6 where / your dad / keep / the car keys?
....

7 you / do / your homework or you / play / a game on that laptop?
....

8 you / not / listen to me? you / not / understand I'm angry?
....

3 **Complete the email with the correct form of the verbs in brackets.**

Hi Marco,

I'm here in Brighton and I **(1)** .... (have) a great time. We **(2)** .... (have) classes every morning from 9 till 12. My flat is near the school so I **(3)** .... (get up) at 8.30 and **(4)** .... (buy) a coffee on the way in. There are some good guys in my class and we all **(5)** .... (go) to the park and **(6)** .... (eat) lunch at a café there. The waiter sometimes **(7)** .... (give) us free ice creams. In the afternoons we **(8)** .... (choose) what we **(9)** .... (want) to do. This afternoon I **(10)** .... (go) to the beach and tomorrow I **(11)** .... (play) volleyball in a match against another language school. What **(12)** .... (you/do) at the moment? **(13)** .... (you/revise) for your exams? **(14)** .... (you/remember) last summer when we went to the lake? Perhaps we can go again this year. Anyway, I **(15)** .... (come) to Brescia with my dad after my English course, so I can see you then.

Milo

147

UNIT 4

PAST SIMPLE; *USED TO*

Past simple

- The past simple active of regular verbs is formed by adding **-ed** to the infinitive.

  open → opened

- Many common verbs are irregular and the past simple doesn't end in **-ed**.

  e.g. **break → broke; feel → felt; put → put; rise → rose; run → ran; say → said; take → took; think → thought**

- We form negatives and questions with **did** and **didn't (did not)** + the infinitive.

didn't open	**did you open?**
didn't make	**did she make?**
didn't take	**did they take?**

- The verb **to be** has two forms in the past simple.

  was/were   wasn't/weren't

  was she? / were you?

- We use the past simple to talk about:
  - completed events in the past.

    *I **grew** up in California.*

    *I **didn't learn** to drive there.*

    ***Did** your mum **work** in the film studios?*

  - events in the past at a time which is mentioned.

    *I **went** to a football match **last night**.*

    *My friends **didn't send** me a card **on my birthday**.*

    ***Did** you **find** your phone **when you went home**?*

  - regular events in the past.

    *I **went** to my last school by bike.*

    ***Didn't** you **catch** the bus on rainy days?*

Practice

1 Complete the conversation with the verbs in the box in the past simple.

> be   cost   find   happen   have
> pay   take   try   use   want

Kiki: Hi, Kay. What **(1)** .... to you yesterday afternoon? I **(2)** .... to call you several times, but your phone **(3)** .... off.

Kay: Mum **(4)** .... me to the shopping mall. She **(5)** .... to get a new leather bag and I **(6)** .... these amazing boots in a sale.

Kiki: They're really cool! How much **(7)** .... they ....?

Kay: I **(8)** .... £35 for them – they only **(9)** .... one pair left in my size! I **(10)** .... all my birthday money to buy them.

2 Complete the story with verbs in brackets in the past simple.

Last winter we **(1)** .... (not / have) very cold weather but it **(2)** .... (rain) nearly every day for a month. After three weeks, the river **(3)** .... (rise) and the water **(4)** .... (come) into people's gardens. As the water **(5)** .... (continue) to rise, the school **(6)** .... (offer) some families with young children accommodation. They **(7)** .... (sleep) on the floor of the hall and the children **(8)** .... (think) it was a great adventure. Luckily most of the houses **(9)** .... (not flood) and the people **(10)** .... (go) home the next day.

used to

- We use **used to** + verb.

used to go	**didn't used to go**	**did he used to go?**
used to say	**didn't used to say**	**did they used to say?**

  Note that for questions and negative forms it is possible to use either **used to** or **use to**.

- We use **used to** + verb to talk about habits or situations in the past which are not the same now.

  *We **used to live** in a small flat. (= we don't live in a small flat now)*

  *They **used to cycle** everywhere. (= they don't cycle everywhere now)*

  *I **didn't used to like** camping. (= I enjoy it now)*

Practice

3 Complete the sentences with the correct form of *used to* and the verb in brackets.

1 All the children .... to school before the road got so busy. (walk)

2 My dad .... me a story every night before I went to sleep. (tell)

3 At my last school, we .... sport every day. (do)

4 My parents .... me to go out in the evenings with my friends. (not / allow)

5 .... when they were younger? (your brothers / fight)

6 I .... practising the guitar but now I find it relaxing. (not / like)

4 How has the world changed in the last forty years? Use *used to* or *didn't used to* + the verbs in the box to complete the sentences.

> carry   catch   get   go   have

1 There were no mobile phones, so people .... a phone with them all the time.

2 Not everyone had a car and more people .... buses or walk to work.

3 Air travel was extremely expensive so only rich people .... abroad for their holidays.

4 Computers were the size of cars and of course people .... them at home.

5 There was no internet so students .... information online, they had to go to a library.

UNIT 5

PAST SIMPLE AND PAST CONTINUOUS

Past simple

- The past simple regular verb is formed by adding *-ed* to the infinitive.
  open → opened
- In irregular verbs the past simple has different forms.
  e.g. *think → thought; take → took; put → put*
- Negatives and questions are formed with *did* and *didn't (did not)* + the infinitive.
  didn't open   did you open?
  didn't take   did they take?
- We use the past simple to talk about events in the past.
  I lived in Russia.
  Did the river flood last winter?
  I didn't go to a party last weekend.

Past continuous

- All verbs form the past continuous with the past tense of the verb *to be* + present participle.

I/he/she/it **was** you/we/they **were**	opening thinking taking
I/he/she/it **wasn't** (was not) you/we/they **weren't** (were not)	opening thinking taking
Was I/he/she/it **Were** you/we/they	opening thinking taking

- The past continuous is used for:
  - events happening around the time of another past event (in the past simple).
    I was waiting for a bus when you texted.
    At the time the exam started I was sitting in a traffic jam.
  - past events which describe the background to a story.
    We were travelling with some friends and visiting lots of great cities.

Practice

1 Complete the text with the verbs in brackets in the past continuous.

The sun **(1)** .... (shine) and some teenagers **(2)** .... (sit) in the park. One girl **(3)** .... (sing) quietly to her friends and two boys **(4)** .... (take) selfies. They **(5)** .... (not / play) loud music and they **(6)** .... (not / shout).
However, some older people thought they **(7)** .... (not / behave) well and complained. 'What **(8)** .... (do) wrong?' asked the teenagers, but no one could tell them.

2 Choose the correct form of the verb.

1 We **watched / were watching** a film on my computer when it suddenly **stopped / was stopping** working.
2 I **didn't notice / wasn't noticing** what time my sister **came / was coming** home because I **played / was playing** a video game in my room.
3 I **learned / was learning** quite a few words of Spanish in the six months I **travelled / was travelling** in South America.
4 My brother **went / was going** to Africa last year and **climbed / was climbing** Mount Kilimanjaro.
5 Guess who we **saw / were seeing** when we **drove / were driving** to the funfair!
6 **Did you text / Were you texting** when I **talked / was talking** to you? Please don't!
7 How many nights **did you sleep / were you sleeping** in the open when you **went / were going** to that adventure camp?
8 I only left the kitchen for a moment, but I came came back to find that my toast **burned / was burning**.

3 Complete the conversation with the verbs in brackets in the past simple or past continuous.

Barbara: What **(1)** .... (you / do) in the hall cupboard for so long?

Rhiannon: I **(2)** .... (look) for my winter boots.

Barbara: **(3)** .... (you / find) them?

Rhiannon: No, but I'm sure I **(4)** .... (put) them there last spring. I remember when I **(5)** .... (tidy) my room I **(6)** .... (decide) I **(7)** .... (not / want) to keep them there in the summer.

Barbara: I guess Alex **(8)** .... (move) them. He **(9)** .... (use) that cupboard for his sports gear until he **(10)** .... (stop) going to the gym.

Rhiannon: Well, I hope he **(11)** .... (not / throw) my favourite boots away! They **(12)** .... (cost) a lot of money!

UNIT 6

MODALS: OBLIGATION AND NECESSITY

must, should, ought to

- These modal verbs do not change. They go before the infinitive of another verb.
  *I **must have** a shower.*
  *You **should have** a shower.*
  *He **ought to have** a shower.*
  *We **mustn't go** into the house.*
  *She **shouldn't go** into the house.*
- **ought not to** is possible but not often used.

have to

- This modal verb uses the forms of **have**. It goes before the infinitive of another verb.
  *I/You/We/They **have to go** outside.*
  *He/She/It **has to go** outside.*
  *I/You/We/They **don't have to go** outside.*
  *He/She/It **doesn't have to go** outside.*

Necessity

- **Must** and **have/has to** mean that it is **absolutely necessary** to do something.
  *You **must rest** your leg for five days.*
  *I **have to** leave home at seven o'clock to get the bus.*
- **Mustn't** means that it is **absolutely necessary not to do** something.
  *You **mustn't go** into that room.*
  *He **mustn't find** this letter.*
- **Don't/doesn't have to** mean that it is **not necessary to do** something.
  *I **don't have to get** to school before eight.*
  *You **don't have to work** at weekends.*

Advice

- **Should** and **ought to** mean that it is **a good idea to do** something. They are not as strong as **must** and **have to**.
  *You **should try** to relax before your exam.*
  *I **ought to finish** my homework before I go out.*
- **Shouldn't** means that it is **a bad idea to do** something. It is not as strong as **mustn't**.
  *I **shouldn't go** out when I've got homework to do.*
  *He **shouldn't eat** sweets before a meal.*

Practice

1 Do the pairs of sentences mean the same? Mark *S* for same or *D* for different. If they are different, can you explain why?

1 You should get up early and go for a run.
  You must get up early and go for a run. ....
2 I have to buy some new jeans.
  I must buy some new jeans. ....
3 Alan doesn't have to go out this evening.
  Alan shouldn't go out this evening. ....
4 We ought to buy some fruit for our lunch.
  We have to buy some fruit for our lunch. ....
5 You mustn't open that parcel till your birthday.
  You don't have to open that parcel till your birthday. ....
6 In my opinion, Jo should apologise to Amy.
  In my opinion, Jo ought to apologise to Amy. ....
7 Pat must remember to take his phone with him.
  Pat has to remember to take his phone with him. ....

2 Choose the correct modal in these sentences.

1 You look very sleepy. You **shouldn't / don't have to** go to bed so late when you have to get up early the next day.
2 You **mustn't / shouldn't** use your phone during the exam or the teacher will take it away from you.
3 I **ought to / must** finish this work before dinner, but I'm so hungry I can't wait any longer.
4 My dad **doesn't have to / mustn't** come home at lunchtime because there's a good restaurant near his office.
5 We **have to / should** post this parcel before six o'clock or it won't arrive in time for Jane's birthday.

3 Complete the text with the modals in the box.

> don't have to   have to   mustn't
> ought to   shouldn't

I belong to a photography club and it's very interesting. We use all kinds of cameras, some old and some new. There's a darkroom for people who work with black and white film. You (1) .... pay for darkroom time when you book it because it's quite popular and people get annoyed if it's booked and then not used. You (2) .... wear old clothes in the darkroom because you'll probably make marks on them.

You (3) .... buy special equipment, you can borrow it, but you (4) .... borrow anything without signing for it. I've got some great pictures from a trip we took to a mountain village, including some wonderful photos of people. Of course, you (5) .... really photograph people without asking permission, but usually they don't mind if you ask politely.

UNIT 7

PRESENT PERFECT AND PAST SIMPLE

→ **For the past simple form see Grammar reference, Unit 4, p.148**

Past simple

- We use the past simple to talk about actions which began and ended in the past. Sometimes we say when they happened.

  We **spent** hours in the recording studio yesterday.

  I **didn't finish** my song.

  Did they **learn** lots of songs last weekend?

Practice

1 Complete the email with the verbs in brackets in the past simple.

Hi

I really **(1)** .... (enjoy) the course
I **(2)** .... (do) last week. I **(3)** ....
(meet) some amazing people and **(4)** ....
(make) some new friends. We **(5)** .... (work)
hard during the day but we **(6)** .... (have)
fun in the evenings. We **(7)** .... (not / go) to
bed until after midnight every night. **(8)** ....
(you / buy) the music I **(9)** .... (tell)
you about when I **(10)** .... (text) you?
I **(11)** .... (find) some more tracks by
the same singer. She **(12)** .... (record)
them in California last year. They **(13)** ....
(not / be) very good songs but of course her voice
(14) .... (be) beautiful.
See you soon x

Present perfect

- We form the present perfect with **has/have** + the past participle.
- We use the present perfect for actions beginning in the past which continue up to the present or have some link to te present.

  We**'ve spent** hours in the recording studio.
  (so we know a lot about it now)

  I **haven't made** a recording.

  Have you **seen** this website?

Practice

2 Complete the conversation with the verbs in brackets in the present perfect.

Emma: Mum, **(1)** .... (you / see) my phone?

Mum: No, I **(2)** .... (not / see) it since yesterday. **(3)** .... (you / look) in your bag?

Emma: I **(4)** .... (look) everywhere! I think someone **(5)** .... (steal) it.

Mum: I bet you **(6)** .... (check) your bed.

Emma: Oh, yes. I **(7)** .... (find) it under my pillow! Thanks, Mum!

Present perfect with *just, already, yet, ever*

- We use *just, already, yet, ever* with the present perfect.
- *Just* goes before the main verb.

  I**'ve just arrived**. (= a few moments ago)
- *Already* goes before the main verb, or at the end of the sentence.

  I**'ve already made** one recording. (= I made it some time before now.)

  I**'ve made** one recording **already**.
- *Yet* goes at the end of the sentence with a negative verb or a question. It means 'up to now'.

  I **haven't finished** this recording **yet**. (= I'm still making it now.)

  Have you **made** a recording **yet**? (= I think you plan to make one around now.)
- *Ever* goes before the main verb in questions. It means 'at any time in the past up to now'.

  Have you **ever made** a recording? (= at any time in your life)

Practice

3 Rewrite the sentences with the words in brackets in the correct position.

1 The course has finished. (already)

   ....

2 Have you visited a recording studio? (ever)

   ....

3 Have you met your new teacher? (yet)

   ....

4 The singer has arrived. (just)

   ....

5 I haven't listened to that track. (yet)

   ....

4 Choose the correct form of the verbs in this telephone conversation.

Ana: Mina, **(1) have you ever bought / did you buy** clothes online or do you always go to a shop?

Mina: **(2) I've found / I found** a new website last week and **(3) I've ordered / I ordered** some jeans and a jacket. **(4) They've already arrived / They arrived** but **(5) I haven't tried / didn't try** them on yet because I want to have a shower first.

Ana: **(6) I've ordered / I ordered** a T-shirt from a website last weekend but it **(7) hasn't arrived / didn't arrive** yet.

Mina: **(8) Have you paid / Did you pay** for it at the same time?

Ana: Yes, **(9) it's cost / it cost** $50. **(10) There's been / There was** a special offer at the weekend.

UNIT 8

COMPARATIVE AND SUPERLATIVE ADJECTIVES

- One-syllable adjectives form comparatives and superlatives by adding -er and -est.

new	→	newer	→	(the) newest
light	→	lighter	→	(the) lightest

- One-syllable adjectives ending in e add -r and -st.

nice	→	nicer	→	(the) nicest

- One-syllable adjectives ending in vowel + consonant usually double the consonant.

big	→	bigger	→	(the) biggest

- Adjectives ending in consonant(s) + -y change -y to -i.

tidy	→	tidier	→	(the) tidiest
funny	→	funnier	→	(the) funniest

- Adjectives with two or more syllables usually use more and the most.

active	→	more active	→	(the) most active
modern	→	more modern	→	(the) most modern

- A few common adjectives are irregular.

good	→	better	→	(the) best
bad	→	worse	→	(the) worst
far	→	further/farther	→	(the) furthest / the farthest

- Adjectives which are two words use more and the most.

  user-friendly → more user-friendly → (the) most user-friendly

Comparative structures

- When we want to compare things in a positive way, we use the comparative adjective form + than.
  Your bike is newer than mine.
  The grammar book was more useful than the dictionary.
- When we want to say things are not the same, we can use:
  - not as adjective + as
    My bike isn't as new as yours.
    The dictionary wasn't as useful as the grammar book.
  - or less adjective + than.
    My bike is less new than yours.
    The dictionary was less useful than the grammar book.

Superlative structures

- Superlatives compare more than two things. We can say something is (the) ... -est, (the) most ... or (the) least ... .
  Your bike is the newest in the race and mine is the oldest.
  The grammar book was the most useful. (of several books)
  The dictionary was the least useful.
- We use the or a possessive before a superlative.
  The fastest runner in our school is Amy.
  Amy is the school's most successful runner.
  Game shows are my least favourite TV programmes.

Practice

1 Complete the sentences with the comparative form of the adjective in brackets, adding *not as ... as, less* or *than* where necessary.

1 I want to change into .... (smart) clothes before my interview. The clothes won't make me .... (intelligent) but they might make me feel .... (confident)!

2 The modern part of the house is .... (new) the rest of it, so it has .... (big) windows and .... (good) heating.

3 This MP3 player looks .... (modern) mine, but it's .... (expensive) and .... (easy) to carry because it's bigger.

4 I prefer this café. The other one is .... (not / comfortable) this one, and the waiters are .... (friendly) too.

2 Complete the sentences with the superlative form of the adjective in brackets, and use *the* or *least* where necessary.

1 My sister is the world's .... (bad) cook, she can't follow .... (simple) recipe.

2 This website is .... (useful) of all the ones I've looked at. It gives no real information at all.

3 I've just spent all morning sorting out my room. It's now .... (tidy) it has ever been!

4 This phone is .... (cheap) in the shop, but it's also .... (easy) to use, so it isn't good value.

5 Shall I wear my .... (good) boots or will it rain, do you think?

6 Bob's .... (kind) boy in the class, and he's also one of .... (funny), so he's probably .... (popular) too.

UNIT 9

FUTURE FORMS; FUTURE CONTINUOUS

Present continuous for plans

- We use the present continuous, usually with the time mentioned, for definite plans.
  *Charlie **is leaving** on Tuesday.*
  *What **are you doing** in the holidays?*

will

- We use ***will***:
  - for general predictions.
    *The price of phones **will fall**.*
    *Smart watches **won't do** everything laptops can do.*
  - for offers and promises.
    *I'**ll help** you set up the new equipment.*

going to

- We use ***going to***:
  - for plans (this is like the present continuous).
    *Charlie **is going to leave** soon.*
    *What **are you going to do** after school?*
  - for firm intentions.
    *We'**re going to drive** to the south coast.*

Future continuous

- We form the future continuous with ***will/won't** + **be** + **-ing***.
  *I'**ll be working***
  *He **won't be playing***
  ***Will** you **be living** …?*
- We use the future continuous for predictions about things which will happen over a period of time.
  *I'**ll be working** for my dad next year.*
  *He **won't be playing tennis** all morning.*
  ***Will you be living** in a hostel at university?*

Practice

1 Complete the conversation with the verbs in brackets in the future continuous.

Evita: I'm going to England with my brother for six weeks.

Harry: **(1)** .... you .... (stay) in London or **(2)** .... you .... (move) round from place to place?

Evita: We **(3)** .... (spend) a few days in several big cities and we **(4)** .... (visit) as many of our English friends as we can.

Harry: How **(5)** .... you .... (travel)?

Evita: We **(6)** .... (use) public transport most of the time but for the last week we **(7)** .... (borrow) a friend's car. I **(8)** .... (not / drive) because I'm not old enough to have an international licence. But I **(9)** .... (speak) English more than him because I **(10)** .... (not / worry) about making mistakes when I talk, like he always does.

2 Choose the correct form of the verbs.

1 I can't stop now, **I'll meet / 'm meeting** my mum at the station in fifteen minutes.

2 In the next few years, technology **is making / will make** a lot of difference to the lives of people in isolated communities.

3 Let me fix your phone for you, I **won't damage / won't be damaging** it.

4 Our teacher says **we'll be using / we'll use** the new science laboratories for the rest of this term.

5 **Are you going to play / Will you play** volleyball this afternoon or can you help me with the shopping?

3 Complete the conversation with the verbs in brackets in the correct form: present continuous, *will*, *going to* or future continuous. Two forms are possible in some places.

Evan: What time **(1)** .... (we / have) dinner tonight, Mum?

Mum: About seven. Do you have any plans?

Evan: I **(2)** .... (watch) the match at Tom's house later. Is that OK with you?

Mum: Yes, of course. You **(3)** .... (not / go) to school tomorrow. But **(4)** .... (get) home very late?

Evan: Yes, probably, but I **(5)** .... (not / make) a noise.

Mum: Please be very quiet. Your sister **(6)** .... (do) an exam in the morning and your dad and I are tired. We **(7)** .... (sleep) by the time you come home.

Evan: Don't worry, I promise you **(8)** .... (not / hear) me.

UNIT 10

CONDITIONAL SENTENCES

Zero conditional

- We form the zero conditional with:
  - *If* + present tense + comma + present tense.
    *If a lioness **has** cubs to protect, she **is** more dangerous.*
  - or present tense + *if* + present tense.
    *A lioness **is** more dangerous if she **has** cubs to protect.*
- We use the zero conditional to describe a real situation and its result.
  *Wild animals **aren't** dangerous if people **behave** sensibly.*
- *If* usually means the same as *when* in zero conditional sentences.
  *A lioness **is** more dangerous **when** she **has** cubs to protect.*

Practice

1 Complete the sentences with the correct form of the verbs in brackets.

1 Beautiful places often .... too crowded if they .... also popular tourist resorts. (get / be)
2 If river water .... clean, the fish in it .... (not be / die)
3 Travelling to see wildlife .... a great holiday if you .... watching nature documentaries. (make / enjoy)
4 When we .... trees, we .... the birds' environment. (cut down / destroy)

First conditional

- We form the first conditional with:
  - *If* + present tense + comma + *will/won't*.
    *If she **thinks** her cubs are in danger, a lioness **will attack**.*
  - or *will/won't* + *if* + present tense.
    *A lioness **will attack** if she **thinks** her cubs are in danger.*
- We use the first conditional to describe a possible situation and its likely result.
  *If the forests **disappear**, the weather **will be** more extreme.*
  *We **won't be able** to replace ancient trees if we **cut** them **down**.*

Practice

2 Choose the correct form of the verbs.

1 If we **won't do / don't do** something soon, we **will lose / lose** many wild animals.
2 If conservation work **will be / is** successful, there **will be / are** more wild animals in the mountains.
3 Many of our rare birds **will disappear / disappear** if there **won't be / aren't** safe places for them to nest.
4 Future generations **don't see / won't see** any wild animals if we **won't look after / don't look after** them.

Second conditional

- We form the second conditional with:
  - *If* + past tense + comma + *would*.
    *If politicians **cared** about the rainforests, they'd (would) do more to protect them.*
  - or *would* + *if* + past tense.
    *Politicians **would do** more to protect the rainforests if they **cared** about them.*
    *If people **cared** about their planet, they **wouldn't pollute** the sea.*
    *There **wouldn't be** any apples if bees **didn't exist**.*
- We use the second conditional to describe something in the present or future which is unlikely or imaginary.
  *If I **had** a garden, I'd **grow** lots of fruit.*
  (= I don't have a garden so I don't grow fruit.)
  *We **wouldn't eat** honey if we **didn't like** it.*
  (= We like honey so we eat it.)

Practice

3 Complete the sentences with the correct form of the verbs in brackets.

1 Cities .... cleaner if people .... cars for short journeys. (be / not use)
2 If more people .... this nature reserve, there .... more money to spend on conservation. (visit / be)
3 Raising money for wildlife projects .... easier if people .... how important the work is. (be / understand)
4 Some animals .... if people .... them. (not survive / not protect)

unless

- We can use *unless* instead of *if ... not* in conditional sentences.
  *We wouldn't eat honey **unless** we **liked** it.* (= if we **didn't like** it)
  *There wouldn't be any apples **unless** bees **existed**.* (= if bees **didn't exist**)
  ***Unless** we **do** something to protect the rainforests soon, they will all disappear.* (= If we **don't do** something soon ...)

Practice

4 Rewrite the sentences using *unless*.

1 We will lose the rainforests if we don't do more to protect them.

....

2 If we don't look after the planet, future generations will suffer.

....

3 I wouldn't support conservation work if I didn't think it was important.

....

UNIT 11

PAST PERFECT

- We form the past perfect with **had** + the past participle.

had looked	**hadn't looked**	**had he looked?**
had written	**hadn't written**	**had he written?**

- We use the past perfect to talk about events which happened some time before an action or event in the past.
- The past perfect makes the order of the events clearer. The other action is usually in the past simple.

  *I'd never **been** to a live concert so I was really excited when we went to one last weekend.*

- We often use words such as **before** or **after** in sentences with the past perfect.

  *I'd seen the film **before** but I enjoyed seeing it again.*
  ***After** we'd sung Happy Birthday, my sister opened her presents.*

Practice

1 Last Saturday the students of Green Park School gave a surprise party for their head teacher when she retired. Write sentences about what they had and hadn't done when the head teacher arrived on the afternoon of her last day.

1 Decorate the school hall. ✔
  They ....

2 Do their usual lessons. ✘
  They ....

3 Eat lunch. ✘
  They ....

4 Prepare a special meal. ✔
  They ....

5 Write a song to sing her. ✔
  They ....

2 Last summer Leo left school and went on holiday with some friends. Look at the things he had planned to do before he left home. Write questions and answers.

0 running shoes? ✘ / swimming trunks ✔ (pack)
  Had he packed his running shoes?
  No, he hadn't packed his running shoes
  but he had packed his swimming trunks.

1 sun block? ✘ / shampoo ✔ (buy)
  ....
  ....
  ....

2 driving test? ✘ / all his exams ✔ (pass)
  ....
  ....
  ....

3 hotel room ✘ / seat on the train ✔ (book)
  ....
  ....
  ....

3 Complete the text with the verbs in brackets in the past perfect.

When I first came into my new classroom in the village school, the students were sitting in rows. My previous job **(1)** .... (be) in a modern school in the capital city, where the students **(2)** .... (sit) in a circle.

I asked the students to stand up and move their desks. After we **(3)** .... (arrange) the desks in a circle, I asked them to sit down and began the lesson.

After we **(4)** .... (try) the new arrangement for several days, I asked the students what they thought about it. Here's what they said:

'We were surprised because we **(5)** .... (not / sit) in a circle before. We **(6)** .... (always / sit) in rows and the lessons **(7)** .... (often / seem) boring. Now we have more discussions and everyone joins in.'

Luckily the headteacher agreed with them!

'I **(8)** .... (not / realise) that moving the furniture could make such a difference,' he said.

4 Choose the correct form of the verbs.

1 When John arrived late for his exam he **was** / **had been** upset because nobody **told** / **had told** him the time **changed** / **had changed**.

2 The school team **never played** / **had never played** in a real stadium before and they **were** / **had been** very excited to see so many spectators when they ran out onto the pitch.

3 I was at a boarding school before I **went** / **had been** to university so I knew how to look after myself, but some of my classmates **were never** / **had never been** away from home and **found** / **had found** it hard to manage without their parents at first.

4 Last Friday our teacher **gave** / **had given** us a test in biology and I **was** / **had been** able to answer the questions because I **saw** / **'d seen** a documentary on the subject just a week before, not because I **revised** / **'d revised**. In fact I **forgot** / **'d forgotten** that we **had** / **had had** a test that day!

UNIT 12

MODALS: OBLIGATION AND ADVICE

Advice

- We use **should / shouldn't** + verb when the speaker believes this is the right thing to do.

  You **should arrive** at the airport early.

  You **shouldn't take** too much hand luggage.

Practice

1 Give advice in the following situations. Use should(n't) + the words in brackets and add any other words you need.

1 John's got to catch a train in twenty minutes but he can't walk to the station.

  You .... (call / taxi)

2 Amina has a test in school tomorrow. Her sister wants her to play a video game.

  You .... (revise)

  You .... (play / sister)

3 Dmitri is going out later. He's used his phone a lot already today.

  You .... (charge)

4 Tex wants to mend his bike. He's wearing his best sweater.

  You .... (change)

Obligation

- We use **(don't) need to** + verb when the speaker believes something is important, but it's not a law.

  You **need to keep** your passport in a safe place.

  You **don't need to take** any food with you.

- We use **have to** + verb when this is a rule or it is the law.

  You **have to get** a visa.

  You **have to show** your passport when you enter the country.

Lack of obligation

- When something is not necessary, we use:
  - **don't have to** + verb.

    You **don't have to pay** for your food on this flight.
  - or **needn't** + verb (needn't is not followed by to).

    You **needn't pay** for your food on this flight.
  - or **don't need to** + verb.

    You **don't need to pay** for your food on this flight.

Practice

2 Choose the correct verbs.

1 You **need to / needn't** finish your homework, then you can relax.

2 You **have to / needn't** tell the teacher today if you want to go on the school trip.

3 You **need to / should** clean your teeth before you go to the dentist.

4 You **don't have to / need to** walk to school – I can give you a lift.

5 You **needn't / shouldn't** buy a drink; I've already got one for you.

6 You **should / needn't** pack your bag the night before you leave so that you'll be ready when the taxi arrives.

3 Which pairs of sentences mean the same and which are different? Mark *S* for same or *D* for different. Can you explain the differences?

1 You need to book in advance to get a cheap ticket.

  You don't have to buy your ticket in advance, but it costs more on the day. ....

2 You don't have to take a lot of cash with you.

  It's sensible to take plenty of money with you. ....

3 You shouldn't buy tickets on the internet from people you don't know.

  It's a bad idea to buy tickets on the internet from people you don't know. ....

4 You should try to stay with your friends if there are big crowds.

  You have to stay with your friends if there are a lot of people there. ....

5 You have to be with an adult if you're under 16, or you can't go in.

  People aged under 16 can only go in if they're with an adult. ....

6 You don't have to take a phone.

  You needn't take a phone. ....

UNIT 13

THE PASSIVE

The present simple passive

- We form the present simple passive of a verb with the present tense of the verb **to be** + the past participle.
  We're given presents on our birthdays.
  These toys aren't sold in supermarkets.

The past simple passive

- We form the past simple passive of a verb with the past tense of the verb **to be** + the past participle.
  This picture was drawn to illustrate a story.
  The artists weren't told what to paint.

Modal passives

- We form the passive of modal verbs like **can, could, must, may** and **might** with modal + **be** + past participle.
  The writer of the poem couldn't be identified.
  The students may be allowed to film the show.
  Tickets must be booked in advance.

The agent

- The person or thing that does the action of a passive verb is called **the agent**. The agent of the passive verb is the subject of an active verb. We use **by** to introduce the agent.
  Our friends give us presents on our birthdays. (active)
  We're given presents by our friends on our birthdays. (passive)
  The photographer didn't pay that model very much. (active)
  That model wasn't paid very much by the photographer. (passive)
- We often use the passive in English when:
  - we do not know the agent.
    My bag was taken while I was sunbathing.
    A lot of clothes are made in small factories.
  - the agent is not important.
    My new phone was delivered yesterday.
    This room must be cleaned immediately.
  - we want to emphasise the subject of the passive verb.
    I've been asked to sing at the end-of-term concert!
    Your brother must be invited to the party.

Practice

1 Rewrite the sentences using the active form of the verb.

1 The school blog is edited by a group of senior students.
....

2 This kind of box can't be opened by young children.
....

3 This software isn't often used by designers nowadays.
....

4 The paintings in my room were done by my grandfather.
....

2 Rewrite the sentences using the passive form of the verb. Only include the agent if it is important.

1 Several celebrities attended the party.
....

2 Nobody could find the ball at the end of the match.
....

3 I made all these cakes and my sister decorated them.
....

4 My aunt designed these shoes for a famous singer.
....

5 Software can change the shape of a model's eyes in a photo.
....

6 The editor of the magazine couldn't identify the writer of the poem.
....

7 Our parents may allow us to go to a concert on Saturday if we tidy our rooms.
....

UNIT 14

NON-DEFINING RELATIVE CLAUSES

Defining relative clauses

- Defining relative clauses give essential information about things or people. They are never separated from the rest of the sentence by commas.

  *The cakes **that my brother makes** are really good.*

  We need the words *that my brother makes* to know which cakes the speaker is talking about.

- To begin a relative clause we use the pronouns **who** (for people), **which** (for things), **that** (for things and people), **whose** (belonging to).

  *There's the girl **who** won the cookery competition.*

  *She showed me the recipe **which** she invented.*

  *I can email the recipe **that** I told you about.*

  *That's the boy **whose** mum designs sunglasses.*

- **Who, which** or **that** can be the subject or the object of the relative clause.

  *The woman **who/that** runs the café is very friendly.* (who/that is the subject)

  *There's the chef **who/that** I told you about.* (who/that is the object)

  *He showed me a recipe **which/that** he uses.* (which/that is the object)

- We can leave out **who, which** or **that** if it is the object of the defining clause.

  *The cakes **(which/that)** my brother makes are really good.*

  *There's the chef **(who)** I told you about.*

  *He showed me a recipe **(which/that)** he uses.*

  *I can email the recipe **(which/that)** I told you about.*

- We cannot leave out **who, which** or **that** if it is the subject.

  *The woman **who** runs the café is very friendly.*

  not ~~The woman runs the cafe is very friendly.~~

Practice

1 Complete the sentences with *who, which* or *whose*.

1 The first recipe .... I ever tried was soup.

2 Do you remember the name of the chef .... restaurant we visited?

3 I've never met anyone .... could cook as well as my mum.

4 The dishes .... I like best are the ones .... use fresh ingredients.

5 I like working with people .... are interested in food from different countries.

6 The friend .... saucepan I borrowed will be angry when he sees I've burnt it.

2 Look at the sentences in exercise 1.

a Where can you use *that* instead of the word you chose?

b Where can you leave out the relative pronoun?

Non-defining relative clauses

- We use non-defining relative clauses to give extra information about things or people.

  *The cakes on this plate, **which my brother helped to make,** are really good.*

  If we take out *which my brother helped to make*, we still know which cakes the speaker is talking about.

- Non-defining relative clauses are always separated from the rest of the sentence by commas.

  *My birthday cake, **which my mum made for me,** was in the shape of a football pitch.*

- They begin with the relative pronoun **who** (for people) or **which** (for things) or **whose**, but never **that**.

- *My brother, **who** is an excellent cook, has written a cookbook.*

  *The recipes, **which** he tested carefully, require lots of special ingredients. **NOT** ~~The recipes, that he tested carefully, ...~~*

  *My grandparents, **whose** kitchen he uses, are proud of what he's done.*

- We can never leave out the relative pronoun in a non-defining clause.

Practice

3 Rewrite the pairs of sentences using non-defining relative clauses.

1 My grandma taught me to make cakes. She worked in a restaurant when she was young.

....

2 We lit the barbecue half an hour before the guests arrived. We had bought it the day before.

....

3 My friend Daren brought us some fresh fish. Daren's dad is a keen fisherman.

....

4 This Thai food is mild enough for anyone to eat. It doesn't have any chillies in it.

....

5 These sausages are all burnt. I was cooking them for my lunch.

....

4 Explain the difference in meaning between the pairs of sentences.

1 a The biscuits which my brother made were all eaten.

  b The biscuits, which my brother made, were all eaten.

2 a The students who had not had lunch wanted to find a café.

  b The students, who had not had lunch, wanted to find a café.

3 a The lettuces which weren't fresh were thrown away.

  b The lettuces, which weren't fresh, were thrown away.

4 a The bread which was freshly baked smelled delicious.

  b The bread, which was freshly baked, smelled delicious.

UNIT 15

ARTICLES – A/AN, THE AND ZERO ARTICLE

The indefinite article a/an

- We use **a/an** before a singular countable noun:
  - when we mention someone's job or occupation.
    *My mum's **a doctor**, my dad's **an architect** and my brother's **a student**.*
  - when we mention something for the first time.
    *I live in **a flat** near the city centre.*

The definite article the

- We use **the** before any noun:
  - when there is only one of something.
    *My brother likes swimming in **the sea**.*
  - when we talk about particular people or things.
    ***The school** I go to is not far away.*
  - when we refer to a thing or things for the second time.
    *Our flat is near a park. **The park** has several tennis courts.*
  - which is the name of a group of islands, mountains, lakes, states, etc.
    the Azores**, **the Urals**, **the United Arab Emirates
  - which is the name of a desert, ocean or river.
    the Sahara**, **the Pacific**, **the Amazon

The zero article

- We do not use an article:
  - before an uncountable noun or a plural countable noun, when we talk about that thing in general.
    ***Volleyball** is my favourite sport.*
    ***Teenagers** are usually interested in **sport**.*
  - with the names of continents, cities, towns, villages, individual islands, mountains and lakes.
    New Zealand**, **Rome**, **Mount Fuji**, **Lake Issyk Kul

Practice

1 **Choose the correct article or no article.**

1 **The** / – town where I grew up is on **the** / – River Loire.
2 My brother has gone to **the** / – Chile for a mountaineering expedition in **the** / – Andes.
3 There was **a** / **the** thunderstorm yesterday and my cat hid under my bed because he's terrified of **the** / – loud noises.
4 Our maths teacher was **a** / **the** soldier before he trained to be **a** / **the** teacher.
5 On Fridays, my friends and I all meet in **a** / **the** café near **the** / – central bus station to drink **the** / – coffee and chat. **A** / **The** café isn't very smart, but **the** / – music they play there is great.
6 **The** / – cheese is good for you, but too much can give you **the** / – spots.
7 When we went to **the** / – Canada last year, we stayed in – / **a** hostel in **the** / – Vancouver and we also camped near **the** / – Lake Louise in **the** / – Rocky Mountains.

2 **Complete the email with a/an, the or – if no article is necessary.**

We had a great holiday in **(1)** .... West Indies last February. We went to **(2)** .... Grenada and stayed in **(3)** .... hotel near **(4)** .... amazing beach of white sand. **(5)** .... hotel had **(6)** .... beautiful garden with **(7)** .... good sports facilities and we played **(8)** .... tennis every morning. We also did **(9)** .... tour of **(10)** .... island and wandered round **(11)** .... market in **(12)** .... St Georges, which is **(13)** .... capital. But the best thing was swimming in **(14)** .... warm sea every day when **(15)** .... sun was rising over **(16)** .... mountains behind our hotel.

3 **Find the mistakes with articles in the sentences and correct them.**

1 The petrol is very expensive in this country.
   ....
2 I'm not very interested in the science but I enjoy learning a new language.
   ....
3 A football match we watched last night was very exciting and my team won!
   ....
4 I went to good sports club when I was on holiday.
   ....
5 The vegetables are an important part of a balanced diet.
   ....
6 I was so embarrassed in the meeting yesterday when I realised phone that was ringing was in my bag!
   ....

UNIT 16

REPORTED SPEECH

Verbs in reported speech

- The tense of the verbs in direct speech changes when the reporting verb (*said, told, explained,* etc.) is in the past tense.

Direct speech		Reported speech
present simple *'I **enjoy** watching films.'*	→	**past simple** *He said he **enjoyed** watching films.*
present continuous *'That girl **is acting** well.'*	→	**past continuous** *He said that girl **was acting** well.*
past simple *'She **studied** at film school.'*	→	**past perfect** *He said (that) she'**d** (**had**) **studied** at film school.*
present perfect *'I **haven't seen** her before.'*	→	**past perfect** *He said he **hadn't seen** her before.*
will *'She'**ll** be famous one day.'*	→	**would** *He said she'**d** (**would**) be famous one day.*
can *'She **can** sing well too.'*	→	**could** *He said she **could** sing well too.*

- We do not change **could, would, should, might, used to** and past perfect when they are reported.
  *'You **could visit** her website.'* →
  *He said I **could visit** her website.*
  *'She **used to be** in a TV series.'* →
  *He said she **used to be** in a TV series.*
  *'She **hadn't appeared** on TV before that.'* →
  *He said she **hadn't appeared** on TV before that.*

Pronouns in reported speech

- Pronouns often have to change when they are reported.
  *'**I** enjoy watching films,' said Tom.* → *Tom said **he** enjoyed watching films.*
  *'**You** can watch a film after dinner,' said the boys' mum.* → *Their mum said **they** could watch a film after dinner.*

Reporting verbs

- We introduce reported speech with reporting verbs like **said, told, insisted, announced, demanded, explained.**
  *She **said** she enjoyed acting.*
- There must be an object after **told.**
  *She **told us** she enjoyed acting.*
- Reporting verbs are often followed by **that.**
  *She **said that** she enjoyed acting.*
  *She **told us that** she enjoyed acting.*
  *She **explained that** she enjoyed acting.*
- **Insisted, suggested** and **demanded** can be followed by **that ... should do** instead of a past tense.
  'You must give us your autograph.' → *We insisted that she **gave** us her autograph.*
  *We insisted **that** she **should give** us her autograph.*
  'Let's watch the film again.' → *I suggested **that** we **should watch** the film again.*

Practice

1 Change the sentences from reported to direct speech.

1 The director told the actors he would pay them a lot of money.
  The director said, '..'

2 One of the stars insisted that she needed a special diet.
  One of the stars said, '..'

3 The cameraman complained that the lights were too weak.
  The cameraman said, '..'

4 The leading actor told me he didn't enjoy working with that director.
  The leading actor said, '..'

5 The make-up artist explained that the star was feeling ill.
  The make-up artist said, '..'

6 The actors told the director they hadn't worked in such a beautiful place before.
  The actors said, '..'

7 The writer said he'd completed the film three years ago.
  The writer said, '..'

2 Complete the reported sentences.

1 'We made a film at school last term.'
  The students announced that ....
  ....

2 'We're making another one this term.'
  They told us ....
  ....

3 'I hadn't been in a film before.'
  The leading actor said ....
  ....

4 'I enjoy directing but I don't like acting.'
  The director explained that ....
  ....

5 'Everyone must learn their words by next week.'
  Our drama teacher insisted that ....
  ....

6 'You can't be in the film because you didn't learn your words.'
  The teacher told me that ....
  ....

7 'We've learned a lot in drama classes.'
  The students said ....
  ....

UNIT 17

REPORTED QUESTIONS

- The word order of the reported question is like a statement, not a question.
- The verbs change after a reporting verb in the past tense in the same way as in reported statements.
- The auxiliary verbs *did*, *didn't* are not used in reported questions.
- Pronouns change in the same way as in reported statements.
- For reported **yes/no** questions we use **if** or **whether**.
  '*Are you busy?*' → *She asked if I was busy.*
  '*Did he send an email?*' → *I asked whether he'd sent an email.*
  '*Do you often play video games?*' → *He asked whether we often played video games.*
  '*Have you seen my website?*' → *She asked if I'd seen her website.*
- For reported **Wh-** questions the reported question begins with the same question word as the direct question.
  '*What time is it?*' → *She asked what time it was.*
  '*When are you coming home?*' → *He asked when we were coming home.*
  '*Where can I charge my phone?*' → *He asked where he could charge his phone.*
  '*Which websites have they looked at?*' → *I asked which websites they'd looked at.*

Reporting verbs

- We can introduce reported questions with verbs like **ask, want to know** or **wonder**.
  Are you busy? → *She asked if I was busy.*
  Did he send an email? → *I wanted to know whether he'd sent an email.*
  Do you often play video games? → *He wondered whether we often played video games.*
- The reporting verb **asked** is sometimes followed by a noun or pronoun.
  What time is it? → *She asked the nurse what time it was.*
  When are you coming home? → *He asked us when we were coming home.*
  Which websites have they looked at? → *I asked them which websites they'd looked at.*

Practice

1 Change the questions from reported to direct speech.

1 My friends asked me why I hadn't texted anyone all day.
They said, '...?'

2 They wanted to know whether I was coming out with them.
They said, '...?'

3 I asked them what time they were leaving.
I said, '...?'

4 My brother asked me if he could come with us.
He said, '...?'

5 My dad wanted to know whether I had finished my homework.
He said, '...?'

6 My mum wondered how long I would be out.
She said, '...?'

7 My sister asked whether I wanted a lift to town.
She said, '...?'

2 Change the questions into reported speech.

1 Why haven't you texted me?
My mum wanted to know ....

2 Have you seen my car keys?
My dad wondered ....

3 Where will you stay in London?
My teacher asked me ....

4 How many tweets have you sent today?
The reporter asked the actor ....

5 Why is everyone shouting at me?
The footballer wondered ....

6 Do the students often use the website?
We wanted to know ....

7 Can you get superfast broadband in your town?
The film-maker asked us ....

3 Find and correct six mistakes in the reported questions in this email.

Hi Jan,
I went to see a careers adviser yesterday. He asked me what were my favourite subjects and did I prefer playing video games or taking part in sport. He wanted to know what languages did I speak and which foreign countries I visited in my life. He asked could you imagine working in an office. He also wanted to know how much did I want to earn. He didn't suggest a career but he helped me to think more clearly about the decisions I have to make in the next two years.
Hope you're well. Write soon,
Kai

UNIT 18

HAVE SOMETHING DONE

- We use tenses of **have** + object + past participle of the verb which describes the action.

I'm going to have my hair We **had** our hair They**'ve never had** their hair You **should have** your hair He**'ll** probably **have** his hair She needs **to have** her hair	**coloured / cut / done**.

- We use **have something done** when someone else does something for us.

  We want **to have** our hair cut. (= We want someone **to cut** our hair for us.)

  I'm **going to have** my hair **done**. (= Someone **is going to do** my hair for me.)

- We do not usually mention who the person is that does something for us, unless that's important.

  I **had** my hair **done**. (= Someone, probably a hairdresser, **did** my hair for me.)

  I **had** my hair **coloured by my mum**. (emphasises that my mum did it for me)

Practice

1 **Match the sentence halves.**

1 Do you go to the supermarket every week?
2 What did your brother do for his girlfriend's birthday?
3 Is that your grandfather?
4 Your sitting room looks different from last time I visited you.
5 Your mum's car looks very smart!
6 Where's your computer?

a Yes, we've just had it decorated.
b I'm having it checked for viruses at a shop in town.
c No, we have our food delivered.
d Yes, she's had it washed at last.
e Yes, he had his portrait painted and my dad had it framed.
f He had flowers delivered to her.

2 **These people want someone to do something for them. Complete what they say, using have + object + past participle of the verbs in brackets.**

1 My room is a boring colour. I want to
.... (paint)
2 My phone isn't working properly. I'll
.... (check) at the shop.
3 My little sister can't reach the front door bell. We're going to .... (move)
4 Our kitchen is very old-fashioned. We'd like to
.... (modernise)
5 I can never find clothes to fit me. I wish I could
.... for me by a personal shopper. (choose)

3 **Complete the sentences with the correct form of have + the words in brackets.**

1 I ....
at a nail bar. Do you like them? (just / my nails / do)
2 We ....
after our last party. (all the carpets / clean)
3 I bought some jeans but I need to ....
....
(them / shorten)
4 You must ....
(your bike / mend)
5 ....
in your new dress yesterday? (you / your photo / take)

UNIT 19

DIFFERENT TYPES OF CLAUSE

Contrast clauses

- We can join clauses which give different or surprising information about something with words like *although*, *whereas* and *while*.
- *Although* and *whereas* can go in the middle of a sentence, or at the beginning for extra emphasis.
  *I enjoyed my holiday job **although** it was hard work.*
  ***Although** my holiday job was hard work, I enjoyed it.* (= my holiday job was hard work but I enjoyed it)
  *I prefer to get up early, **whereas** most of my friends like to sleep late.*
  ***Whereas** most of my friends like to sleep late, I prefer to get up early.* (= unlike most of my friends, I like to get up early)
- *While* usually goes at the beginning of a sentence.
  ***While** I don't enjoy going for a run, I know it's good for me.* (= I don't enjoy going for a run but I know it's good for me)

Purpose clauses

- We can use a clause beginning with *so that* or *in order to* when we want to explain the purpose of something.
- *In order to* can go in the middle of a sentence, or at the beginning for extra emphasis.
  It is followed by the infinitive form of the verb.
  *I want to work in the office **in order to** learn about business software.*
  ***In order to** learn about business software, I want to work in the office.*
- *So that* goes in the middle of a sentence. It is followed by a tense of the verb, or *can*.
  *I want to work in the office **so that** I **can** learn about business software.*

Reason clauses

- We can use a clause beginning with *because* or *as* when we want to explain the reason for something.
- *Because* and *as* can go in the middle of a sentence, or at the beginning for extra emphasis.
  *I needed to get a job **because** I wanted to save money for my holiday.*
  ***Because** I wanted to save money for my holiday, I needed to get a job.*
- *As* has the same meaning as *because* but it is not so strong.
  *I decided to walk to work **as** it was a fine morning.*
  ***As** it was a fine morning, I decided to walk to work.*

Practice

1 Which of the pairs of sentences mean the same thing? Mark *S* for same and *D* for different. Can you explain the differences?

1. **a** I need to get good exam results because I want to go to college.
   b The reason I need good exam results is that I want to go to college. ....

2. **a** My dad likes to read on holiday, whereas my mum prefers going for a swim.
   b My mum enjoys going for a swim when my dad is reading. ....

3. **a** It's important to leave early so that we avoid the rush hour traffic.
   b To avoid the rush hour traffic we need to leave early. ....

4. **a** While most teenagers enjoy parties, not all of them like dancing.
   b Teenagers who can't dance don't enjoy parties. ....

5. **a** The company offers good training programmes in order to attract the best students.
   b The company wants to attract the best students so they offer good training programmes. ....

6. **a** As I don't enjoy swimming, I'm not so keen on seaside holidays.
   b I quite like seaside holidays despite the fact that I don't like swimming. ....

7. **a** Although it was a cold day the sun was shining.
   b It was a cold day, but the sun was shining. ....

2 Match the sentence halves and join them with linking words from the box. Can any of the words fit in more than one place?

> although   as   because   in order to
> so that   whereas

1. I can afford new trainers
2. I passed the exam
3. Most students have long summer holidays
4. It's a good idea to talk to a careers advisor
5. I've got the afternoon off
6. We're usually given half an hour

a. some of the questions were really hard.
b. I was paid yesterday.
c. you know what kind of jobs might suit you.
d. I worked late yesterday evening.
e. medical students have to work all through the year.
f. prepare for our final race.

1. ....
2. ....
3. ....
4. ....
5. ....
6. ....

UNIT 20

VERBS WITH TWO OBJECTS

- An active verb usually has a subject and often has a direct object.
- The direct object is usually a thing.

Subject	Verb	Direct object
I	sent	a text.
Maisie	wrote	a note about the volleyball match.

- Some verbs can have two objects, a direct object and an indirect object.
- The indirect object is usually a person.
- When the direct object comes first, we say **to** or **for** before the indirect object.

Subject	Verb	Direct object	Indirect object
I	sent	a text	to my aunt.
Maisie	wrote	a note about the volleyball match	for the teacher.

- When the indirect object comes first, we do not say **to** or **for**.

Subject	Verb	Indirect object	Direct object
I	sent	my aunt	a text.
Maisie	wrote	the teacher	a note about the volleyball match.

- Verbs which can have two objects include: **bring, buy, cook, choose, fetch, give, lend, make, offer, owe, pay, send, show, take, teach, tell, throw, write.**

Practice

1 Complete each sentence with to or for.

1 I bought some flowers .... my mum.
2 Did you show your presents .... your friends?
3 Alex gave a silver necklace .... his girlfriend.
4 Bettina told her story .... the police officer.
5 Dad paid ten euros .... the taxi driver.
6 Give that phone .... me now!
7 Charlie cooked a pizza .... himself.
8 Debbie taught a new song .... the children.
9 Can you fetch a clean towel .... me?
10 My brother took his notebook .... the teacher after the lesson.

2 Rewrite each sentence in exercise 1 with the indirect object before the direct object.

1 *I bought my mum some flowers.*
2 ....
3 ....
4 ....
5 ....
6 ....

3 Write the words in the correct order.

1 twenty dollars / Wilfred / his / owes / sister
....
2 Yolanda / cake / a / I'll / for / nice / choose
....
3 you / me / a / make / sandwich / can / ?
....
4 threw / the / sister / to / Tom / his / ball
....
5 of / mum / photo / gave / Zoe / a / and her friends / herself / her
....
6 Paul / has / to / address / his / you / texted / new
....

4 Rewrite each sentence in exercise 3, changing the order of the direct and indirect objects.
You will need to add or leave out to or for.

1 *Wilfred owes twenty dollars to his sister.*
2 ....
3 ....
4 ....
5 ....
6 ....

List of irregular verbs

Infinitive	Past simple	Past participle
be	was were	been
beat	beat	beaten
become	became	become
begin	began	begun
bleed	bled	bled
break	broke	broken
bring	brought	brought
build	built	built
burn	burnt/burned	burnt/burned
buy	bought	bought
catch	caught	caught
choose	chose	chosen
come	came	come
cost	cost	cost
cut	cut	cut
dig	dug	dug
do	did	done
draw	drew	drawn
dream	dreamed/dreamt	dreamed/dreamt
drink	drank	drunk
drive	drove	driven
eat	ate	eaten
fall	fell	fallen
feel	felt	felt
fight	fought	fought
find	found	found
fly	flew	flown
forget	forgot	forgotten
get	got	got
give	gave	given
go	went	gone/been
grow	grew	grown
have	had	had
hear	heard	heard
hide	hid	hid
hit	hit	hit
hold	held	held
hurt	hurt	hurt
keep	kept	kept
know	knew	known
lead	led	led

Infinitive	Past simple	Past participle
learn	learned/learnt	learned/learnt
leave	left	left
lend	lent	lent
lie	lay	lain
lose	lost	lost
make	made	made
mean	meant	meant
meet	met	met
pay	paid	paid
put	put	put
read	read	read
ride	rode	ridden
ring	rang	rung
rise	rose	risen
run	ran	run
say	said	said
see	saw	seen
sell	sold	sold
send	sent	sent
shine	shone	shone
show	showed	shown
shut	shut	shut
sing	sang	sung
sit	sat	sat
sleep	slept	slept
speak	spoke	spoken
spell	spelled/spelt	spelled/spelt
spend	spent	spent
stand	stood	stood
steal	stole	stolen
swim	swam	swum
take	took	taken
teach	taught	taught
tell	told	told
think	thought	thought
throw	threw	thrown
understand	understood	understood
wake	woke	woken
wear	wore	worn
win	won	won
write	wrote	written

Acknowledgements

The authors would like to thank Jo Hunter for her vision and encouragement in the development of this level of the course. Warm thanks also go to Diane Hall and Sheila Dignen for their creative suggestions and editorial support, and to Alyson Maskell for her helpful comments.

The authors and publishers are grateful to the following for reviewing the material during the writing process:

Colombia: Ellen Darling; Mexico: Paty Cervantes and Louise Manicolo; Russia: Catherine Lee and Lynn Pollard; Spain: Laura Clyde; Turkey: Kamil Koc

Development of this publication has made use of the Cambridge English Corpus, a multi-billion word collection of spoken and written English. It includes the Cambridge Learner Corpus, a unique collection of candidate exam answers. Cambridge University Press has built up the Cambridge English Corpus to provide evidence about language use that helps to produce better language teaching materials.

This product is informed by English Profile, a Council of Europe-endorsed research programme that is providing detailed information about the language that learners of English know and use at each level of the Common European Framework of Reference (CEFR). For more information, please visit www.englishprofile.org

The authors and publishers acknowledge the following sources of copyright material and are grateful for the permissions granted. While every effort has been made, it has not always been possible to identify the sources of all the material used, or to trace all copyright holders. If any omissions are brought to our notice, we will be happy to include the appropriate acknowledgements on reprinting.

The Register for the text on p. 24, listening exercise(2) adapted from a forum blog by Mark Budden, *The Register* 21/11/201 on p. 24, and for the text on p. 25 adapted from '500 homes destroyed by fire so powerful it spawned intense storms' by Simon Sharwood, APAC Editor, *The Register* 21/11/2012. Reproduced with permission;

Daily Mail for the text on p. 27 listening exercise adapted from 'Teenager lost on snowy mountain survives thanks to skills learned from Bear Grylls' Man vs Wild' by Paul Thompson, *Daily Mail* 4/1/2011. Copyright © Daily Mail;

James Geary for the text on p. 37 adapted from 'The Man Who Was Allergic to Radio Waves', *Popular Science,* 3.4.2010. Reproduced with permission of James Geary;

Steve Rees, Minddrive, org for the quote on p, 55. Reproduced with permission. Copyright © 2013 All Rights Reserved;

Liberal Democrat Voice for the text on p. 77 adapted from 'Advertising watchdog upholds Jo Swinson MP's complaints about overly airbrushed ads' by Helen Duffet, *Liberal Democrat Voice* 27/7/2011. Copyright © Liberal Democrat Voice, www.libdemvoice.org. Reproduced with permission;

ABCNews. Com for the text on p. 81 'Teen Chef Flynn McGarry Makes Debut at Beverly Hills Restaurant' by Lawrence Dechant, ABC News 27/1/2013. Copyright © ABCNews.Com. Reproduced with permission.

For the sound recording on p. 36, Track 1.14: *Darktronic,* artist – Exalton. Copyright © Pump Audi/Getty Images; p. 42, Track 1.19 (2) *Dirty Indie Rock*, artist - Pete Min. Copyright © Pump Audio, Exclusive/Getty Images, 1.19 (4) *Get Up and Run*, artist – Seeking Sui. Copyright © Pump Audio/Getty Images, Track 1.19 (5) *Hot Launch*, artist - City Wide Walkie Talkie. Copyright Pump audio/Getty Images.

Photo acknowledgements

p.10 (a): Andrew Fox/Alamy, (b): Alex Segre/Alamy, (c): Roberto Herrett/Alamy, (d): Kumar Sriskandan/Alamy, (e): Fanatic Studio/Alamy, (BR), p. 43 (TR), p. 115 (CL): naluwan/Shutterstock; p.11: Janine Wiedel/Photofusion; p.12: Radius Images/Alamy; p.13 (TR): Alexander Mak/Shutterstock, (BL): Carolyn Jenkins/Alamy, , (BR): Dean Pictures/Corbis ; p.14 (TL): Kaponia Aliaksei/Shutterstock, (CL): Steve Mason/Getty Images, (CR): Ted Foxx/Alamy, (B): Pitu Cau/Alamy; p.15; p.17 (TR): Richard G. Bingham II/Alamy; p.19 (TL): william casey/Shutterstock, (TR): ZouZou/Shutterstock, (CL): Mark Bassett/Alamy, (CL-Esen): ART DIRECTORS & TRIP/Alamy (CR): Sarfraz Abbasi/Getty Images, (CR-Thomas): WilleeCole Photography (BL): Alexander Tolstykh/Shutterstock, (BR): Lucas Oleniul/Getty Images; p.20 (TL): JeffG/Alamy, (TR): Glow Asia RF/Alamy, (CL): PCN/Corbis, (CR): Gavin Hellier/Alamy, (BL): Jarous/Shutterstock, (BR): Beyond Fotomedia GmbH/Alamy; p.21: Jim West/Alamy; p. 22 (TR): VIGE.CO/Shutterstock; p.23 (TL): Ariel Skelley/Corbis, (TR): 145/Gary S Chapman/Ocean/Corbis; p.24 (TR): A.T.Willett/Alamy, (C): Mirvav/Shutterstock, (BL), p.40 (L), p.41 (CL), (B), p.76 (BR), p.90 (f), p.107 (B): ZUMA Press, Inc./Alamy, (BR): Ellen McKnight/Alamy; p.25: DANIEL MUNOZ/Reuters/Corbis; p. 26: Bear Grylls Survival Academy; p.27 (T): Karl Weatherly/Getty Images, (B): Alexander Chaikin/Shutterstock; p.28 (TL), (B): Bob Krist/Corbis, (TR): PabloVieta/Getty Images, (CL): Jon Arnold Images Ltd/Alamy, (CR): pumkinoie/Alamy; p.28-29 (B): Bob Krist/Corbis; p.32 (T): paul abbitt rml/Alamy, (C), p.49 (B), p.85 (TR), p.102 (T), p.107 (L): WENN Ltd/Alamy, (BL): Jason Cox/Alamy, (BR): Joe Seer/Shutterstock; p.33 (TR): Image Source/Getty Images, (CL): Todor Tsvetkov/Getty Images; 34 (T): novkota1/Shutterstock, (B): marilyn barbone/Shutterstock; p.35 (L): Ksenila Perminova/Shutterstock, (R): David Crausby/Alamy; p.36 (TL): kokanphoto/Shutterstock, (TR), p.54 (T), p. 91 (BL): Agencja Fotograficzna Caro/Alamy, (BL): Leah-Anne Thompson/Shutterstock, (BR): Aleksandr Markin/Shutterstock; p.37 (TL): Umberto Shtanzman/Shutterstock, (TR): David J. Green - technology/Alamy, (B): Robert Matton AB/Alamy; p. 40 (TL): Simon Littlejohn/Alamy, (TR): James A. Sugar/Getty Images, (CL): B. Leighty/Photri Images/Alamy, (CR): Murray Hayward/Alamy, (BL): Enigma/Alamy, (BR): Daniel Teetor/Alamy; p.41 (TR): Gunter Marx/Alamy; p.42 (TL): keith morris/Alamy, (CL): Ross Gilmore/Alamy, (BL): Wavebreak Media Ltd/Alamy, (BC): Anna Lubovedskaya/Shutterstock, (BR): Lisa Maree Williams/Stringer/Getty Images; p.44 (TR): REUTERS/Carlos Barria; p.45: Gino's Premium Images/Alamy; p.46 (TL): Aflo Co. Ltd/Alamy, (TR): Bruno Ismail Silva Alves/Shutterstock, (CL): Dave Porter/Alamy, (CR): AP Photo/Alik Keplicz; p.48: LUKE MACGREGOR/Reuters/Corbis; p.49 (T): Picture Partners/Alamy; p.51 (TL): Ollyy/Shutterstock, (TC): Africa Studio/Shutterstock, (TR): Anna Omelchenko/Shutterstock, (CL): dwph/Shutterstock, (C): Kip Evanas/Alamy, (CR): Michael Kemp/Shutterstock, (B): Armin Staudt/Alamy; p.54 (C): Tribune Content Agency LLC/Alamy; p.55 (T): Kumar Sriskandan/Alamy, (B): Dan Saunders Photography/Alamy; p. 56 (BR): AP Photo/Andy Wong; p.57 (TL): Natalia rex/Shutterstock, (TR): Sergio Azenha/Alamy, (B): Oleksiy Mark/Getty Images; p.58 (T): Scott Camazine/Alamy, (C): holbox/Shutterstock, (B): skynavin/Getty Images; p.59 (TR): Paula Bronstein/Stringer/Getty Images, (B): Sergey Uryadnikov/Alamy; p.61 (T): AP Photo/Al Grillo, (B): Phil Cole/Getty Images; p.62 (a): Betty Shelton/Shutterstock, (b): CreativeNature R.Zwerver/Shutterstock, (c): Karel Gallas/Shutterstock, (d): Maggy Meyer/Shutterstock, (e): Pyty/Shutterstock, (f): Holly Kuchera/Shutterstock, (g): Darren Foard/Shutterstock, (h): lightpoet/Shutterstock; p.63: Chris Humphries/Shutterstock; p. 64 (TR): epa european pressphoto agency b.v./Alamy, (CL): REUTERS/Beawiharta, (BR): STRINGER/CHINA/Reuters/Corbis; p.65 (T): imaginechina/Corbis, (C): Douglas Peebles Photography/Alamy, (B): Chris Hammond Photography/Alamy; p.66 (TR): Nicram Sabod/Shutterstock; p.67 (B): Willy de l'Horme/Photononstop/Corbis; p.68 (a): Danita Delimont/Alamy, (b): Justin Kase zsixz/

lamy, (c): Tim Graham/Alamy, (d): ianmurray/Alamy, (e): vladimir akharov/Getty Images; p. 71 (T): Loop Images Ltd/Alamy, (C): ack Sullivan/Alamy; p.72 (TL): Aurora Photos/Alamy, (TC): MAX AREY/Alamy, (TR): Getty Images, (CL): Mark Hamilton, (CR): ge footstock/Alamy; p.73 (BR): PhotoAlto/Alamy; p.75: The Bedol ater Clock www.bedol.com; p.76 (T): MJTH/Shutterstock, (C): ris Mercer/Alamy; p.77: Everett Collection/Shutterstock; p. 78: at Hayward/Shutterstock; p.79 (T): 360b/Shutterstock, (C): Marc ielemans/Alamy, (B): Liquid Light/Alamy; p.80 (TL): Isantilli/ hutterstock, (TR): Ingrid Balabanova/Shutterstock, (B): Martin arnham/Alamy; p. 81: NBC/Lloyd Bishop/Getty Images; p. 84 (a): lichelaubryphoto/Shutterstock, (b): Massimiliano Trevisan/Alamy, :): Performance Image/Alamy, (d): inxti/Shutterstock, (e): Carlo ollo/Alamy; p.85 (L): David Grossman/Alamy; p.86 (T): Yurchyks/ hutterstock, (C): Doug Houghton/Alamy, (B): littleny/Shutterstock; .87 (TL): Andrew Palmer/Alamy, (TR): Karen D.Silva/Getty nages; p.88 (T): Daniel Kaesler/Alamy; p.89 (TL): Moxie roductions/Getty Images; p.90 (a): Danjaq/EON Productions/ he Kobal Collection, (b), p. 95 (TL), (TC): AF Archive/Alamy, (c): ionsgate/The Kobal Collection, (d): Lucasfilm/20th Century Fox/ he Kobal Collection, (e): Photos 12/Alamy, (g): REUTERS/Mario nzuoni; p.91 (TL): Dave Stevenson/Alamy (CR): Jiri Hubatka/ lamy, (BR): Pavel L Photo and Video/Shutterstock; p.93 (B): plash News/Corbis; p.95 (TR): Constantin Film Produkion/The obal Collection; p.97: Mirka Markova/Shutterstock; p.98 (TL): anon Boy/Shutterstock, (TR): Anatolii Babii/Alamy, (CL): OJO nages Ltd/Alamy, (CR upper): Jeff Metzger/Getty Images, (CR ower): Bloomua/Shutterstock, (BR): Alex Segre/Alamy; p.99: ngelo Cavalli/Getty Images; p.100: Directphoto Collection/ lamy; p.101: michaeljung/Shutterstock; p.102 (C upper): REX/ ichard Young, C lower): David Osuna/Demotix/Press Association nages, (B): PjrNews/Alamy; p.103 (TL), (BL): Allstar Picture ibrary/Alamy, (TR), (BR): Pictorial Press Ltd/Alamy, (CL): REX/ en Queenborough/BPI, (CR): Sydney Alford/Alamy; p.106: pa picture alliance/Alamy; p.107 (T): WFPA/Alamy; p.108 (TR): noodboard/Corbis, (CL): Blend Images - KidStock/Getty Images, C): Bart Coenders/Getty Images, (BR): Claudia Wiens/Alamy; .111 (T): JeffG/Alamy, (B): 2/Alistair Berg/Ocean/Corbis; p.112 T): Melvyn Longhurst/Alamy, (C): Oli Scarff/Getty Images, (BL): lesya Z/Shutterstock, (BR): Murray Hayward/Alamy; p.113 B/G): Taras Vyshnya/Shutterstock, (L): Cultura Creative (RF)/ lamy; p.114: Lena Granefelt/Johner Images/Corbis; p.116 TL): alexmillos/Shutterstock, (TC): PSL Images/Alamy, (TR): etastock/Alamy, (BL): Luis Louro/Shutterstock; p.117: Jan Thijs/ etty Images; p.122 (T): Sielemann/Shutterstock, (B): Monkey usiness Images/Shutterstock; p.126: Erin Fotos/Getty Images; .129 (CR): wdeon/Shutterstock, (BR): Bob Martin/Getty Images; .130 (BL): moodboard/Getty Images; p.131 (TL): PACIFIC RESS/Alamy, (BL): James Leynes/Corbis.

Commissioned photography by Gareth Boden: p.10 (Eva), Bonnie), (Marty), (Elena); p.15; p.17 (CR), (BR);p. 69 (TR); p.71 B); p.76 (BL), (BR inset); p.91 (TR);p. 113 (TR); p.115 (TL), (TC), TR), (CR)

Front cover photo by Phase4Studios/Shutterstock

Illustrations

Mark Duffin pp. 38, 50, 69; emc design ltd p. 39 (T); Stuart Harrison pp. 16, 22, 67, 104, 105, 110, 118; Martin Sanders Beehive Illustration) p. 87; Alek Sotirovski (Beehive Illustration) pp. 39 (B), 83, 115, 123, 129, 130, 131.

The publishers are grateful to the following contributors: text esign and layouts: emc design Ltd; cover design: Andrew Ward; icture research: Ann Thomson; audio recordings: produced by H Sound and recorded at DSound, London; Culture and cross- urricular sections: Diane Hall, Robert Quinn; Grammar reference ection: Louise Hashemi.